CHINESE LINEAGE AND SOCIETY:
FUKIEN AND KWANGTUNG

WITHDRAWN

LONDON SCHOOL OF ECONOMICS
MONOGRAPHS ON SOCIAL ANTHROPOLOGY

Managing Editor: Anthony Forge

The Monographs on Social Anthropology were established in 1940 and aim to publish results of modern anthropological research of primary interest to specialists.

The continuation of the series was made possible by a grant in aid from the Wenner-Gren Foundation for Anthropological Research, and more recently by a further grant from the Governors of the London School of Economics and Political Science.

The Monographs are under the direction of an Editorial Board associated with the Department of Anthropology of the London School of Economics and Political Science.

Annual Worshipping at the Tombs of Ancestors

LONDON SCHOOL OF ECONOMICS
MONOGRAPHS ON SOCIAL ANTHROPOLOGY
No. 33

CHINESE LINEAGE AND SOCIETY: FUKIEN AND KWANGTUNG

BY

MAURICE FREEDMAN

UNIVERSITY OF LONDON
THE ATHLONE PRESS
NEW YORK: HUMANITIES PRESS INC.

Published by
THE ATHLONE PRESS
UNIVERSITY OF LONDON
at 2 Gower Street, London W C 2

Distributed by Tiptree Book Services Ltd
Tiptree, Essex

First edition, 1966
First paperback edition, with corrections, 1971

© *Maurice Freedman* 1966, 1971

U.K. SBN 0 485 19633 6

U.S.A. SBN 391 00199 X

First printed in Great Britain by
WESTERN PRINTING SERVICES LTD
BRISTOL

Reprinted by photo-litho by
WILLIAM CLOWES & SONS, LTD
LONDON, BECCLES AND COLCHESTER

PREFACE

I published *Lineage Organization in Southeastern China* in 1958.[1] It was an attempt to bring together what I then knew about its subject, mainly from published work, and to discuss the role of unilineal descent grouping in China against the background of anthropological theory. When I finished it I knew it was not ended, for I was conscious of having failed to tap the existing sources in Chinese and Japanese, and I was confident that my exercise in the armchair anthropology of China would fairly soon be improved on both by people sinologically better equipped than I and by field workers able to take advantage of the possibilities for research open in the New Territories of Hong Kong.

My confidence, especially in respect of the field work, was well placed; several anthropological studies have been made in the New Territories in the last five years or so (my own very brief one among them); and I have decided to continue the argument begun in *Lineage Organization*. But this new book is no more conclusive than its predecessor. It is able to call on more facts and I can write about them with greater assurance now that I have myself explored the New Territories and established from the evidence of my own eyes what, in timorous moments, I had earlier feared might be the product of a too enthusiastic imagination. Yet this second instalment is by no means the end of the story. The great bulk of the field work in the New Territories is still unpublished. The same is true of the field research in Taiwan which has an important bearing on the provinces of Fukien and Kwangtung. And we are merely at the beginning of the period during which the written genealogies and gazetteers (*fang-chih*) laid up by Chinese society and the documents produced by Japanese administrators and scholars in Taiwan will be fully exploited. A third instalment will be necessary in a few years' time, although it is very unlikely that I shall be its author.

It will be clear that I have not been able to remedy in this book

[1] London School of Economics Monographs on Social Anthropology, no. 18 (reprinted with typographical corrections, London and N.Y., 1965).

209601

all the defects of the first, but since 1957, when *Lineage Organization* went to the printer, my view of Chinese social organization has been enlarged by several experiences. First, I have read in the new Western work on the sociology and social history of China. In recent years this literature has greatly increased, and, coming mainly from the United States, it places us deeper in debt to American scholarship. Second, during the years 1962 to 1964 I was lucky enough to take part in a series of seminars on the sociology and anthropology of China organized by the cumbersomely named but very agreeably conducted 'Sub-committee on Chinese Society of the Joint Committee on Contemporary China of the American Council of Learned Societies and the Social Science Research Council'. In these seminars, as well as in other, less formal, settings, I was privileged to have access to the learning and experience of specialists whom, along with the people responsible for organizing the seminars (especially Mr Bryce Wood of the Social Science Research Council, New York), I should like very warmly to thank. Third, I have done more reading in the older literature on China – and re-read much of it, finding (the pleasure must surely be common) that it comes alive all over again as new questions are put to it. Finally, I was given the opportunity in 1963 to make a short field trip to the New Territories; it tied my earlier speculations to a living reality and gave me the chance to look more deeply into the documented past of the Kwangtung county of Hsin-an from which the New Territories were created in 1898.

This book draws on the newer literature, on older writings which I had not previously used, and on my field work in 1963. I have resisted the temptation to set out the results of this field research in great detail because they will be better presented independently of a work intended to be about southeastern China in general.[1] But I think it will be clear that many of the changes that have taken place in my view of society in Fukien and Kwangtung are attributable to my experience in the New Territories. It is for that reason that I must stress its importance.

[1] A preliminary account of my field research was given in a mimeographed report prepared to be read by officers of the New Territories Administration: *A Report on Social Research in the New Territories*, Hong Kong, 1963. A sketch of some aspects of New Territories society is given in my paper, 'Shifts of Power in the Hong Kong New Territories', *Journal of Asian and African Studies*, vol. 1, no. 1, 1966, Leiden.

In February 1963 I began a period of field study in the New
Territories. It was cut short after three months by my falling sick,
but in that time I had come near completing a general survey of
social conditions and research needs. The survey was carried out
under the auspices of the then newly created London-Cornell
Project for the study of Chinese and South-East Asian societies, an
enterprise financed jointly by the Carnegie Corporation of New
York and the Nuffield Foundation. My work was in addition
financed partly out of a Ford Foundation grant made to the
London School of Economics and Political Science, and I was in
several ways assisted by the New Territories Administration. I
acknowledge all this aid with gratitude and record my appreciation of the help and advice given me in Hong Kong by Mr J. B.
Aserappa, District Commissioner New Territories, and his
officers and staff, especially Mr G. C. M. Lupton (District Officer
Tai Po) and Mr Tsang For Piu; by Mr K. M. A. Barnett; by
Mr J. W. Hayes; by Mr C. T. Leung; by Mr K. W. J. Topley;
by Dr Marjorie Topley; and by Mr P. K. C. Tsui. In writing
these names I acknowledge only some of my debts to the people
who made it possible for me to move freely and profitably in the
New Territories.

In the course of carrying out the survey I was able to confirm my
earlier opinion that some of the guesses made in *Lineage Organization* could be tested by both historical research and anthropological
field work in the New Territories. True, the historical materials
are thinner than I had expected. There appears to be only a small
amount of Chinese documentation bearing directly on the New
Territories. But there is more than has yet been collected in the
way of land deeds, genealogies, and engraved inscriptions. In an
ideal world of historical and anthropological scholarship somebody would be paid to gather in or copy all that remains. (It is not
only paper that perishes; inscribed stones and boards are removed
and lost. It is more than an antiquarian and nostalgic *cri de coeur*
that appeals for the rescue of the monuments of what, in the
present state of the world, is a privileged part of China.) When
the information to be culled from these Chinese sources is com-
bined with the data from British documents and the memories
of old men, there will be an opportunity to say something illumin-
ating about a corner of southeastern China in the last years of the
Ch'ing dynasty. An impressive example of what can be achieved

by using these varied sources of information on the past is given in a series of papers by Mr J. W. Hayes, a Hong Kong civil servant who was at one time a District Officer in the New Territories.[1]

As for anthropological field research, there are abundant opportunities for work on lineage organization and topics germane to it. The groundwork for the study of New Territories rural society has already been laid by Miss Barbara E. Ward, Miss Jean A. Pratt, Professor Jack Potter, Mr H. D. R. Baker, and Mr R. G. Groves. Other anthropologists will certainly follow them, and I should like to help dispel the notion that the New Territories have been so far affected by British rule and modern changes in population and economic life that they are no longer capable of being useful to anthropologists interested in the study of traditional Chinese institutions. Of course the New Territories have been profoundly changed since they were brought into the Colony of Hong Kong. Of course they are not a mere fossil of the nineteenth century. Of course they show many 'modern' problems worth investigating (especially as they arise from the industrial and agricultural revolutions of the last decade and a half), and we should be very foolish to ignore them. But old lineages still exist; power is exercised within them; land is still held in ancestral trusts; rites of worship continue to be held in ancestral halls. . . . We may see something of what went on under the Chinese Empire, but, just as important, we have the chance of understanding how lineages adapt themselves to the modern world.

A further preliminary point needs to be made on this sequel to *Lineage Organization*. The new book gets its focus from the one it is designed to supplement. It takes up an interest in the Chinese lineage which I developed many years ago. From this it does not follow that I think the lineage to be the paramount form of

[1] The first of these to be published are: 'The Pattern of Life in the New Territories in 1898', *Journal of the Hong Kong Branch of the Royal Asiatic Society*, vol. 2, 1962; 'Cheung Chau 1850–1898: Information from Commemorative Tablets', *Journal of the Hong Kong Branch* . . ., vol. 3, 1963; 'Peng Chau between 1798 and 1899', *Journal of the Hong Kong Branch* . . ., vol. 4, 1964 (published 1965); 'Settlement and Development of a Multiple-Clan Village' and 'A Mixed Community of Hakka and Cantonese on Lantau Island' in Royal Asiatic Society, Hong Kong Branch, *Aspects of Social Organization in the New Territories*, Hong Kong [1965]. This last publication is a pamphlet printing a series of seven short papers, by H. Baker, R. G. Groves, J. Hayes, and R. Ng, read at a symposium held in Hong Kong in May 1964 under the chairmanship of Dr. Marjorie Topley.

Chinese local grouping, or local grouping to be the chief topic in Chinese society for anthropologists to study. As some of the remarks I have made elsewhere will perhaps have shown,[1] I am aware of the need for anthropologists to take a larger view of Chinese society and to raise their eyes (or at any rate stretch their imagination) to wider limits than those of the village. For the moment, however, I am concerned primarily with the local scene. I propose to reconsider the problem of how corporate descent groups in China fitted into a complex society, looking at that society from the point of view of the local group.

Finally, I have several debts to acknowledge in connexion with the writing of this book. Dr Chêng Tê-k'un made a number of comments on the typescript of *Lineage Organization* which I unfortunately received too late to take account of in that book; I have tried to profit from them in this one. On several sinological points I have been lucky enough to be able to consult Mrs H. M. Wright and Professor D. C. Twitchett. Professor Lucy Mair did me the great service of reading a draft of the book; she helped me to remedy many faults in argument and style. For his encouragement (it was a remark he made two years ago that gave me the idea of returning to the theme of *Lineage Organization*), intellectual help, and penetrating criticism of both earlier and later drafts I am deeply in debt to Professor G. William Skinner, my transatlantic colleague in the London-Cornell Project. My thanks to him are accompanied by an expression of regret that in this second attempt at the subject I am still very far below the standard of scholarship he has himself set for sinological anthropology. With Professor Skinner's name I must couple those of his colleagues in Chinese studies at Cornell University who many times since 1960 have offered me hospitality, intellectual and other. Among these colleagues I should like to single out Professor Arthur P. Wolf with whom I have had the privilege of discussing at length problems in the analysis of Chinese society, and who criticized an early draft of this book. From the correspondence I

[1] See 'A Chinese Phase in Social Anthropology', *The British Journal of Sociology*, vol. XIV, no. 1, March 1963. On the general issue of the anthropologist's place in the study of Chinese society see the Symposium on Chinese Studies and the Disciplines in *The Journal of Asian Studies*, vol. XXIII, no. 4, August 1964, especially G. William Skinner, 'What the Study of China can do for Social Science', and my own complementary contribution, 'What Social Science can do for Chinese Studies'.

have maintained with Mr Baker and Mr Groves while they have been at work in the New Territories, I have been able to settle a number of doubtful points and supplement my own all too short field experience of the things on which I write. And I have profited by Mr Baker's criticism of a late draft of this book. My wife went over the last two drafts in detail, helping me to remove a number of obscurities and giving me editorial aid without which this would have been even less of a book than it is.

The frontispiece (redrawn from an illustration in George Smith, *A Narrative of an Exploratory Visit to Each of the Consular Cities of China, and to the Islands of Hong Kong and Chusan*, London, 1847) and the maps were prepared by the staff of the Department of Geography, London School of Economics and Political Science. I wish to thank them warmly for this and for some preliminary work on the photographs from which the plates have been made.

London School of Economics   M. F.
and Political Science
August 1965

PREFACE TO THE PAPERBACK EDITION

In this reprint I have corrected a few typographical errors and, by the alteration of one word, a minor ethnographic-sinological blunder – which I alone, I am happy to note, seem to have detected. Otherwise the book is exactly as it was in 1966. Since then, of course, the published work that bears on the subjects dealt with has grown at such a pace that the 'third instalment' referred to on page v is now overdue. There seems little point in printing a list of the new works in the absence of an attempt to assess their precise relevance; and I have been prevented, by the cost involved, from adding to the length of the book. I may offer some indication of the scope and significance of a good deal of the newer work by simply referring to *Family and Kinship in Chinese Society*, published by Stanford University Press in 1970, which I edited.

All Souls College, Oxford
May 1971   M. F.

CONTENTS

PLATES

MAPS

I

Village, Lineage, and Clan

With the exception of the county of Shun-tê and perhaps a few scattered pockets in other counties (of which the Wun Yiu area of the Tai Po District in the New Territories is an example),[1] the villages of the provinces of Fukien and Kwangtung are compact. Many of them are communities composed of the male agnatic descendants of a single ancestor together with their unmarried sisters and their wives. To begin with, the chief problem to be discussed is the relationship between settlement pattern and patrilineal grouping.

The literature published since 1957 can be made to serve as a point of departure. C. K. Yang has given us the results of the last village study to be made in mainland China (it concerns a community near the capital of Kwangtung province) before Communism had come upon the face of Chinese society.[2] And we have been afforded glimpses of two other village studies relevant to southeastern China, one of them being carried out in a Hakka community in the New Territories,[3] the other in a Hokkien-speaking village in Taiwan.[4]

[1] Chinese place names in Hong Kong have official spellings (based on the Cantonese pronunciation), and I have thought it wise to follow Hong Kong usage here even though other place names are given in their Mandarin form. The Hong Kong names are readily identifiable in *A Gazetteer of Place Names in Hong Kong, Kowloon and the New Territories*, Hong Kong, Foreword dated 1960, which gives the Chinese characters for the romanized versions.

[2] C. K. Yang, *A Chinese Village in Early Communist Transition*, Cambridge, Mass., 1959.

[3] Jean A. Pratt, 'Emigration and Unilineal Descent Groups: A Study of Marriage in a Hakka Village in the New Territories, Hong Kong', *The Eastern Anthropologist*, vol. XIII, no. 4, June–August 1960. This brief and not too readily accessible paper is full of interesting things; one hopes that Miss Pratt will soon be able to publish more fully.

[4] Bernard Gallin, 'Matrilateral and Affinal Relationships of a Taiwanese Village', *American Anthropologist*, vol. 62, no. 4, August 1960; 'A Case for Intervention in the Field', *Human Organization*, vol. 18, no. 3, 1959; 'Cousin Marriage in China', *Ethnology*, vol. II, no. 1, January 1963; 'Land Reform in

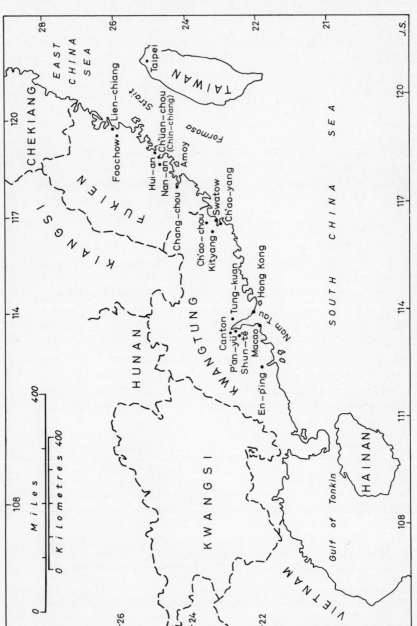

MAP I: South-Eastern China

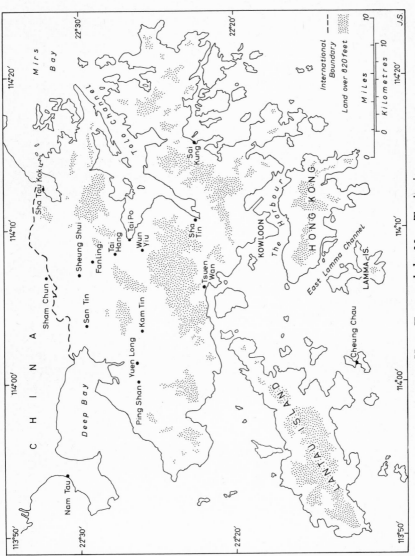

MAP 2: Hong Kong and the New Territories

Yang's sociological field study was begun before the village of Nanching came under Communist government, and continued during the first phase of the new regime. The remarkable 'choice' of time at which to make observations of modern village life in China gives the book one of its major interests, but for the moment we are concerned with the data in the first part of the study where the traditional organization is described. In 1948 Nanching had a population of some 1,100 and was dominated by two 'clans', as Yang calls them, which accounted for the overwhelming majority of the inhabitants. The two main 'clans' and the three minor ones severally occupied distinct parts of the village. Moreover, segments of the larger entities were also spatially separated. 'Each branch within a clan also had its own street. . . . Thus the physical plan of the village was blocked out into many individual cells on a kinship basis.'[1]

One of the main 'clans' had ancestor tablets for members of the forty-second generation; the first ancestor had made his home in the village in 1091. The most recently dead of the other main 'clan' were members of the thirty-seventh generation.[2] It would appear that the counting of generations starts from a point genealogically much higher than the ancestors first settling in Nanching. As many as forty-two generations are unlikely to have elapsed since 1091. A genealogical framework wider than that of the localized lineage was evidently involved and, as we shall see presently, the 'clan' founded in Nanching at the end of the eleventh century was at the time it was studied a segment of a scattered lineage. Yang cites a written genealogy relating to this 'clan',[3] but he does not discuss its contents or its significance.

The village community studied by Miss Pratt in the New Territories is a small Hakka lineage of some forty families. This is a relatively isolated and poor hill community which we shall

Taiwan: Its Effect on Rural Social Organization and Leadership', *Human Organization*, vol. 22, no. 2, Summer 1963; 'Chinese Peasant Values towards the Land', in Symposium on Community Studies in Anthropology, *Proceedings of the 1963 Annual Spring Meeting of the American Ethnological Society*, Seattle.

[1] Yang, *op. cit.*, pp. 11, 14, 81. The larger of the two main 'clans' numbered fewer than 600 souls: p. 93. (Yang's figures are approximate; he wrote his book from memory, his notes having been kept in China.) It is important to remember that there were large lineage villages in the area, despite the fact that Nanching itself was of mixed lineages. Yang mentions one of over 10,000, 'Chen Tsun, about forty miles down the Pearl River': p. 93.

[2] *Ibid.*, p. 12.   [3] *Ibid.*, *loc. cit.*, and p. 271 (note 13).

need to consider later as a close approximation to the theoretical model A discussed at pp. 131 f. of *Lineage Organization*. The lineage is sixteen generations deep and divided into three ancestral hall groups which 'tend to live in discrete areas of the village'.[1]

When we come to Gallin's Taiwan village we are dealing with a community of very heterogeneous lineage elements. The population of 650 (in 115 households) has twelve surnames in all, but there are in fact more than twelve lineages (if indeed we may legitimately use the term in this context), for families bearing a single surname are not all members of one lineage. Despite the heterogeneity, people bearing four of the surnames account for some 80 per cent of the village population. Most of the members of a lineage 'live in the same house or at least the same part of the village', and the genealogies of such units are of course very shallow. In this village 'with its relatively short history, almost all *tsu* [lineage] relatives in the village are related through a grandfather or at most a great-grandfather which they have in common'. It is a characteristic of the area of Taiwan in which this village is situated (the west-central coastal plain) that 'large clans' are lacking.[2]

These new cases raise again the problem of the emergence of single-lineage communities. One of the three villages is a single-lineage community: the small Hakka community in the New Territories. Nanching is in an area where single-lineage settlements are common, but is not itself one. The Taiwan village is mixed and fairly recent. Now, people have tended to interpret multilineage villages and shallow lineage organization in China as being the result of a breakdown of single-lineage communities by migration, the southern part of the country displaying a higher degree of deep and single-lineage settlement because of its relative immunity from invasion.[3] Van der Sprenkel, for example, in a recent re-appraisal of Max Weber's work on China, writes: 'The evidence shows that lineage organizations were more numerous, better organized and more influential in South China than in the North. This may be partly due to southward population

---

[1] Pratt, *op. cit.*, pp. 147–9.

[2] Gallin, 'Matrilateral and Affinal Relationships', pp. 633 f. In 'A Case . . .', p. 140, Gallin gives the total of surnames as 'about nine' and says the village has been settled some 150 years. The discrepancy in the number of surnames is apparently accounted for by changes during the period of the field study.

[3] *Lineage Organization*, p. 1.

movements of the Han Chinese under "barbarian" pressure. Such internal migrations were important as early as the Six Dynasties period, and notably after the fall of the Northern Sung and during the Mongol conquest.'[1] That is to say, there is a temptation to look upon the single-lineage settlement as the historically prior form and mixed settlements as evidence of a later disturbance of the primordial pattern.[2]

It must be true that migration and the different conditions in which it took place account in some measure for the pattern of distribution of large localized lineages in China; the problem will need to be dealt with later. But it would be a great mistake to think that the only direction of change is that in which what were originally in lineage terms homogeneous local settlements became heterogeneous. On the contrary, the process is reversible, single-lineage settlements emerging from mixed ones. The proof is contained in the New Territories genealogies which speak (with some evident relish) of earlier neighbours in the village territory (their surnames are usually given) now thrust into oblivion by those who have supplanted them, and, more surely and convincingly, in the abandoned ancestral halls belonging to surnames now no longer represented in what have become single-lineage settlements. Some of these derelict halls, to judge by their appearance, must have been in use in fairly recent times (say, even two or three generations ago), and we have no reason to suppose that the process of elimination has come to a stop. There is of course nothing special about the New Territories in this respect. Evidence of extinct lineages is to be found everywhere. Of Nanching, Yang says that, according to old villagers, 'in the dim past there was a Hua clan and a Fang clan who inhabited the northern end of the present village site. Apparently both of them were crowded out by the late comers, and there were no descendants of either clan in the village.'[3]

---

[1] Otto B. van der Sprenkel, 'Max Weber on China', *History and Theory*, vol. III, 1964, p. 367. But the passage continues: 'There are also strong grounds for associating developed lineage structures with local prosperity. The areas of fertile soil, productive agriculture, and dense population, conditions which are found predominantly in the southern and south-eastern provinces, are also those where clan organization is most frequently met with.'

[2] Cf. Hsiao Kung-chuan, *Rural China, Imperial Control in the Nineteenth Century*, Seattle, 1960, p. 328. But at p. 329 Hsiao stresses the correlation between strong lineage organization and economic prosperity.

[3] Yang, *op. cit.*, p. 12.

Weaker and less prosperous lineages may 'die'. Their numbers may fall away by sickness and failure (again through sickness or because of poverty) to reproduce. The sad remnants depart. (Declining natural population will not by itself account for the disappearance of a lineage, for gaps in the ranks of a rich lineage could always be filled by stocking up with adopted sons. Chen Ta, writing of rural Fukien, says that formerly, when 'feuds between clans' were frequent, sons were sometimes adopted as a means of increasing manpower for defence.[1] There was, incidentally, much more buying of sons in southeastern China than the legal rules governing adoption might lead one to suppose. Merchant venturers in Fukien, for example, sometimes adopted sons to send out on their trading expeditions overseas. The law was in fact concerned with adoption aimed at continuing the line of succession in the ancestor cult – whence the stress on the need for the adopted son to be of the correct agnatic and generation status – and did not affect the adoption of sons taken only to swell the ranks of the family; they could be got from any convenient source.[2]) The happy survivors might attribute the ill fortune of their lost neighbours to disaster springing from geomancy, but it

[1] *Emigrant Communities in South China. A Study of Overseas Migration and its Influence on Standards of Living and Social Change*, London and N.Y., 1939, p. 131.

[2] The point needs glossing. In inheritance (or, as the lawyers put it, succession to property) all sons were on an equal footing, except in regard to a special portion connected with the maintenance of the ancestor cult. In respect of this cult a distinction must be made between the standing of the sons as defined in law and their status as it was in fact determined by custom and regular practice. 'In theory – and the theory formed the background of enacted law until the end of the Manchu dynasty – the duty of offering . . . [ancestral] sacrifice was not only transmitted through the male line of descent but was concentrated in one person in that line, namely the eldest son by the wife.' – Henry McAleavy, 'Varieties of Hu'o'ng-hoa . . .: A Problem of Vietnamese Law', *Bulletin of the School of Oriental and African Studies*, vol. XXI, pt. 3, 1958, p. 609. To show how in reality the theory of the statute law was departed from, McAleavy goes on to translate a passage from the *Taiwan Shihō*, 1910–11, a Japanese compilation of the private law of Formosa: 'The old clan law has decayed. Sacrifice to the ancestors is not a privilege of the eldest son by the wife, but all sons are competent to perform it . . . [In] the provinces of Fukien and Kwangtung, and especially in Formosa . . . [the] ancestral temple and tombs and the business of sacrifice are in charge of all the sons or grandsons either jointly or one at a time.'—*ibid.*, pp. 609 f.; and cf. *ibid.*, pp. 613 f. That is to say, if a man lacked a son, he was in the eyes of the law obliged to adopt one from among his nearest agnates in the generation next below his in order to provide a legally satisfactory substitute in the interests of succession to the cult. The distinction drawn here between theoretical primogeniture and the practical equality of the sons is crucial to our understanding of ancestor worship, as we shall see.

is easy to understand how, once their numbers and riches are declining, a minority must soon find itself subject to political and economic pressure from its more fortunate fellow villagers to force it finally to abandon its crumbling foothold. The economic pressure on a weakening minority was not, however, always exerted directly by its stronger rivals. The climatic hazards of the area of China we are concerned with – typhoons, floods, and droughts – must certainly have borne more heavily on those with fewer accumulated resources and have led to their being the first to give up the struggle.

I think we must assume that the desire to form a single lineage in one village territory is a motive given in the system. Where there is enough land, a nucleus of agnates strive to build themselves up to form a large homogeneous settlement. If to begin with they must share a territory with members of one or more other lineages, they will await their opportunity to dominate and eventually drive out their neighbours. In many cases it is not clear why in the first place strangers are permitted into the village territory or how the newcomers manage to establish a strong position for themselves.[1] As far as I know, the historical evidence bearing on these questions does not exist; it is a deficiency which might conceivably be made good by a careful analysis of the recent past of certain lineages in the New Territories, but for the most part we shall probably always need to have recourse to speculation. (In present-day circumstances in the New Territories the 'invasion' of lineage territories by outsiders is taking place on entirely new terms; the refugees from Communist China admitted as tenants to the lands and houses of long-established lineages are unlikely to consolidate themselves to form agnatic groupings.)

It may be that, in the past, outsiders taken on as tenants of agricultural land were sometimes successful and contrived to organize to the point where they could begin to challenge their longer-established neighbours. Good fortune, and with it the power to drive off unwanted fellow-villagers, may perhaps on occasion have come from ties built up with the bureaucracy. The fighting between lineages, to which the study of southeastern China has

[1] Professor Skinner has pointed out to me that some outsiders admitted to a lineage-village will have been occupational specialists (shopkeepers among them), although one would not expect that such people would normally be able to consolidate their position to the point where they might rival their hosts.

accustomed us, may have played its part; if one lineage failed to meet the regular challenge of arms it perhaps went under, its handing over of land to its rivals as part of the terms of truce being the first step along the road to the disaster of final capitulation by retreat. (There was, however, a way of retreating without leaving the village: men could marry into the families of the dominant lineages, abandoning their right to transmit their surname to their children. And, as a quotation from a nineteenth-century Western source will presently show, the process of absorbing the weak may have sometimes taken place by a simple change of surname.)

But it is important to realize that a few particularly powerful lineages dotted over the whole region were not subject to challenge by outsiders. They certainly admitted strangers to their land as tenants, for even if they had wished to cultivate their own fields, diverting their energies from the more prestigeful and productive occupations of scholarship, administration, and business, they could never have rallied the necessary manpower. The tenants they took were held in a state of subjection to masters of unquestionable and unchallengeable political and economic power, and formed satellite villages which were called upon to support the dominant lineages in their fights and pay taxes through (and perhaps largely to) their landlords.[1] In some cases the subordinate tenants were thrust into the status of servile families (*sia-wu*, hereditary tenants, as Chen Han-seng calls them)[2] 'who look upon the members of the clans that harbour them as their masters and who, in addition to farming the fields assigned to them, render additional services as labourers, servants and watchmen, for which they are paid no wage, though here and there their wretched condition is occasionally alleviated by perquisites of

---

[1] This appears to have been the situation in, e.g, the Tang lineage of Ping Shan in the western part of the New Territories. I am greatly indebted to Professor Jack M. Potter of the University of California, Berkeley, for his kindness in allowing me to see and make use of his Ph.D. thesis, *P'ing Shan: The Changing Economy of a Chinese Village in Hong Kong*, University of California, Berkeley, 1964. As this thesis is likely soon to be published, I have been sparing in my use of it in this book, despite the temptation which its rich material has offered me. The MS of this book was finished before I received from Professor Potter a copy of his paper, 'The Structure of Rural Chinese Society in Hong Kong's New Territories', which is soon to appear in a symposium on Hong Kong edited by I. C. Jarvie.

[2] *Agrarian Problems in Southernmost China*, Shanghai, 1936, p. 57.

various kinds'. In one district of Kwangtung, with a total population of some ten thousand, about 30 per cent were *sia-wu* in the 1930s.[1]

The process of the decline and elimination of agnatic groups becomes even more interesting to us as soon as we realize that it can be seen at work not only in the relations between different lineages, but also in the relations between different segments of one localized lineage. Again, geomancy may 'explain' why segments disappear, and political and economic pressure account for their elimination. Let me illustrate from the case of a Hakka village only a few miles from the one described by Miss Pratt.

It has now about four hundred inhabitants divided among three primary segments of a lineage. Local 'history' has it (no written genealogy survives, if it ever existed) that the lineage was founded over three hundred years ago, since when fourteen generations have appeared. The founder's father had left his native place in the northern area of the county of which the New Territories were formerly part and had tried to settle on the island of Lantau. He died there. The surviving members of his family did not fare well, so that, with his father's bones over one shoulder and his little son on the other, the founder made his way to the present home of the lineage. Here there were already established two other lineages, with whom the newcomers settled down. The three groups decided to build ancestral halls and align them so that they faced in one direction. The alignment having been agreed upon, the ancestor of the surviving lineage (whether he was the founder himself or a later figure is not clear in the story) took advantage of the workmen's temporary absence to make a slight adjustment to the angle at which his own hall was to stand, and the subterfuge worked so well that the two longer-established lineages died away; their geomancy had been ruined. The ancestor tablets which they abandoned were in recent time removed by the surviving lineage and placed in a 'vegetarian hall' in another part of the New Territories so that the derelict ancestral halls might be made use of.[2] (There is in reality no detectable

[1] *Ibid.*, p. 58. Potter, *P'ing Shan*, mentions the presence of servile families in the village he studied, where they were known by the Cantonese term *ha fu*.

[2] Cf. Jacques Amyot, *The Chinese Community of Manila: A Study of Adaptation of Chinese Familism to the Philippine Environment*, Research Series no. 2, Philippine Studies Program, Dept. of Anthropology, Univ. of Chicago, 1960 (mimeo.), p. 44: 'The Ting lineage has occupied Ch'entai [Chin-chiang *hsien*, Fukien] for

difference in the alignment of the ancestral halls; the villagers simply assume – and assert – it to exist.)

Geomancy is thought to have destroyed the two older lineages, but it is also credited with having broken off one segment of the triumphant lineage, for the three major segments now in the village are the second, third, and fourth. Facing their ancestral hall there is a dip in the line of the hills which is interpreted geomantically as bringing ill fortune to seniors: younger sons fare better than older and junior segments better than senior. The fourth sub-lineage is the most successful (in the Chinese restaurant business in England, among other things); the first has disappeared. Some fifty years ago the last surviving family in the senior sub-lineage, resigning themselves (it is said) to the inevitability of their geomantic misfortune, went off to South-East Asia where one last member is thought to live on. When the family departed it pawned its land to the second sub-lineage, which has now taken full possession of it; the senior sub-lineage has ceased to exist. (Compare Chen Ta's reference to a lineage in eastern Kwangtung in the 1930s of which the second branch had declined while the fourth was growing more prosperous. The village head explained the change in fortune: 'The southern mountain has the shape of a monster lobster. The graves of the second branch are located at its head and thus far have had numerous offspring and plenty of money. Recently, the fourth branch has unfortunately placed a grave on the right claw of the lobster and caused disharmony to the graves of the second branch. This is why the latter is not doing so well these days.'[1] I shall have more to say on geomancy in a later chapter.)

Migration has been a constant feature of southeastern Chinese society. Sometimes whole villages have moved when continuing sickness, lack of sons, or some other kind of misfortune has convinced their inhabitants that their geomancy is wrong. J. W. Hayes has demonstrated for Lantau Island in the New Territories some seven hundred years. It was originally Ch'en territory and still retains the Ch'en name. It is said that the founders of the lineage first came to Ch'entai attracted by a burial site considered to be particularly propitious according to the principles of geomancy. They obtained the site from the Ch'ens by their astuteness, settled close by, and their descendants eventually displaced the Ch'ens completely.' (In this study Father Amyot presents some very important data on Fukien lineage and local organization which he collected from informants in Manila.)

[1] Chen Ta, op. cit., p. 247.

that several villages have moved their sites in the last fifty years, giving geomantic unsuitability as the reason for their drastic decision.[1] More usually, however, individual men or families have gone off to seek a living elsewhere; and during the last hundred years or so there has been a steady drain of people, especially men, away to South-East Asia and the United States, to mention only the major areas of overseas migration. So that while the population of the provinces of Fukien and Kwangtung has risen as a whole,[2] there have been striking disparities in increase between local settlements.[3] Some have expanded to number several thousands while others have shrunk to, or failed to grow beyond being, small hamlets. Where economic conditions have been favourable, lineages have tended to exclude outsiders or cast out their neighbours of other surnames and to develop into massive single-lineage settlements, as we can see very clearly in the part of Hsin-an county which became the New Territories. There the largest and most powerful lineages occupy the most fertile stretches of land. We have a description of Hsin-an in the middle of the nineteenth century from the pen of a missionary who spent several years in it; he writes: 'The villages in the plain of San-keaou [outside the area later to become the New Territories] are almost exclusively inhabited by four clans, – Man . . ., Mak . . ., Tsang . . ., and Chang. . . . The villages inhabited by other clans are of no importance, and gradually either become absorbed in the more powerful clans, or are ruined by their hostility, and forced to remove to some other part of the country. For instance, the villagers of Hung-tiu changed their name and adopted that of the powerful clan which inhabited San-keaou. This was done

---

[1] 'Movement of Villages on Lantau Island for *Fung Shui* . . . Reasons', *Journal of the Hong Kong Branch of the Royal Asiatic Society*, vol. 3, 1963, pp. 143 f.

[2] Ho Ping-ti, *Studies on the Population of China, 1368–1953*, Cambridge, Mass., 1959, gives Fukien a population of 12 millions and Kwangtung of 16 millions in 1787, with an increase in Fukien to 13 millions and in Kwangtung to 35 millions by 1953: p. 283. The low increase in Fukien must be due to overseas emigration and movement across the Formosa Strait to Taiwan: p. 287. It will be seen that the figure of 50 millions for the population of Fukien and Kwangtung given in *Lineage Organization* at p. vii is too high. See also John D. Durand, 'The Population Statistics of China, A.D. 2–1953', *Population Studies*, vol. XIII, no. 3, March 1960, p. 251.

[3] Chen Ta, *op. cit.*, p. 23, writing of his field investigations in Fukien and Kwangtung in the mid-thirties, says that people frequently commented on the fact that large population increases had taken place in some villages and substantial decreases in others.

to extricate themselves from the endless feuds, which the aggres-
sive conduct of their neighbours enclosed them in.'[1]

Outsiders may gain a foothold in lineage territory (perhaps
first only as tenants) and, in consequence, a multilineage settlement may develop; such a heterogeneous community may survive
for a long time (as appears to be the case in the village of Nanching
as described by Yang); but then one lineage, either lately come or
long established, gets the upper hand and a single-lineage settlement emerges once more.[2] Indeed, as I have tried to illustrate
from the case of a New Territories village, the process of ex-
clusion may cut away part of the victorious lineage itself.

It may be that some of the very mixed settlements to be found
in Fukien and Kwangtung were formed by the gathering together
of elements pushed out of communities by oppression (or what
the excluded took to be oppression). Chen Ta, speaking in the
1930s of a community composed of seven villages and one town
in the Swatow region of Kwangtung and made up of people of
many different surnames, says that in the past many families must
have moved there from the surrounding area. He quotes an old
woman: 'We came here from a neighbouring *hsien* [county]
about twenty-three years ago. In our former home village we
were members of the minority and frequently ill-treated by those
who belonged to the majority of the clan. In this little community
here people do not show that kind of discrimination.'[3]

[1] Rev. Mr [Rudolf] Krone, 'A Notice of the Sanon District [i.e., Hsin-an
hsien]', Article V, *Transactions of the China Branch of the Royal Asiatic Society*,
Pt. VI, 1859, Hong Kong, 1859, pp. 91 f. I am indebted to Mr J. L. Cranmer-
Byng and Mr J. W. Hayes for telling me of the existence of Krone's informative
paper. Strangely enough, there appears to be only one copy of it in the United
Kingdom – in Cambridge University Library. As this book goes to press I am
reading the extensive reports made by Krone and his colleagues of the Rhenish
Mission on northern Hsin-an. I am hoping to publish translations from them.
They were discovered by my colleague Professor I. Schapera in the course of his
researches into the Rhenish Mission sources on southern Africa!

[2] Hsiao, *op. cit.*, pp. 327 and 663 (note 23) gives the balance between 'monoclan'
and 'multiclan' villages in Hua Hsien, Kwangtung. In a total of 398 villages 40
per cent were 'monoclan'. There were some very large 'monoclan' villages
in the area, the largest being about 10,000, but the smallest villages of this kind
'contained about a dozen clansmen each'. Krone, *op. cit.*, p. 80, says that the Punti
villages in Hsin-an sometimes numbered from 10,000 to 30,000 inhabitants. Of
course, settlements of this size were in reality composed of several villages; and
they were probably referred to as single villages because each complex was occupied by one lineage.

[3] Chen Ta, *op. cit.*, pp. 199 f.

Clearly, geomantic ideas in the Chinese south-east enshrine, explain, and justify the attachment of particular lineages to their territory. By the same token they demonstrate the unsuitability of the territory for people of other lineages. Okada Yuzuru, the Japanese sociologist, studying villages on Amoy island in 1940, found that it was said of two villages (it is not clear to me whether they were settlements belonging to one lineage or to two lineages of one surname) that their natural features were not suitable for members of other clans. Outsiders who had moved in had for the most part fallen sick, and none of them had settled down there. Even the schoolteachers from other villages returned home after school hours, never attempting to live in the village territory.[1] On the one hand, people may use unfavourable geomantic influences to explain retrospectively why they have not settled in a particular place. On the other hand, a dominant lineage may prevent or discourage outsiders from trying to establish themselves in its territory by predicting geomantic disaster for them.

Lineage settlements differ greatly in their prosperity, past and present, and in the extent to which they have lost members by migration and gained them by 'marrying in' sons-in-law and by adoption. Consequently, there is no simple relationship between the generation-depth of a lineage and its numerical size. We tend to think, as do the Chinese themselves, that a lineage is a kind of genealogical pyramid with the founding ancestor at the apex and a broad base representing the living generations. But even though population as a whole may be increasing,[2] many lineages may be able to do no more than simply replace their losses by death, and others may well, because of epidemics, poverty, and migration, diminish greatly in numbers, even to the point of extinction.

It follows that not all very deep lineages are very large. Not all shallow lineages are small. A lineage may have been long established and yet failed to be fruitful. It may have only a few generations behind it and yet have fared so well that early and universal marriage, high fertility, and adoption have brought its numbers to a bustling prosperity. The lineage in Nanching which goes

[1] 'Kinship and Village in South China: Village Life on Amoy Island' (in Japanese) in the author's *Kiso Shakai*, Tokyo, 1949. I have to express my gratitude to Professor Ch'en Ch'i-lu of the National Taiwan University who translated this interesting source of material for me. And I should like to thank Professor Okada himself for sending me a copy of his paper.

[2] Cf. p. 12 above, fn. 2.

back to the late eleventh century numbered fewer than 600 people when Yang studied it in the late 1940s. The New Territories village I have referred to has two-thirds of this population but only a third of its time-span. Obviously, a lineage which starts off small and has only a very few generations behind it (compare the groups in the village studied by Gallin) cannot have many people in it. But it does not follow that a lineage with a small population must have been in existence only a short time.[1] Disease, poverty, migration, and desertion to other lineages may keep its numbers pruned, but the generations go on increasing, in memory as well as in fact, for lack of the genealogical amnesia, discussed by anthropologists studying non-literate societies, by means of which the record of the past is tailored to fit the present.[2] Certainly, by no means all Chinese lineages kept written genealogies; probably only a minority did;[3] and in many lineages there was not even a stock of ancestor tablets to provide a genealogical framework for the past. But even without the tangible evidence of writing or tablets Chinese still count generations, so that extension in time cannot be simply translated into population size. And in this connexion it is worth noting the interesting case of the lineage discussed by Miss Pratt in which, despite the absence of an agreed genealogical framework to explain the precise relations among the segmentary divisions, 'all the males traced their common descent back to the founding ancestor sixteen generations before'.[4]

In his study of Manila Chinese, Amyot quotes some very interesting data from a clan record, published in Manila in 1953,

[1] In a review of *Lineage Organization* (*The British Journal of Sociology*, vol. xiii, no. 4, December 1962, p. 372) Miss Barbara E. Ward, commenting on the characteristics of the model A lineage, says: 'Dr Freedman might have added that it was also of shallow time-depth.' I might well have added this qualification, but I should have been wrong.

[2] Cf. *Lineage Organization*, pp. 69 ff.

[3] But it may well have been a substantial minority. In a brief survey carried out in 1956–7 of 'emigrant' communities in Ch'üan-chou, Fukien, the investigators collected 80 genealogies, some manuscript and some printed. See Chuang Wei-chi, Lin Chin-chih, and Kuei Kuang-hua, 'Investigation into the History of the Overseas Chinese of Ch'üan-chou' (in Chinese), *Hsia-men Ta-hsüeh Hsüeh-pao She-hui K'o-hsüeh Pan* (Journal of Amoy University, Section of Social Sciences), no. 1, 1957, pp. 31 ff. I should like to thank Mrs H. M. Wright for her translations of a number of articles in this journal. The investigation reported in the article cited is one of the very few field studies made in Communist China.

[4] *Op. cit.*, pp. 148 f.

which provides material on the distribution of lineages of the Hung surname in Ch'üan-chou, Fukien.[1] I shall draw on one section of this material (for Ying-ling *hsiang* of Chin-chiang *hsien*) to illustrate the great variation in time-depth and size of local settlements. In the first village listed we can see the full time-extension of Hung settlement in that area and the number of generations associated with it; but in the case of the other villages, while we may assume that the number of generations elapsed since first settlement is correct, the time-depths of settlement are clearly very rough, to say the least. (It will be noted that thirty-five generations have emerged in 950 years in the first village and thirty in only 500 years in villages 23 and 24!)

Village[2]	Years of occupation	Generations elapsed	Present Population
1	950	35	2,000
2	500	22	720
3	100	4	570
4	400	14	500
5	100	6	270
6	500	18	700
7	300	12	100
8	300	12	130
9	500	16	200
10	100	5	190
11	400	24	350
12	500	22	320
13	500	20	200
14	200	7	410
15	60	3	340
16	300	12	150
17	190	6	150
18	90	5	340
19	150	4	90
20	60	3	200
21	400	21	200
22	400	21	260
23	500	30	700
24	500	30	2,400
25	520	9	250
26	220	8	680
27	580	19	100
28	400	20	100

[1] Amyot, *op. cit.*, pp. 166 ff.
[2] *Ibid.*, p. 166. The largest population shown in this material is 14,000 (p. 169).

Village	Years of occupation	Generations elapsed	Present Population
29	400	20	50
30	400	20	220
31	400	20	50
32	400	20	50
33	400	20	90

At pp. 6 f. of *Lineage Organization* I said that 'the southeastern Chinese lineage commonly extended to about twenty-five generations in recent time'. I am more cautious now, for I am aware of the constant movement within the area and the consequent establishment of many local lineages of time-spans considerably shorter than twenty-five generations. About 1955 the District Commissioner of the New Territories sent out a questionnaire which sought information on the dates when 'surnames' first settled in their present villages and on the numbers of the generations counted since. Replies came in from a high proportion of the villages, and it is possible to get from the data a fairly clear idea of the range of lineage depth.[1] They also provide an indication of the balance between single-lineage and multilineage settlements. I shall draw two examples from these data.

The first example consists of the villages in the Sha Tau Kok area, which abuts the Chinese frontier in the eastern part of the New Territories. (I have excluded the data on the islands which fall in this area, because I am concerned here with agricultural settlements; the analysis of communities which get their living from the sea raises different problems.[2]) Twenty-six single-surname villages are listed, one of 26 generations, four of 12, six of 11, six of 10, five of 9, one of 8, two of 7, and one of 5. There are eighteen multi-surname villages, although one of them might better be classified as a single-surname settlement because only

---

[1] I am very grateful to the District Commissioner New Territories for access to this information.

[2] A Tanka fishing community in the New Territories has been exhaustively studied by Miss Barbara E. Ward. See her 'A Hong Kong Fishing Village', *Journal of Oriental Studies* (Hong Kong), vol. I, no. I, January 1954; 'Floating Villages: Chinese Fishermen in Hong Kong', *Man*, vol. LIX, art. 62, March 1959; and 'Varieties of the Conscious Model, The Fishermen of Hong Kong', in *The Relevance of Models for Social Anthropology* (= M. Banton, ed., *A.S.A. Monographs*, vol. I), London, 1965. Despite what has been often said about them, the Tanka are thoroughly Chinese in their culture, but their estrangement from the land makes for a great difference in their kinship structure.

two or three families of a second surname are reported to have remained, the rest having moved away – a single-surname settlement has perhaps almost emerged. The generation-depths of the 'surnames' found in these multi-surname settlements are as follows: one of 16 generations, two of 14, four of 13, thirteen of 12, thirteen of 11, eight of 10, five of 9, two of 8, three of 7, two of 6, two of 5, one of 4, four of 3, and two of 2. It will be seen that there is an average of three and a half surnames per village in the multi-surname settlements, although it would of course be unrealistic to count as lineages the recently established 'surnames'.

The Sha Tau Kok area is predominantly Hakka territory and it is important to note that the only very old lineage listed (of 26 generations) is in fact an outlier of the Punti (Cantonese-speaking) clan of Tang (Mandarin: Têng) whose heartland is the Yuen Long plain in the western part of the New Territories. My second example is taken from the Ping Shan area of this plain. Thirty-four villages are listed of which seven are multi-surname settlements. The twenty-seven single-surname villages show the following distribution of generation-depths: one of 29 generations, one of 28, eight of 27 (all but one of these are Tang settlements), one of 26, one of 25, two of 23, two of 22, one of 16, one of 15, one of 14, one of 11, one of 9, one of 4, two of 3, two of 2, and one of 1. In fact, the last six cases ought really to be removed from the list, for they are not deep enough to be lineages and must be far too small to be villages. Generation-depths are given only for one 'surname' in each of the multi-surname villages. They are as follows: two of 28 generations, one of 27, one of 23, two of 11, and one of 1. There is an average of just under three surnames per village in the seven multi-surname villages.[1]

These data cannot of course be fully understood unless we know the relevant population figures and the agnatic connexions between the units listed. Which of the 'surnames' are lineages, which segments of lineages? Clearly we have come to a point in the argument when we must abandon the use of the word 'lineage' in a loose sense and try to give it a meaning precise enough to help in the analysis of the complex forms assumed by

---

[1] Cf. 'The Chinese Clans and their Customs, etc.', *The Chinese and Japanese Repository*, no. XXIII, 1 June 1865, p. 282: '. . . sometimes we see 10, 13, 19, 25, or at most, 30 generations recorded on the tablets' in the ancestral halls of (presumably) coastal Kwangtung.

agnatic grouping in China. Let us take the case of the Tang settlements mentioned briefly in the last paragraph. It happens that they formed the subject of Potter's study in 1962–3, and we are able from his material to get a clear picture of the agnatic and territorial constitution of the Ping Shan Tang lineage.[1]

It is in fact made up of a cluster of eight, not seven, villages, with a total population of about three thousand, although this figure includes various non-Tang residents (servile families and recent immigrants among them). All Tang in the eight villages form a single descent group focused upon the central ancestral hall of the complex and nominally under a single lineage head, who is the oldest man in the most senior surviving generation. The relation at a lower level between territory and agnatic grouping can be seen from the example of the village of Hang Mei, the one most closely studied by Potter. Hang Mei is both a village and a sub-lineage. As a village it contains (in addition to the outsiders) 80 Tang households; but as a sub-lineage it over-flows into two neighbouring villages of the complex, where a further 32 of the households belonging to the Hang Mei sub-lineage are found. Hang Mei and its co-ordinate sub-lineages, each with its territorial base, compose the Ping Shan lineage, but this in turn is part of a wider corporate agnatic group embracing Tang lineages scattered widely in the region. The founder of Ping Shan is given in the genealogy as being one of the grand-sons of the Tang who first established himself in the county. Two of the Ping Shan ancestor's brothers founded other lineages, one at Kam Tin and the other at Tai Po (the latter being a group of Tang which will concern us later on). All the Tang local lineages tracing their descent to the first ancestor in the county have a share in an estate held in that ancestor's name.

Now, we may take the Ping Shan lineage to belong to a large class of such lineages in the New Territories – and, by extension, in southeastern China in general. Some of them, as earlier quotations will have indicated, are very much larger in numbers than the Ping Shan Tang group; the figure of 10,000, although it may be suspect as a good round Chinese number, is probably not always very misleading, and it may be recalled that Krone gave 30,000 as the upper limit for the size of Punti villages in Hsin-an county.[2] Each group of this class occupies a compact

---

[1] Potter, *P'ing Shan*. [2] Cf. p. 13 above, fn. 2.

cluster of settlements which have grown up around the original central settlement. One at least of the settlements is likely to be walled and moated, or was so fortified in the past. (The word *wai* – Mandarin: *wei* – still appears in the names of many villages in the New Territories, indicating that at some time they have been walled enclosures and may still be so today. I have calculated from the official *A Gazetteer of Place Names in Hong Kong, Kowloon and the New Territories* that of some 1,600 traditional Chinese names in the Colony as a whole, about 110 include the character for *wai*. It is important to add that not all forms of enclosure earn the description of *wai*, which usually implies the existence of a brick wall and tower; some fortifications were humbler and rougher; and not all *wai* have that word as part of their name. It will be seen, therefore, that a very considerable proportion of settlements were huddled behind their walls in pre-British times.) Traditionally at any rate, the different settlements in one complex belonged to different agnatic segments of the total group, and there may have been a further residential discrimination within each settlement such that it was divided up among segments of lower orders. To this kind of group I propose to apply the term 'local lineage'.

But it is in fact only the extreme case of the local lineage. The great majority of local lineages are much smaller and less spectacularly sited and defended. Some share their village not only with a few outsiders but also with other local lineages. What defines the whole class of local lineages, great and small, is that they are corporate groups of agnates (minus their married sisters and plus their wives) living in one settlement or a tight cluster of settlements. It will be obvious that 'local lineage' does not exhaust 'lineage'. There are two different sets of conditions in which the members of a local lineage may be linked by lineage bonds to people not living in their local community. First, as will be fairly common among poorer groups, some of the descendants of the ancestor who defines the local lineage will be resident in other local communities; we have in such cases what may conveniently be called dispersed lineages. Those of its members, forming a local lineage, who occupy the main settlement (where the ancestral hall and its associated property are likely to be found) are, so to say, the headquarters group of the dispersed lineage.

Second, a local lineage may be grouped with other local

lineages on the basis that the ancestors of these lineages are all
descended agnatically from a common ancestor, the whole unit
in turn being focused on an ancestral hall or other piece of property.
For this larger scale of group (of which we have just seen an
example in the Tang) I propose to use the term 'higher-order
lineage' because I cannot for the moment think of a more
appropriate one. (It seems to me that terms such as 'compound
lineage' and 'composite lineage'[1] suggest, wrongly, that the
unit has been formed by the banding together of local lineages.
In some cases, indeed, they may have come about in this manner,
but it is just as likely that they will have emerged by a process of
segmentation, new local lineages being formed as part of the
development by which what was once a local lineage is now
differentiated and dispersed.)

Agnation does not stop at the higher-order lineage. As every-
body knows who has read a book about China, the mere sharing
of a surname is by itself a fact of agnatic kinship. But once we get
above the level of any unit we call a lineage we are in the realm
of clanship, where lineages of like surname may be tied together
genealogically but are not members of an enduring group with
common interests and activities. The ties of clanship may be
almost devoid of significance. They may, on the other hand,
be used for genealogical reference and for forming temporary
alliances. But if several local or higher-order lineages in fact combine and establish a common ancestral hall or estate, then clanship
has once more been condensed into lineage bonds. The difference
between a system of physically dispersed segments of a single
corporation and a network of historically – or at any rate genealogically – related but independent lineages turns upon the maintenance of common property and the ritual obligations and privileges entailed in that property. If a common estate is kept up in
which the geographically distinct units continue to share, then
a total lineage exists. Otherwise the proliferated segments turn
into autonomous lineages linked only by ties of clanship.

It might be argued that there is an important difference between
clan and lineage in the ways in which they are genealogically
justified. In general terms, the genealogical information on a

---

[1] The latter term is used by G. William Skinner in 'Marketing and Social
Structure in Rural China, Part I', *The Journal of Asian Studies*, vol. XXIV, no. 1,
November 1964, p. 37.

local or higher-order lineage is relatively complete and relatively fixed; that on a clan grouping is comparatively tenuous and subject to change. I shall return to this question in a later context; what needs to be shown now is that the genealogical difference between clan and lineage is contingent, not necessary; for some of the local lineages, lacking written genealogies, have no 'demonstrated descent'[1] – indeed, their genealogical frameworks may be very much in debate, as we shall see presently – and yet they function as effectively as other, genealogically better endowed, local lineages.

Let us consider some of the ethnography. Yang provides an example which I interpret to be a case of a higher-order lineage. In Nanching the 'clan land' of the Lee was in another county, some eighty miles away, 'where the headquarters of the Lee clan were located, the clan in this village being only one of the branches. Every year the Lee clan of Nanching received over 10,000 catties of unhusked rice from the income of the headquarter's clan land. In addition, the subdivisions of the Lee clan did possess altogether about twenty mow of sacrificial land within Nanching.'[2] A wide range of relevant material is to be found in Amyot's study of the Chinese in Manila. He was able to collect a good deal of information on Ch'üan-chou, Fukien, from documentary sources and from emigrants.[3] It is worth looking, however briefly, at the evidence he presents on Hui-an county.

Amyot says that its 'several hundred villages and hamlets' are grouped into about fifty hsiang, a term which he translates as 'township'. '. . . the term hsiang may designate either a complex of villages and hamlets forming some kind of unity, or again, the largest village of this complex from which the latter derives its name. It is usually a market center. . . . An average hsiang can be crossed on foot in a couple of hours.'[4] Most of the population of Hui-an is divided among ten major surnames ('lineages'), each of which 'occupies predominantly at least one of the Hsien village complexes. There are twelve such lineage hsiang. The

---

[1] This expression is used by Morton H. Fried, 'The Classification of Corporate Unilineal Descent Groups', *Journal of the Royal Anthropological Institute*, vol. 87, pt. 1, January–June 1957. Fried classifies the Chinese descent group (*tsu*) as a lineage because it has 'demonstrated descent' (p. 26). My argument is that China has both clans and lineages, and that 'demonstrated descent' is crucial to neither.

[2] Yang, *op. cit.*, p. 42.   [3] Amyot, *op. cit.*, pp. 37 ff.   [4] *Ibid.*, p. 40.

others are shared by two or more surname groups. . . . The Ch'en lineage occupies two. . . . It has an ancestral hall in both places. Membership runs to about ten thousand distributed into six *fang* or sub-lineages.'[1] And so on. In his summary of his findings on southeastern China Amyot says that 'lineage organization is constantly associated with a specific district or *hsiang* of relatively small dimensions. . . . Considering now the spatial distribution of surname groups in relation to one another, no significant pattern appears from the point of view of social organization. Groups with the same surname can show up in ten different places. There is no immediate organizational connection between them, certainly not merely from the fact that they have the same surname. There is none even when they belong to the same lineage as sub-branches having migrated away from the founding village. Their populations do not have the same kind of interrelationship across spatially separated sub-branches as they have within the limits of one territory or between contiguous territories.'[2]

I think Amyot uses the word 'lineage' rather too vaguely, but his analysis is extremely interesting and important. The essence of it is that what I have called higher-order lineage relationships are likely to be confined to the small areas formed by *hsiang* (which 'can be crossed on foot in a couple of hours'). Amyot translates *hsiang* as 'township', but since both the Chinese and the English words have often been administrative terms, implying formal divisions laid down by governments,[3] and since the areas within which higher-order lineage systems are likely to develop may have little to do with bureaucratically dictated areas, I suggest that we refer to our crucial territories as 'vicinages'.[4]

I am able to offer another example, on a smaller scale, from Taiwan. Wolf, setting the background to his study of a village near Taipei, tells us that the villagers orient themselves towards the outside world in terms of the village's status as one of the five *lún* (a Hokkien word) which make up the 'district' of Chi-chou. This 'district' has never been recognized by the bureaucracy, but its boundaries are those which 'mark the line between the villagers' immediate private world and the larger impersonal

[1] *Ibid.*, p. 43. [2] *Ibid.*, pp. 52 f.
[3] On the meanings of the term *hsiang*, see Hsiao, *op. cit.*, pp. 11 f.
[4] I planned to use the word 'neighbourhood', but I was warned that it might carry the wrong connotations for Americans.

world of society at large'. Chi-chou appears to have been settled in the late eighteenth century by men of the surname Ong (presumably, Mandarin: Wang) and in early times the inhabitants of the 'district' made up a single lineage. In time it segmented and spread, and people of other surnames began entering the district to settle. As a result, today Chi-chou 'consists of five independent Ong lineages each of which occupies a community in which a third of their neighbors are families of another surname'. The unity of Chi-chou rests on the common origin of the Ong people, while the separate identity of each of the five *lún* is a product of the fact that it is built around a core of Ong families who make up a local lineage.[1] I take it that the five Ong local lineages together form (or formed) a higher-order lineage, which, as the dominant agnatic group in the 'district', provides it with its organizational framework.

Arguing with cogency and great scholarly elegance for the significance of marketing areas in the non-official structure of Chinese rural society, Skinner has seized upon Amyot's remark that the largest village in a *hsiang* (itself also called by that term) is usually a market centre. And he has put forward the view very persuasively that lineage organization above the level of the village depends for its conformation on the catchment area of the lowest level of market town. 'My suggestion here is that, since peasant families have much social intercourse within their standard marketing community but little outside it, interlineage ties contained within a single marketing system are likely to be perpetuated whereas bonds between localized lineages sited in different standard marketing areas tend to erode with time.' And he pushes the argument a step further, drawing on some information about a Fukien 'standard marketing community', by suggesting that 'the dominant localized lineage within a composite lineage

[1] Arthur P. Wolf, *Marriage and Adoption in a Hokkien Village*, unpublished Ph.D. thesis, Cornell Univ., September 1964. I am profoundly grateful to Professor Wolf for his gift to me of a copy of the thesis and permission to make use of it for this book. It is a remarkably original analysis of Chinese marriage and adoption, and in many ways a pioneering study of these subjects, however strange this assertion may seem in the light of the material already published. I have not plundered the material which Professor Wolf, his generosity matching his scholarship, has placed at my disposal. But I have drawn on it at a few points in my argument, limiting myself severely and hoping that the book which is now being written on the basis of the thesis will appear at about the same time as my own.

may arrogate preponderant control in the marketing community'.[1]

It may well turn out, after the matter has been fully explored, that in fact vicinage and standard marketing area are usually congruent and that they provide us with the key to understanding how local lineages are normally grouped together. There is contrary evidence (how explain, for example, that units of the higher-order lineage of which the Nanching Lee, in Yang's account, were members, were separated by eighty miles?), but it may well be that most of this evidence relates, not to lineages which are predominantly peasant in their composition, but to those whose affairs are in the hands of gentlemen and merchants of substance. It is part of Skinner's argument that men with wider political and economic horizons will operate within areas defined in relation to higher-order market centres;[2] and it may follow from this that the great lineage groupings maintained in the case of the few dominant 'surnames' in the southern part of Hsin-an county (such that local lineages very widely separated were grouped together) were dependent on the fact that the influential leaders of these local lineages had an active interest in the superior market town of Sham Chun, which now lies just to the north of the frontier between China and the Colony of Hong Kong. Some (perhaps all) of the local lineages belonging to the surnames Tang and Man (Mandarin: Wên) were members of geographically wide-ranging higher-order lineages.[3]

The Chinese term *tsu* is applied to both lineages and clans (as these terms are used by anthropologists); so too are *tsung* and *tsung-tsu*; the Chinese nouns by themselves are not unambiguous pointers to the precise nature of the groups and quasi-groups for which they are used. Yet Creel has recently argued that in ancient China the terms *hsing* and *shih* (which in modern Chinese are both translatable as 'surname') indicated precisely the distinction between clan and lineage which needs to be made in the analysis of modern Chinese agnatic organization. 'The *hsing*

[1] Skinner, *op. cit.*, pp. 36 f.   [2] *Ibid.*, p. 27.

[3] The example cited above from Wolf's work on Taiwan of a small-scale vicinage shows lineage organization working within a framework much more restricted than that of a standard marketing area; but Skinner ('Marketing and Social Structure in Rural China, Part II', *The Journal of Asian Studies*, vol. xxiv, no. 2, February 1965, p. 221) cites this case to illustrate how communities contract when marketing systems are modernized.

was a large and rather loose "common descent group", showing an attitude of solidarity which in a specific situation might or might not produce united action. But the much smaller *shih* was, in the fullest sense of Max Weber's terminology, a "corporate group".[1] Not being a sinologue and knowing very little about ancient China, I cannot say how far Creel's distinction is justified by the evidence, but it may be that if a sinologue turned a critical (and anthropologically focused) eye on the modern Chinese terminology for descent groups, he might be able to assert, as Creel has done for the ancient usage, that there is in fact a clearer linguistic distinction in Chinese between what we call clans and lineages than we have thought. (It has been suggested to me by one Chinese scholar that in some parts of China clans are *hsing* and lineages *tsu*; but I do not think that the southeastern Chinese usage of these terms would generally show this kind of distinction.) Lacking the requisite sinological knowledge, I regretfully leave this problem of terminology hanging in the air.[2]

Descent and genealogies justify both lineages and clans, but while it is easy enough to interpret the genealogy of a lineage both structurally and historically, the genealogies linking lineages together to form clans may be a puzzle. What do they do? What do they say? Why do they exist? Written genealogies embracing enormous populations and spanning a thousand or more years are by no means uncommon in China. In a recent major work Eberhard has analysed two such compilations of direct interest to students of southeastern Chinese society.[3]

In trying to understand what these giant genealogies are about, we may ask which of the following two assumptions is correct. First, the genealogies are statements of historical truth, documents for studying the geographical flow of population by the constant ramifying of agnatic branches. Second, the genealogies are retrospective constructions of the relations between lineages, making 'historical' sense of the present distribution of lineages on the ground. In reality both assumptions seem partly to be borne out. On the one hand, some of the data on the geographical movement

[1] H. G. Creel, 'The Beginnings of Bureaucracy in China: The Origin of the *Hsien*', *The Journal of Asian Studies*, vol. XXIII, no. 22, February 1964, p. 168.

[2] Mrs Hui-chen Wang Liu, *The Traditional Chinese Clan Rules*, Locust Valley, N.Y., 1959, pp. 25 ff., makes some interesting notes on this terminology.

[3] Wolfram Eberhard, *Social Mobility in Traditional China*, Leiden, 1962. Despite its general title, the book rests very heavily on the two genealogies.

of branches are supported by historical evidence of another kind. On the other hand, there are good reasons for supposing that some of the links 'established' in the genealogies are fabricated. The great genealogies are scholarly works, and the scholarship put into their compiling seems to have ensured a mixture of historical accuracy and creative imagination.

Consider the genealogy which Eberhard treats at length: the General Genealogy of the Wu Clan of Ling-nan in its latest edition (c. 1933). The Wu clan of south China is spread widely in the provinces of Kwangtung and Kwangsi. The author of the genealogy thought that all the Wu came of a single 'family' tracing its origin back into the first millennium B.C., but confined himself in his compilation to the eight 'great houses' of Wu in the two provinces just mentioned. He knew that there were in this region more Wu than he could account for genealogically, but he tried to find all the villages where Wu lived and to establish the names of their first settlers. Through Eberhard's account we can see how the compilers had to struggle to fit together various kinds of genealogical data to make a coherent system.[1]

The genealogy reaches down to the eighty-fifth generation, but the 'great houses' themselves trace back their individual origins to twenty-eight generations, in the case of the deepest, and fourteen, in the case of the shallowest.[2] All the 'great houses' are arranged to show how branches ramify within them, but while the compilers 'constructed a frame which would accept all Wus now existing, disregarding their ethnic origin', there are other branches 'which the genealogists could not integrate into this framework, and where they admit that the degree of relationship remains unclear'.[3] Each of the 'great houses' has by further ramification produced a number of settlements, some concentrated, some scattered, and at this level of the genealogy it is possible that the 'facts' are historical: 'We have no reason to doubt the assertion of the genealogy that each of these settlements was created by a member of the main house, or a member of a known daughter settlement.'[4]

A genealogy such as this is concerned with what some anthropologists prefer to call fission. That is to say, it aims to record, or to 'reconstruct', the manner in which branches send out further branches, each resulting new unit being independent of its parent

[1] *Op. cit.*, pp. 50–8.   [2] *Ibid.*, p. 57.   [3] *Ibid.*, p. 67.   [4] *Ibid.*, p. 118.

unit and only potentially forming with it a system of articulated groups. The 'great houses' and their subdivisions are not groupings for action (although they may in some circumstances come to be); they presuppose common origin and not joint interest; they explain 'history' and not 'sociology'. In contrast, within the local or higher-order lineage the genealogical justifications of division refer to segmentation: how within the largest unit lesser and lesser units are contained in an unfolding series, all units being corporate and distinct precisely because they are part of a system of units.[1] The significance of the genealogical background to segmentation is simple enough to grasp. What motivates the production of a panorama of fission?

There must be several answers to this question. The genealogy may look back to an ultimate origin of glory. (The Wu clan 'came from the ancient, mythical emperor Chuan-hsü'.[2] Genealogies often begin thus proudly and remotely.) In chronicling many generations and enumerating vast numbers of men, the genealogy must of necessity document some success for the clan: somebody, somewhere, at some time has been a scholar, held office, or otherwise brought honour to his agnates. (When lineage ancestral halls put up boards showing high honours and examination successes, they need not confine themselves to the achievements of their own members; the general genealogy provides them with evidence of clan achievements on which they can draw.) But the general genealogy also makes a bid for prestige on the grounds of sheer numbers. A line has prospered and spread. So that while the scholars who edit and compile the genealogy fulfil a pious obligation in acknowledging the root from which the clan sprang, at the same time they bask in the warmth of an intrinsic virtue demonstrated by fruitfulness. Filial piety, hunger for prestige, and scholarly appetite for writing history converge to produce the great genealogy.

The need to form effective social relationships among them may stimulate the members of scattered lineages to produce a general genealogy. Contrariwise, once the general genealogy is given it may lead people to base their social relationships on it. Charter and grouping may interact. Individuals from lineages linked in a clan framework may make political claims on one another; if a man needs protection or favour from the bureau-

[1] *Lineage Organization*, chaps. 4 and 6.　　[2] Eberhard, *op. cit.*, p. 58.

cracy he may perhaps find it through a clansman and be able to cite a valid claim to it in genealogical terms. But, more significantly, the genealogical arrangement of lineages into wider and wider clan groupings may furnish the basis for joint action between them. And it is at this point that the logic of Chinese genealogy may go beyond the limit of state tolerance.[1]

The state cherished kinship. Family and lineage were morally good and politically useful. They laid the foundations for proper social attitudes and relieved the state of a great part of the burden of social control. But let agnatic kinship come to represent too strong a concentration of local power and the state was on the alert, for the delicate balance between people and government seemed to be threatened. The useful could turn into the dangerous. If lineages took steps towards forming effective clan-groupings, danger might be sniffed in the air; the benign encouragement of limited agnation was then converted into the wrathful disapproval of its organizational extension.

In the first place, the state was suspicious of claims to high ancestry. 'One kind of undesirable behavior exhibited by some clans was making "fraudulent claims" concerning ancestry. Apparently desiring to enhance their prestige or extend their influence, these kinship groups resorted to the dubious expedient of claiming direct descent from well-known celebrated personages (real or imagined) of antiquity.'[2] If the genealogies smacked of dangerous pretension the state might bring its machinery of repression into play. Hsiao cites a late eighteenth-century case of genealogical records being destroyed by imperial order when the local magistrate reported that they contained ' "outrageous and

---

[1] Cf. the south Chinese case given (improbably in a book with this title) in E. W. Burgess and H. J. Locke, *The Family, from Institution to Companionship*, 2nd edn., N.Y., 1953, pp. 33 f. The Chu lineage, descended from an ancestor who lived some 300 years ago, are the sole occupants of X Village, which is one of six villages making up 'the Chang River clan of Chus'. Besides this group of Chu lineages there is 'the South River clan of Chus with nine villages and the Stone River clan of Chus with fifteen villages. . . . The Chu county clan has no definite organization.' They combine only in some extraordinary circumstance. Some fifty years ago a Chu with a grievance against the magistrate of a neighbouring county complained to the members of the Chang River Chu 'and they decided to take revenge'. Chu men from two 'districts' of the county came together and about a thousand people marched to seize the offending magistrate and haul him off to the prefect, who consented to the demand that the magistrate be dismissed.

[2] Hsiao, *op. cit.*, pp. 351 f.

seditious" statements which implied that the kinship group in question had its origin in the imperial family of the Han dynasty'.[1] To lay claim to great ancestry was not only an illegitimate arrogation of status; it might be the first step towards making a political claim on the basis of the status.

Again, the establishment of ancestral halls and common estates, good things in themselves, ceased to be tolerable if they were made the foci of large higher-order lineages. 'When local inhabitants realized that organization spelled influence or power and that the extent of power varied proportionally to the size of the clan organization, they were soon persuaded to extend their kinship groups, by fraudulent means if necessary, and to build "common ancestral halls" as a visible symbol and operational base of their groups.'[2] Worse still, if people of one surname but who 'did not actually belong to the same clan' set up ancestral halls, official anger was the greater.[3] Hsiao cites a number of imperial edicts which thundered against large-scale agnatic organization: it was fraudulent, conducive to banditry, and subversive of peace in the countryside.[4] The Confucian values of kinship having been carried a step further than a Confucian state could tolerate, the clan or higher-order lineage became criminal and its genealogy treason.

The official objections to 'fraudulent' genealogies are, it seems to me, best viewed as political reactions to what were imagined to be political threats; they were not simply the cries of an outraged historical conscience wounded by the genealogical distortion of the past. The attempts to form wider and wider groupings of agnates is perfectly consistent with the logic of Chinese patriliny, and the invention or discovery of genealogical justifications for them was unacceptable to officialdom only because it implied a political threat. D. C. Twitchett, surveying the development of 'clan' organization from Sung times on, has written: 'The new respect for the clan organization which arose in Sung times led first to an increased sense of obligation towards the clan community on the part of its members, then to the proliferation of clan institutions . . ., and gradually, to an ever-widening conception of what constituted the clan – a conception which ended in the absurdity of many clans from Kwangtung and Kwangsi claiming

---

[1] *Ibid.*, p. 352.   [2] *Ibid.*, *loc. cit.*   [3] *Ibid.*, pp. 352 f.
[4] *Ibid.*, pp. 354 f. Hsiao also deals with genealogies at pp. 333 f.

as clansmen all local residents with the same surname.'[1] It seems to me that what Professor Twitchett is discussing can be called absurd only if we start from assumptions about the need for genealogies to be historically true or if we are infected across time and distance by the official Chinese panic in the face of massive social combinations.

The study of Chinese clan and lineage genealogies from a sociological point of view has barely begun. The few people engaged in exploiting the material tend to look at genealogies merely as sources of demographic, institutional, and biographical data – in short, as texts of social history. A genealogy is much more than that, as we can see. It is a set of claims to origin and relationships, a charter, a map of dispersion, a framework for wide-ranging social organization, a blueprint for action. It is a political statement – and therefore a perfect subject for the anthropologist.[2]

I should like to return now to the question of lineage and settlement patterns. I have assumed that virtually all villages in Fukien and Kwangtung are highly nucleated. Except where post-war immigrants have scattered their huts, the villages of the New Territories nearly always conform to the standard pattern. The houses in the large settlements are densely packed; in walled villages they form blocks on what look like the streets of a miniature rectangular town. Even a small village usually has streets which divide up groups of terrace houses.[3] It is interesting,

[1] 'The Fan Clan's Charitable Estate, 1050–1760', in David S. Nivison and Arthur F. Wright, eds., *Confucianism in Action*, Stanford, Calif., 1959, pp. 131 f.

[2] In the West, Chinese genealogies have recently been studied by Eberhard, *op. cit.*; Twitchett, *op. cit.*, and 'Documents on Clan Administration, I: The Rules of Administration of the Charitable Estate of the Fan Clan', *Asia Major*, n.s., vol. VIII, pt. I, 1960; Mrs Hui-chen Wang Liu, 'An Analysis of Chinese Clan Rules: Confucian Theories in Action', in Nivison and Wright, eds., *op. cit.*, and *The Traditional Chinese Clan Rules*. Otto B. van der Sprenkel has been drawing on genealogies in connexion with his studies of the civil service; see his 'The Geographical Background of the Ming Civil Service', *Journal of the Economic and Social History of the Orient*, vol. IV, pt. 3, December 1961, p. 315. I have also seen his paper 'New Light on the Chinese Gentry Clan from Genealogical Registers', mimeographed paper, Anthropological Section of A.N.Z.A.A.S., Perth, 1959. A general guide to Chinese genealogical materials is to be found in Akigoro Taga, *An Analytic Study of Chinese Genealogical Books* (in Japanese), Toyo Bunko Publications, series A, no. 45, Tokyo, 1960. I am greatly indebted to Professor Ch'en Ch'i-lu for his having translated parts of this work for me.

[3] Cf. Thomas R. Tregear, *A Survey of Land Use in Hong Kong and the New Territories*, Hong Kong, 1958, pp. 52 ff. Plate 51 in E. A. Gutkind, *Revolution of*

therefore, to discover that there appears to be one area of Kwangtung in which a quite different pattern of settlement has emerged.
In Shun-tê, which is (or at least was) the centre of the Kwangtung
silk industry, and where nearly every inhabitant was engaged in
some way in producing silk and 70 per cent of the total land area
was given over to the mulberry, 'the disseminated pattern of rural
settlement predominates in the midst of what is otherwise a
region of rural villages'. The farm houses 'stand alone and isolated'.[1] It would be interesting to know what consequences in
social organization flow from this unusual pattern. I suspect that
lineage organization and the system of land tenure must have been
of a different order; and it may be no accident that Shun-tê was
the home of a movement ('Girls who do not go to the family')
in which young women, after unconsummated marriage, set
themselves up in special houses to lead an independent female
existence.[2] Independent wage-earning in sericulture, relative
lack of control over women by their men, and a weak form of
lineage organization may prove (if we can succeed in getting
closer to the facts) to be three facets of an unusual, and therefore
informative, variant of society in southeastern China. (I am not,
of course, saying that lineage organization was uniformly weak in
Shun-tê. This was clearly not the case, since we know from Chen
Han-seng's work that the proportion of 'clan land to cultivated
area' was in fact very high – 60 per cent – in this county.[3] But the
figure is a general one and may tell us little about the precise parts
of Shun-tê where both the dispersed pattern of settlement and the
peculiar marriage system were to be found – for we must assume

Environment, London, 1946, shows how Kwangtung houses may be huddled
together. In an area of Fukien province the walled villages, typically rectangular,
become circular: 'Occasionally you see one of massive proportions, being in some
instances 600 feet in circumference, sixty feet high, and walls ten feet thick.' –
Philip Wilson Pitcher, *In and About Amoy*, Shanghai and Foochow, 1909, p. 45.
Photographs of a circular walled village in Yung-ting, Fukien, at the present time
will be found in plates 131 and 132 in Andrew Boyd, *Chinese Architecture and
Town Planning, 1500 B.C.–A.D. 1911*, Chicago, 1962. See J. J. M. De Groot,
The Religious System of China, vol. II, Leiden, 1894, plate XVI, facing p. 771,
for an illustration of a walled and moated village in (presumably) southeastern
Fukien. And note De Groot's comment, p. 771: 'Now-a-days, fortified villages
surrounded by moats or walls are the exception in China, and to be found in those
parts of the Realm where feuds and strifes are rife between different clans.'

[1] Glenn T. Trewartha, 'Field Observations on the Canton Delta of South
China', *Economic Geography*, vol. XV, no. 1, 1939, pp. 8 f.

[2] See e.g. Olga Lang, *Chinese Family and Society*, New Haven, 1946, pp. 108 f.

[3] *Agrarian Problems*, p. 34; cf. *ibid.*, pp. 36 f.

that they were very unlikely to have fallen neatly within the boundaries of a county and to have covered its extent.)[1]

In the second chapter of *Lineage Organization* I dealt with certain aspects of land tenure, stressing the significance of holdings by lineages and their segments. Land was the most important material focus of any agnatically constituted group. The general picture of land tenure in the region we are concerned with has been filled in historically by the data in Hsiao's *Rural China*[2] and added to ethnographically by Yang's information on Nanching and some of its neighbouring villages. The latter source has the advantage of showing us how the traditional land system was working on the eve of the advent of the Communist regime.[3]

Hsiao rightly puts emphasis on the connexion between status-making and the creation or enlargement of lineage estates. 'The institution or augmentation of clan property was often regarded by successful men as the crowning achievement of their careers.' He proceeds·to cite evidence drawn from local gazetteers. 'Ch'en Chang, a *sheng-yuan* scholar of Tung-kuan (Kwangtung), did not do well in the provincial examinations but had a good deal of success in business. When he had eventually amassed a considerable fortune, he remarked with satisfaction: "This will enable me to realize my ambition!" Thereupon he bought additional ritual land for his clan and built a new ancestral hall. T'ang Yuan-liang, a trader who became rich and purchased an official title of the fifth rank, constructed in his native village in Hua Hsien (Kwangtung) a shrine for the "first ancestor" of his clan and gathered the village gentry to draw up a set of community regulations for the guidance of his kinsmen.'[4] And so on. But while Hsiao notes how social status and control of lineage affairs were bound up with the institution of estates,[5] he fails to show that landed property was used to differentiate within the lineage between groups of

---

[1] Settlement patterns in China have not been well studied. A brief survey is to be found in Hartmut Scholz, 'The Rural Settlements in the Eighteen Provinces of China', *Sinologica*, vol. III, no. 1, 1951. Skinner, 'Marketing and Social Structure. . . . Pt. II', pp. 196 ff., has recently made some extremely important points on the typical modes of settlement formation.

[2] Pp. 335–8.   [3] *A Chinese Village*, pp. 40–53.   [4] *Op. cit.*, p. 335.

[5] 'At any rate two things are clear: first, ritual land was invariably instituted by members of a clan who enjoyed gentry status and possessed some wealth; second, the control or management of the clan property was usually placed in the hands of propertied and privileged clansmen.' – *op. cit.*, p. 337.

unequal status.[1] True: 'The ancestral hall and ritual land complex was correlated with the economic circumstances of the localities in question.' Where people were poor, halls and lineage land were not likely to be so much in evidence.[2] But in rich lineages with extensive ritual estates there was, as I have argued, a further correlation: between the standing of a segment and the importance of its own estate, such that the distribution of common estates within a lineage was an index of the differential power and social status of their respective owning segments.

In Nanching, collectively owned land was of three kinds: 'clan', education, and temple land. In all, being about eighty *mow* in extent, it accounted for only 6·2 per cent of the village land under cultivation. But the low figure for 'clan' land is to some degree explained by the fact that the common land on which the big 'clan' in Nanching could draw was in another county, some eighty miles away, 'the subdivisions' of the 'clan' holding a mere twenty *mow* in the village itself. Yang comments that Nanching was unusual in its low figure for collective land, pointing out that a village only two miles away had some 70 per cent of its total cultivated area under 'clan' ownership in 1948, and that 'clan' land 'averaged about 30 per cent of all the cultivated land in the whole Panyu County in which Nanching was located . . .' It would seem that the Wong 'clan', now holding a mere thirty *mow* of 'clan' land, once had much larger common estates; but 'according to the elders, . . . different crises befalling the clan during the past century had led to the sale of most of the land to defray emergency expenses.' And discussing the matter more generally, Yang says that, while the value set on retaining common land was very high, for both economic reasons and reasons of prestige, it was nevertheless at times disposed of, 'especially by clans of declining economic and organizational strength such as the Wongs'.[3]

This last point needs to be underlined. While a common estate was intended to be kept for all time, we must assume that, just as new estates could come into existence or be augmented, so

[1] Cf. *Lineage Organization*, pp. 48 f.   [2] Hsiao, *op. cit.*, p. 336.
[3] Yang, *op. cit.*, pp. 42 f. At p. 47 Yang refers to another neighbouring village, some four miles from Nanching, in which about half the total cultivated area was the common land of one 'clan'. Chen Han-seng, *op. cit.*, p. 32, gives the percentages of 'clan' land in total cultivated area for 10 'representative' villages in P'an-yü, Kwangtung. The average percentage is 35, but the range is 6 to 75.

old ones were constantly being reduced or dismantled. The fortunes of any estate-holding unit (a lineage or lineage-segment) rose and fell. Hsiao seems to lean to the view that the disintegration of lineage estates was an aspect of the decline of lineage organization in the nineteenth century.[1] But I can see no reason for not assuming that common estates were always unstable. (And I may add, since Hsiao speaks of the ruins of ancestral halls as a further sign of lineage decay in the last century,[2] that derelict and apparently neglected halls must have been a permanent feature of the system, partly because some lineages always disappeared, and partly because – as my experience in the New Territories has suggested to me – the Chinese do not regularly maintain their halls but merely renovate them. Between one renovation and the next – the interval being determined by the need to accumulate the necessary funds – a hall gets shabbier and shabbier, even to the point of dilapidation, and although still in use may wrongly suggest to a casual observer that it has ceased to be of interest to its owners.)

The figures for common lands in Fukien and Kwangtung are often very impressive,[3] as in the case of the two villages near Nanching, but, having seen something of the land records of the New Territories, I would now suggest that the data given in the various published sources may well understate the extent to which land was held on other than individual tenure. Below the level of the lowest ancestral hall segment there might be many smaller land 'trusts', designed to benefit small groups of people descended from a close common ancestor and subject to rapid disintegration. Precisely because these smaller common estates were not attached to ancestral halls, they lacked the ritual commitment which, in the case of the lands attached to halls, could act as some brake on dismantling. In other words, we cannot understand the differential development of minor segments within the lineage unless we take account of the perpetual ebb and flow of small 'trusts' – a movement which cannot be studied in the literature but only in a systematic collection of land records. Those in the land offices of the New Territories provide an opportunity. (They are not by themselves adequate, but they offer a set of clues to be followed up in the field.)

[1] Hsiao, *op. cit.*, pp. 358 ff.   [2] *Ibid.*, p. 358.
[3] Cf. *Lineage Organization*, pp. 11 f.

3

Land has a further bearing on lineage structure that I have not hitherto considered. Large settlements could continue to develop only when it was possible to reach the furthest fields within an economic time. Where, in the absence of large stretches of cultivable land in the immediate village area, people wanted to make new fields, they had to set up house elsewhere. And in broken agricultural country, villages (and ultimately with them local lineages) must of necessity have been small. It follows from this argument that in the course of the settlement of the region the early occupation of the best continuous stretches of land made it difficult for later comers to build their villages into equally large units. Once all the good land was taken up, a new local lineage could not normally expect to expand to great size, and the general picture in the contemporary New Territories suggests how date of first settlement, agricultural advantage, and size of local lineage are connected in such a manner as to distribute the great Punti local lineages on the rice plains and the smaller local lineages, both Punti and Hakka, by and large on poorer land.[1] The picture is, however, only rough; original settlers may have yielded their place to later arrivals, as we have seen, and smaller lineages may often have wedged themselves in between larger neighbours; but the special agricultural advantage of the best lands has clearly favoured the growth on them of the traditionally largest and most powerful New Territories local lineages. The topography of the New Territories is in fact so differentiated that one can see quite clearly how the smaller settlements may have been limited by their hilly terrain and the larger ones able to spread out in the broader valleys. And in these fertile valleys the big common estates were built up, as both the result and the cause of large local lineage populations.[2]

The suitability of the terrain explains in some measure how large local lineages came into existence. As I have already argued, we must assume that it was the ambition of every local lineage to

[1] Cf. Charles J. Grant, *The Soils and Agriculture of Hong Kong*, Hong Kong [1960?], pp. 114 ff.; K. M. A. Barnett, 'The People of the New Territories', in J. M. Braga, compiler, *Hong Kong Business Symposium, A Compilation of Authoritative Views on the Administration, Commerce and Resources of Britain's Far Eastern Outpost*, Hong Kong, 1957; and S. F. Balfour, 'Hong Kong before the British', *T'ien Hsia Monthly* (Shanghai), vol. XI, nos. 4–5, 1941. And on the general point cf. Eberhard, *op. cit.*, p. 277.

[2] Cf. *Lineage Organization*, pp. 127 f. And cf. Skinner, 'Marketing and Social Structure. . . . Pt. II', pp. 198 ff.

rid its territory of other such units, unless it needed them as tenants and clients. The members of a successfully installed local lineage were driven on by the desire to expand their strength (of which manpower for fighting was an important component) up to the limits imposed on them by the extent of their agricultural land. But, of course, while in this fashion local lineages depended for their size on their terrain, the lack of large continuous areas of land could not inhibit the growth of dispersed and higher-order lineages. On the contrary, it promoted it. When local lineage land became scarce, some men moved away, perhaps to the next valley. For a time they probably remained members of their home lineage; a dispersed lineage had come into being. After a while, if they prospered, their descendants might come to constitute a new local lineage on their own, now forming a higher-order lineage along with those in the original settlement. Segmentation had taken place. But the very conditions leading to segmentation could also produce fission. If on leaving their home settlement men had to move so far that it was difficult or even impossible to keep in touch with those left behind; and if, moreover, the original settlement was so poor that its ancestral property was not worth maintaining an interest in; then the local lineage in the home settlement, instead of proliferating segments, lost members by fission. Naturally enough, we come back to the question of vicinages. Migration within a restricted area was likely to lead to the multiplication of local lineages grouped together in higher-order lineages. Movement far afield produced a definitive break which could be repaired only when, the scattered local lineages having prospered exceptionally, they formed themselves into a higher-order lineage on a geographical scale much wider than that dictated for their humbler neighbours by the limits of the vicinage.

To conclude this discussion of agnatic grouping I want to return to the local lineage in order to deal with its internal differentiation in genealogical structure. In *Lineage Organization*[1] I hazarded the guess – it could not be more, given the nature of the evidence I was then using – that segmentation was likely to be asymmetrical when the lineage was so differentiated that it embraced groups of unequal social status. From what I have seen of local lineages in the New Territories I think my guess was

[1] P. 49.

substantially correct. (It certainly seems to be richly confirmed by Potter's analysis of Ping Shan.) A segment may emerge which marks out a special identity for its members in contrast to the other members of the larger segment which encompasses them all, even though these other members are not likewise organized in a formal segment. We are presented with an irregular segmentary pattern now more clearly recognized in the anthropological literature than it was a few years ago. Evans-Pritchard's classical work on the Nuer[1] set anthropological minds working on systems of symmetrical segmentation and exercised a dominating influence on ideas about lineages. *The Nuer* was concerned with a society in which social homogeneity and the absence of political centralism could be shown to be associated with a kind of political and legal order made possible by the balancing of segments. The people who gave their name to the book were converted into a model to which the accounts of other peoples were assimilated. But the newer work on lineages in centralized political systems has led to an understanding of how, when power is exercised from a centre, a different conformation of segments appears.

In a recent textbook of social anthropology the 'lineage system based on the principle of segmental opposition' is sharply contrasted with that 'based on the principle of the spinal cord'.[2] In this latter form of lineage, 'organization . . . centers around a specific piece of property. It forms a single line with various sublineages tying in at various points of the line. . . . The organization usually centers around a kingship or around some other piece of indivisible heritable property.'[3] In the diagram used to illustrate the form of such a system, a main line is shown from which other lines branch off, and from which in turn yet others branch off, in an irregular fashion. 'In the lineage system of the spinal-cord type, built around an office or a piece of property, one lineage is senior in wealth, status and rank, and the others hook into the main line of descent.'[4] It is clear that while this characterization of a second major class of lineages catches some of the features of the Chinese system, it is not completely satisfactory. It assumes

---

[1] E. E. Evans-Pritchard, *The Nuer, A Description of the Modes of Livelihood and Political Institutions of a Nilotic People*, Oxford, 1940.
[2] Paul Bohannan, *Social Anthropology*, N.Y., 1963, pp. 137 ff.
[3] *Ibid.*, p. 138.   [4] *Ibid.*, pp. 138 f.

the necessity for a central trunk in relation to which all other lines are branches. There is no such trunk in the Chinese system. In fact, the imagery drawn from trees is not suitable to it. So far from the lesser (that is, socially inferior) units ramifying from the trunk, the greater units draw away from the lesser. They create a separate identity for themselves around a newly established piece of property. The property of a unit is its focus, but lesser foci can come into being for smaller units not arranged in a set order. The essential point about the Chinese case is that political and economic power, generated either within or outside the lineage itself, urges certain groups to differentiate themselves as segments and provides them with the material means to persist as separate entities through long periods of time – as long, that is to say, as their common property is held intact. How far this interpretation of the Chinese system is correct the results of future detailed research will be able to say. Except for my abbreviated observations in the New Territories I cannot yet add substantially to what I said on the matter in *Lineage Organization*. (Nanching might well have proved an interesting source of data, but Yang is in fact vague about the segmentary order of the lineages in the village, for he speaks of the main ancestral halls of the two chief lineages and then merely refers en passant to the 'many small ancestral halls set up by the subdivisions'.[1])

There is, however, one modification to be made to my earlier treatment of the subject. As I have already said in referring to land tenure, the New Territories material shows that while the hierarchy of ancestral halls is a hierarchy of segments, in fact below the level of the lowest segment based on an ancestral hall there may well be lesser land-owning segments. These, because they are not anchored to ancestral halls, tend to be unstable. If their common property is dispersed they are in effect erased from history, and we cannot know about them retrospectively except in so far as the land 'trusts' are recorded in official registers. The members of erstwhile segments of this kind appear in a written genealogy as collections of individuals with nothing to indicate that they are in any way different from other collections of individuals which have never formed property-based units.

It will be convenient now to review an aspect of the two models,

---

[1] Yang, *op. cit.*, pp. 78 f. Potter, *P'ing Shan*, has very full data on asymmetrical lineage segmentation and estates.

A and Z, which I proposed in *Lineage Organization*.[1] In model A the community is relatively undifferentiated in social status and segmentation is rudimentary. A great number of New Territories local lineages seem to come close to this model. They would have come closer if the model had provided (as I now think it should have done) for some degree of segmentation on the basis of common estates not linked to ancestral halls. It is worth going back to Miss Pratt's material on the New Territories Hakka village she studied. The local lineage there, it will be remembered, is divided into three units centred on ancestral halls. The interesting feature of these three sub-lineages, as we may call them for convenience, is that the genealogical relationship between them is not agreed in the lineage as a whole. 'According to the largest numerical group . . ., there were originally two brothers . . . who settled in the valley, but after some time they quarrelled . . . and set up their own lineage halls. . . . Then some fifty years ago . . ., a small group hived off from that of the younger brother and set up their own lineage hall. . . . According to this group they are really descended from the elder brother, and the younger brother left the village to settle in the local market town. (When asked to trace their genealogy they jump from the generation of the fathers of the men at present living in the village straight back to the founders.) A third version . . . is given by the last group in the village, who claim that they originally owned all the valley and the other people came as landless dependants but have gradually usurped their masters' position until they became the dominant group. . . . There was, however, no open conflict between [the sub-lineages] for the story would only be told when no one of the other groups was present.'[2] Since there is neither a written genealogy nor any oral genealogy going back through all links to the founders, the three versions of descent can co-exist. Each version makes a claim to high status for one sub-lineage at the expense of the other two. But it would appear that the rival versions are never brought to a confrontation. We are in fact dealing with a local lineage something like model A; the equality of its members is reinforced by suppressing public discussion of the relative genealogical status of the primary segments. The fact that there are ancestral halls for each of the sub-lineages (and not simply a hall for the lineage as a whole) may perhaps mean that

[1] Pp. 131 ff.   [2] Pratt, *op. cit.*, pp. 148 f.

formerly the lineage, being then better off, had been launched on a career of asymmetrical segmentation which was later arrested by a decline into poverty. (It might at first sight appear from what Miss Pratt writes that the lineage is a segment of a wider unit, for we are told that at the New Year all the men of the village go 'to the lineage hall in a village across the valley, where they claim their ancestors originally lived.'[1] But Miss Pratt tells me that the people in this other village are not agnates of the inhabitants of the first village, so that the latter is in fact a self-contained lineage with a main and three sub-lineage ancestral halls.[2])

There are many poor and small lineages in the New Territories (and presumably throughout the region), and we must be prepared to find that genealogical vagueness is common among them. What light does this matter throw on Chinese agnation? Miss Pratt herself, at the end of her paper, puts forward one possible point of view. Having laid great stress on the importance of adoption into the lineage from outside, she goes on to say: 'In spite of its outward appearance, which deluded many early writers into assuming that the Chinese descent groups were a pure form of patrilineal lineage, other principles could and did come into operation. I am not trying to decry the patrilineal nature of these groups, but suggesting that they were centred on the idea of common descent rather than in actual genealogy.'[3] But in reality few unilineal systems are likely to be based on 'actual genealogy'. Genealogy is the tracing or creating of links between individuals and groups in such a way as to arrange them in a coherent framework in accordance with accepted principles of descent. Slaves and other outsiders get absorbed into a system and are allotted genealogical positions. What is true of Miss Pratt's village is true everywhere, at least where genealogies are not written down.

But many Chinese genealogies are put into writing, and one naturally asks how they cope with 'anomalies'. The first and most obvious point to make is that competing versions of the segmentary order, such as those described by Miss Pratt, are impossible

---

[1] *Ibid.*, p. 149.
[2] This is presumably evidence of a case in which the local lineage has been completely eliminated from its home settlement. The new lineage across the valley, probably having begun as an offshoot and being a potential new local lineage, has in fact ended up by becoming the successor local lineage in default of other survivors.   [3] Pratt, *op. cit.*, p. 158.

when the genealogy is recorded, for one version of a public lineage genealogy must be generally acceptable. I am still under the same impression that I was formerly[1] that the written genealogy of a local lineage (but not of a higher-order lineage or clan) was more or less immune to fudging. If a man was adopted then his special status was likely to be noted. A written genealogy may commit many sins of omission (consigning ignominious men to oblivion), but it is unlikely in the case of a local lineage to be allowed to carry a positive statement of untruth.[2] It follows therefore that, while on the one hand a local lineage armed with a written genealogy looks more lineage-like in that it commands a complete (or virtually complete) knowledge of the steps of descent from a founder to the present generation, on the other hand it is also in a sense less patrilineal than a local lineage lacking a written genealogy, for it is deprived of the means of rephrasing anomalies in the 'true language' of patrilineal descent.

[1] *Lineage Organization*, pp. 70 ff.

[2] Eberhard, *Social Mobility*, pp. 46 ff., presents some interesting material on the accuracy of written genealogies. It is clear that lineages differ both in their practices of recording and in their efficiency in gathering in the data they consider fit to be recorded.

2

Family

The study of the Chinese lineage is not the study of Chinese kinship, even though it embraces a great deal of it. No more is it the study of Chinese family organization, but in fact there are several aspects and problems of the family which are highly relevant to the lineage, especially in regard to its internal differentiation and the modes of its linkage with other lineages. I turn now to these questions, opening the discussion by an appeal to what Yang says about the family in the village of Nanching.

There the family 'where parents and all married sons maintained a common unit of living was in a minority . . ., occurring mainly among the wealthy'. The 'size of the family increased with the accumulation of wealth'. Poverty and disease kept the families of the humbler villagers down to small numbers: 'the poor considered it fortunate if they were able to raise two children to maturity out of six or seven live births.'[1] But if in fact a poor family was lucky enough to have several married sons, one of them would continue to live with the parents and the rest set up households of their own, 'thus creating a three-generation family and several two-generation conjugal families counting the married sons' children'.[2] The pattern is very familiar to us. The poor raise few children to maturity, the rich many. Among the poor, marriage brings into the domestic family merely one bride in each generation; among the rich it brings in several. The typical (usual) family is small and morphologically either elementary or stem; the ideal family is 'joint' – and rare.

This is not only a summary of the family in Nanching but also a general statement about the family in China. The units which, so to say, create human beings and provide the personnel for manning the wider institutions, the lineage among them, have certain demographic properties that shape agnatic grouping. Poor men, if they marry at all, marry late; consequently, the

[1] Yang, *op. cit.*, pp. 17 ff.　　　　　　　　[2] *Ibid.*, pp. 81 f.

generations in a poor lineage or segment are chronologically slowed down. The members of a rich lineage or segment produce men of any given numbered generation (which is known both by counting in a written or oral genealogy, and by the middle characters of formal personal names[1]) earlier than do their counterparts in humbler lineages or segments. Ritual headships, based on seniority in generation, naturally tend to fall to men in less prosperous units, but the membership of rich units is greater than that of poor, so that on the basis of size alone the better-off local lineage in a higher-order lineage or better-off segment in a local lineage enjoys one of the means to dominate co-ordinate units within the same group. Very poor units run the risk of dying out altogether, leaving their rights in lineage property to be enjoyed by the fortunate survivors. Again, by being greater in their membership and their economic resources, richer units segment at a faster rate than their less fortunate counterparts; they set up ancestral halls and land 'trusts' which not only confer prestige and material benefit on their members but also mark them off in their social status and life-chances from their less happily placed agnates.

In *Lineage Organization*[2] I discussed factors underlying the differences between, as it were, rich and poor versions of the Chinese family. There is certainly no need to go over exactly the same ground again, but it may be possible to get a clearer perspective on the differences involved by considering schematically how various forms of the family may be relative to different cycles of development and to different phases of these cycles.[3]

A poor family might in the extreme be unable to raise a son to marriageable age and ensure that he stay at home to recreate the domestic unit. The chances were that at most one son would marry and continue the family in the same house. As soon as this son begot a child three generations were present, but the senior generation, represented by the elderly parents, were very unlikely to see a fourth emerge. As soon as these parents died a two-generation family appeared again. The process was repeated: elementary family grew to stem and was reduced once more to elementary. Even though there might be two married brothers

[1] See *Lineage Organization*, p. 7. [2] Pp. 27 ff.
[3] Anthropologists will not need to be referred to Jack Goody, ed., *The Developmental Cycle in Domestic Groups*, Cambridge, 1958; others might well be.

at any stage in the evolution of a family, they rarely lived together, with the consequence that no joint family appears in the typical cycle.

A rich family produced several sons and retained them, perhaps adding to their number by adoption. The sons remained in an undivided family as long as the parental generation survived. And since these sons married young and the seniors might live long, a joint family of four generations could appear. When the senior generation had gone, the family was partitioned among the men in the next generation. One of these men might then already be in a position to preside over a joint family of his own, having two married sons living with him. Another might become the head of a stem family. A third, being most recently married, might form an independent family along with his wife and children. But if high social status was to be maintained, then the stem and elementary families resulting from the division of the joint family would in turn grow into joint families as quickly as possible. It follows that the elementary and stem families in this 'rich' cycle are temporary stages in the development of joint families. In contrast, the elementary and stem families in the 'poor' cycle are repetitive and final: they cannot broaden out into more complex units.

It is important to ask why partition occurred as each generation of a joint family died off. In law a son was not supposed to separate himself from the family estate against the wishes of his parents; during their lifetime he could take out his share of the family property only if they agreed. In practice this kind of secession sometimes occurred. The answer to the question must be looked for in the complex of relationships between the men in the same and adjacent generations. The relation between father and son was overtly one of severe dominance and submission; a son owed obedience and deference; and a distance was called for between the two men which would allow them to maintain a common front to the world without their entering into great intimacy. But the filial relation was in a sense self-defeating as soon as the son assumed a role which made his position ambiguous: the role of father to his own children. Once married and *pater*, a man was potentially *paterfamilias*, but of course he could realize this status to the full only at the expense of his father, either by breaking away from him (which was legally forbidden if the father was unwilling), or by superseding him.

But in order to supersede a living father and dominate him and the remainder of the family, a man needed to reckon with his brothers. Now, it might seem at first sight that the hierarchy of seniority among brothers, well marked by the manner in which they were differently treated by their parents and expressed in the kinship terms and other behaviour they adopted in respect of one another, would allow an eldest son to exercise full authority over the younger sons if he assumed the role of family head. But in fact the fraternal relationship was one of competition, and potentially of a fierce kind. Order was kept among brothers by the presence of an effective father. He not only held them in check individually, but forced them by the exercise of his power to preserve some solidarity among themselves. If, however, the father was dead, or living but displaced to a secondary position by senility or more youthful incompetence, the oldest brother could not for long assume the headship of the family for fear of the hostility that would be released against him by his juniors. A superannuated father was no father, and the joint family could not for any length of time survive; he was as though already dead.

The competition between brothers was economic; they were entitled (except for the eldest son's special share in respect of the ancestor cult) to equal shares in the family estate, and they anticipated their individual shares of this property by showing jealousy for their separate rights. (When partition finally took place each brother was more than careful to see that his arithmetical share was adequately represented in the quality and position of the land and living quarters he was to take for his own.) The competition was domestic; but here it was the wives of the brothers who, so to speak, competed actively on their husbands' behalf. The quarrelsomeness of Chinese women (a socially reprobated but expected quarrelsomeness) was in part a reflex of their position as the unappointed representatives of their husbands' interests in domestic life. As the result of a marriage system in which women were bodily and jurally transferred to the families which acquired them as brides, when a married woman fought, she fought for herself, for her children, and for her husband.[1]

---

[1] It happens that the New Territories village described by Miss Pratt is, to use an expression almost traditional by now in modern studies of China, an 'emigrant community': large numbers of the men are absent, some for short terms, others

This analysis singles out three crucial domestic relationships: between father and son, between brother and brother, and between husband and wife. They formed different configurations in different forms of the family and at different points in their development. In a rich family, where the father was politically and economically strong, he could dominate his sons and hold them in check; the competition between the sons was muted. They paid relatively little attention to the affairs or interests of their wives and aimed at domestic peace by refraining from siding with them when they were in conflict with their sisters-in-law and mother-in-law. But if for some reason the father was displaced from effective headship of the family, fraternal solidarity was lessened and the individuating interests of the wives were encouraged; the sons began to pay that heed to women's grumbles and grievances which Chinese moralists have held to be the death of domestic harmony. A joint family was on the point of breaking.

In poor families the father was politically and economically weak. If in fact there was more than one son, the fraternal bond was fragile and often broken; husband and wife were closely identified with each other. Since there was little family property at stake and few people in the family to share what there was, the wife was not in the position of one asserting her rights and those of her husband and children. Her quarrelsomeness was less in evidence.

This argument may be summarized by saying that three central family relationships varied together: a change in one of them induced changes in the others.[1] Of course, it is artificial to attempt

for long. And the question arises whether, on the theory that it is the men who more fundamentally cause family quarrels and the women who are commonly accused of doing so, the absence of men means an increase in domestic harmony. In fact, Miss Pratt's account (*op. cit.*, p. 154) appears to confirm the theory. She writes: 'The husband is the focus of strain and most quarrels seem to centre around him, except for the eternal complaint of laziness. His removal to cash employment elsewhere forces co-operation in farming and domestic matters upon the women left behind.'

[1] This is a very bald statement of an analysis I have set out elsewhere and hope to develop more fully in a later essay. See 'Problems in the Analysis of the Chinese Family', *Bulletin, Philadelphia Anthropological Society*, vol. XIV, no. 2, 1961; 'The Family in China, Past and Present', *Pacific Affairs*, vol. XXXIV, no. 4, Winter 1961–2; and 'The Chinese Domestic Family: Models', *Actes du VIe Congrès International des Sciences Anthropologiques et Ethnologiques, Paris 1960*, tome II, 1er volume, Paris, 1963. The analysis has an important bearing on the interpretation of changes in family structure in Communist China; see 'The Family in China', *op. cit.*, and 'The Family under Chinese Communism', *The Political Quarterly*,

to explain the dynamics of the Chinese family by reference only to the relations between father and son, brother and brother, and husband and wife; but it is quite legitimate and, as I contend, a restricted framework of this sort does in fact carry us a long way to understanding the essential features of the Chinese domestic group. Naturally, in a fuller analysis the other relationships of the family would have to be dealt with, especially that between the married woman and her mother-in-law, in order to account for things that the restricted model does not.[1]

The terms 'elementary', 'stem', and 'joint' are common-places in the writing on the Chinese family.[2] The first two terms, although ambiguous enough, raise no problem of immediate concern to us. The last term most certainly does, for it leads on from questions of morphology to the nature of the rights and duties entailed in the estates which all but the poorest families

vol. 35, no. 3, July–September 1964. Since the Second World War there have been several attempts at a general treatment of the Chinese family. Of these Marion J. Levy, *The Family Revolution in Modern China*, Cambridge, Mass., 1949, remains the most interesting. Among more recent works on the subject are: C. K. Yang, *The Chinese Family in the Communist Revolution*, Cambridge, Mass., 1959; Morton H. Fried, 'Trends in Chinese Domestic Organization', in E. F. Szczepanik, ed., *Symposium on Economic and Social Problems of the Far East*, Hong Kong, 1962; and W. J. Goode, *World Revolution and Family Patterns*, Glencoe, Ill., and London, 1963. Some idea of the value of the Japanese field studies of the Chinese family can be got from Tadashi Fukutake, *The Structure of Chinese Rural Society*, Tokyo, 1951, in Japanese with brief English summary.

[1] The model assumes patrilocal marriage, but in fact many marriages were of one of the matrilocal varieties, a variation which makes for a great difference in the working out of the family cycle. Furthermore, when in patrilocal marriage a child 'bride' is brought in as a prospective daughter-in-law, her role as an adult is different from that of the bride who comes into the family already grown up. In the village he studied in Taiwan, Wolf collected genealogical data on a population of 843 for the period 1870–1960. In that population, of 196 people leaving the village on marriage only 31 per cent went out in the 'standard' form of Chinese marriage, and of the 236 people who came into the village on marriage only the same percentage fell into the category. No doubt this may be regarded as an extreme case, but it should by no means be dismissed as one, for it is clear that the 'little daughters-in-law' and the married-in sons-in-law play a very important part in the family life of southeastern China as a whole.

[2] For some sinological, sociological, and anthropological examples of the use of some or all of these terms, see: Derk Bodde, *China's Cultural Tradition, What and Whither?*, N.Y., 1957, p. 44; Hu Chang-tu et al., *China, Its People, Its Society, Its Culture*, London [1960?], pp. 158 ff.; Levy, *op. cit.*, pp. 55 ff.; Liu Hui-chen Wang, *The Traditional Chinese Clan Rules*, pp. 2 f.; Lang, *op. cit.*, pp. 136 ff.; G. William Skinner, 'A Study in Miniature of Chinese Population', *Population Studies*, vol. v, no. 2, November 1951, p. 100; Cornelius Osgood, *Village Life in Old China, A Community Study of Kao Yao, Yünnan*, N.Y., 1963, p. 202; *Lineage Organization*, pp. 18 ff.

have in some form. The objection to the word 'joint' in this context is that it confuses the composition of the family with its property rights. 'Elementary' says that a family consists of two generations; 'stem' says that a family consists of three generations, the middle one of which is composed of only one married pair. In one sense 'joint' says that a family is made up of three or more generations, the intermediate ones (or at least one of them) comprising more than one married pair; in another sense it says that the family is an economic unit, owning an estate which is the property of all the male members jointly. But in the latter sense a 'stem' family is also joint, for the father and son and son's son in it are no less coparceners than are the men in a 'joint' family, and *mutatis mutandis* with an 'elementary' family. It becomes important, therefore, to match 'elementary' and 'stem' with some more suitable term of morphology. 'Composite', 'extended', and 'expanded' have been used as alternatives; they are all open to objections (for example: is not a 'stem' family also extended?); my own choice is 'grand'; but let us leave the word-play behind to turn to the serious problem underlying the term 'joint'.

The expression 'joint family' is apparently out of Hindu society by English law.[1] The lawyers, naturally enough, have been concerned with the Hindu family primarily as a property-owning unit; the sociologists and anthropologists have mixed up this aspect of the Hindu family with its ideal morphology; and students of other 'large-family' systems, the Chinese among them, have followed suit. Like the Hindu family, the Chinese contains any number of men (from two upwards to several tens) who together form a coparcenary unit. The estate of which they are joint owners has resulted typically from the partition of some larger unit or from inheritance by a single heir.

At this point I leave the Hindu case behind (for lack of know-ledge) and confine myself to the Chinese family. Every male born or fully adopted into the family is, from the moment of his existence as a son, a coparcener. As long as the estate remains intact (that is to say, no member of the coparcenary unit has

[1] There is, needless to stress, a great literature on the Hindu joint family in its legal and sociological aspects. Among the recent contributions, I have been impressed by T. N. Madan, 'The Joint Family: A Terminological Clarification', in John Mogey, ed., *Family and Marriage*, Leiden, 1963. See also A. M. Shah, 'Basic Terms and Concepts in the Study of Family in India', *The Indian Economic and Social History Review*, vol. I, no. 3, January–March 1964.

taken out his share), every man is an owner of it. The estate may be increased by good luck or enterprise, or diminished by economic failure; every coparcener's right is thereby enlarged or contracted. In theory, at any rate, no part of the estate may be disposed of without the assent, even if only implied, of all the owners.[1] The head of the unit is not a sole owner of property the rights to which pass on his death to his heirs; he is the holder of a trust, the rights of his heirs having been established at their birth or adoption.

When a man dies, his sons may keep the estate unbroken, the management being assumed by the oldest. But in fact, as we know, partition is likely to follow hard upon the father's death, or at any rate upon that of his widow. The shares then taken out are, if we may for the moment roughly generalize about China as a whole, equal, the members of the grandson generation succeeding to a dead father's share *per stirpes*. But, as we have seen, a senior son is often allotted an extra share of the estate in virtue of his role in the ancestor cult.

The history of this eldest son's share is an interesting one, for it demonstrates how primogeniture has waned in Chinese society. In a paper already cited,[2] McAleavy has shown how in the theory underlying statute law the duty of sacrificing to the dead ancestors was concentrated in the eldest son by the wife. 'It was he who offered sacrifice to his dead father and his father's ancestors, while his brothers by his own mother or by his father's concubines assisted only in a very subordinate capacity in the ritual. . . .'[3] (This legally defined role goes back to that of the *tsung-tzu*, the senior son in the senior line of descent, of the pre-imperial stretch of Chinese history.[4]) But in practice, by the time we are concerned with, all that remained of the pre-eminence of the eldest son was his expected role as 'chief actor' in the conduct of the rituals (as McAleavy puts it[5]), a role which stressed the importance of maintaining his direct line of descent (leading to the strict rules governing adoption in this line) and usually entailed the allotment to him of an extra share of the family inheritance. But the extra share, although connected with duties in the

---

[1] See *Lineage Organization*, pp. 14, 22 n.   [2] See above, p. 7 n.
[3] McAleavy, *op. cit.*, p. 609.
[4] See e.g. Ch'ü T'ung-tsu, *Law and Society in Traditional China*, Paris and The Hague, 1961, p. 32.   [5] McAleavy, *op. cit.*, pp. 610 f.

ancestor cult, was not encumbered by those duties, and the man who received it was in fact free to enjoy it as he chose.[1]

To ensure that some part of an estate would be used for maintaining the cult of the ancestors a different provision could be, and sometimes was, made. Either before the partition of the family a special portion was set aside for this purpose, or after partition the sons contributed to such a portion from their several shares. Once established, this 'trust' was the joint property of all the heirs and its management and fruits fell to be enjoyed by them in turn (usually on an annual basis) or collectively. The rights in this 'trust' were transmitted *per stirpes*, so that in the case where there was a rotation of management and benefit, the members of later generations took turns according to the rights of their several ancestors at the point of foundation. And if instead of being rotated the estate was managed in such a way that its annual profits were distributed among the owners, then the sharing of the profits was made on the basis of *per stirpes* shares.[2] It follows that if at the foundation of the 'trust' there were three or more sons, and after the lapse of several generations the male agnatic descendants of these sons differed greatly in number, then the members of the most prolific line enjoyed the smallest shares of the total benefit of the 'trust' and those of the least prolific the greatest. (There is, of course, a problem here which I have not resolved. A continuous transmission of rights down the generations *per stirpes* would obviously be extraordinarily cumbersome, and it is probable that the principle was often applied only at the point of foundation, so that the descendants of any one of the sons of the founding ancestor took their shares *per capita* within their respective branches. It should be added that 'trusts' which came into being in this fashion were not the only kind of indivisible property, for, as I shall argue,[3] some lineage estates were formed by entailing new land brought into cultivation by groups of agnates.)

In theory at any rate, such a 'trust' was a permanent foundation. No individual could shed his rights by disposing of them to

[1] *Ibid.*, pp. 611 f.
[2] *Ibid.*, pp. 612 f. McAleavy's article has made me realize how wrong were the conclusions I drew in *Lineage Organization*, p. 48 n., on the Vietnamese system of cult funds. For some recent field data on the Vietnamese ancestor cult see Gerald C. Hickey, *Village in Vietnam*, New Haven and London, 1964, especially pp. 88 ff.
[3] See below, pp. 160 f., 188.

an outsider. If in fact it became necessary to dissolve the 'trust' then, again in theory, the agreement of all the coproprietors was essential, although it is clear that in the case of large 'trusts', in which stable and powerful managements had developed, the estates were sometimes broken up with scant regard for the opinions of the total membership. It would be very instructive to trace in detail the influence of English law and British rule in the New Territories on the process of building up and dismantling ancestral 'trusts'. From the outset of British administration in 1899 the 'trusts' already in existence were recognized and new ones allowed to be formed; they are being formed at the present day. The land registers and other official and legal documents refer to them under the Cantonese names of *tso* and *t'ong*, the former meaning an estate named after a particular ancestor (whence the term *tso*), the latter an estate owned jointly either by kinsmen or by associates of some other kind (*t'ong*: 'hall'). It seems to me from my reading of the official documents and my observations in 1963 that the bureaucratization of the whole system in this century has on the one hand strengthened the power of the managers in their control of the 'trusts', and on the other hand put a severe brake on their attempts to dismantle them. Section 19 of the New Territories Ordinance, 1910, requires a manager to be appointed for land held in the name of a 'clan', family, or *t'ong* who then handles the land 'as if he were the sole owner thereof, subject to the consent of the Land Officer. . . .'[1] But the Land Officers have been reluctant to give their consent to the dispersion of an estate until they have satisfied themselves that the wishes and interests of all the owners, minors included, have been taken into account. And at the present time some interesting deadlocks arise because universal agreement cannot be reached. In an important case known to me, the several branches of one 'trust' could not be brought to agree on the principle of dividing the assets realizable by sale; the members of the less numerous branches were in favour of the traditional rule of dividing the assets up *per stirpes*, while the members of populous branches were, naturally enough, eager to see some sort of *per capita* division introduced into the scheme for dissolution.

We have moved away from a discussion of inheritance in the

[1] See 'The New Territories Ordinance, 1910', as amended up to September 1950, in *Laws of Hong Kong*, vol. III, Hong Kong, n.d.

family to questions more relevant to the segmentation of the lineage, for the establishment of 'trusts' is the core of the creation of segments. Small segments nest within larger in a constantly developing series of joint estates. The point of differentiation lies in the family. When a family is well-to-do, instead of all its property being dispersed among its successor-families on partition, some of it is jointly entailed in the male agnatic descendants of the partitioners in such a way that what begins as a small segment may grow in time to become a large and prosperous corporate entity (itself in turn being a member of a larger segment and including smaller ones). It asserts its social status against that of less fortunate co-ordinate segments and against that of those people of similar genealogical position who are not lucky enough to be members of a co-ordinate segment.[1]

Let us return to the narrower question of inheritance in the family, beginning with the eldest son's extra share. It is significant for the earlier argument that this share did not always in fact fall to the eldest son, so far had the rule of primogeniture decayed. In her survey of 'clan' rules Mrs Liu writes: 'In dividing family property, it was customarily necessary to decide who among the brothers would assume the responsibility of supporting the living or surviving parent. The custom in some regions was to choose this son by drawing lots at random and to give him a slightly larger share of inheritance.'[2] And she goes on to say that there were local variations in the practice of giving each son an equal share. 'In some places, the eldest son received a double share of inheritance either on the ground of his having more grown-up offspring than his younger brothers, or in partial imitation of the ancient feudal rule of primogeniture. Sons of the wife usually got more than the sons of a concubine. But many localities allowed none of these deviations from the principle.'[3]

But what in reality was the family estate that was to be divided up? Inherited property certainly formed part of it, but did it include the wealth in some sense individually acquired by the sons? Clearly, there was room for dispute on this issue, as Mrs Liu has established. 'A son may claim that a certain piece of property, having come to him from his wife's dowry or entirely from his

---

[1] On asymmetrical segmentation see above pp. 37 ff. and *Lineage Organization*, pp. 48 f.
[2] Liu, *op. cit.*, pp. 68 f.   [3] *Ibid.*, p. 69.

personal career, should not be regarded as a part of the common property. Other sons would retort that whatever he earns himself is not entirely his own fortune, as his personal fortune begins with the initial help of the family. The brothers feel that their sacrifice has made an indirect contribution to his personal success and should share what he mistakenly alleges to be his personal property.'[1] Doubtless, the claims to personal increments of fortune were more likely to arise when men were engaged in business than when they farmed a common estate, and we may recall that this precise question is raised in the famous account of family division given by Lin Yueh-hwa in *The Golden Wing*.[2] When the terms of partition were being discussed one of the contentious issues was 'the disposition of shares in the Hookow store. We remember that the Hwang family had four ordinary shares in the store. [The eldest nephew] demanded an equal division of the shares. But Dunglin, as founder and owner of the store, could insist on reserving more shares for himself. He had already given up one-half of the money and property he had gained from his lifetime of business to the nephews whom he had saved from starvation long ago in the days of the family's first poverty. He kept two and a half shares for himself and let only one and a half shares go to the nephews. [The eldest nephew] was far from satisfied with this arrangement, so the seeds of further future conflict were sown by the old man's refusal.'[3] In fact, we may conclude that the rules for defining the boundaries of the family estate were never so exact as to prevent the very disputes between brothers and between men and their father's brothers which seem to be an outstanding feature of Chinese family life. It cannot be too greatly insisted that the fraternal bond in Chinese society is remarkable not only for the ethical and ideological investment made in its maintenance but also for the forces in the family making for its disruption. Brothers under the dominance of their father keep the peace; without him they are liable to be at one another's throats.

In the second passage I have quoted from Mrs Liu's book there is a reference to a man claiming property as having come to him from his wife's dowry. The discussion up to this point has

---

[1] *Ibid., loc. cit.*

[2] See *Lineage Organization*, pp. 26 f. for a summary of two family partitions described by Lin.

[3] Lin Yueh-hwa, *The Golden Wing, A Sociological Study of Chinese Familism*, London, 1948, p. 125.

assumed that a family estate is in the joint ownership of men and is increased or diminished by the efforts of men. A poor woman going out on marriage is equipped with small items of personal property (her trousseau), some or all of which may have been paid for out of the bride-price received for her. The daughter of a rich family can expect to be sent off with a substantial dowry in the form of jewellery and cash, in addition to the bedroom furnishings that form a standard part of a bride's trousseau. This endowment of the bride by her rich family represents for the men in it a considerable economic sacrifice. They make it not because the girl has any specific economic claims on them (she is not a member of the property-owning unit) but because their own status is at stake; a bride-giving family must, in order to assert itself against the family to which it has lost a woman, send her off in the grandest manner they can afford. And it is no accident, therefore, that dowry and trousseau are put on open display; they are not private benefactions to the girl but a public demonstration of the means and standing of her natal family.

But once she is in her new family, a woman's personal property may after a time become merged with that of her husband. If the relations between the spouses are good and the marriage promises to be stable and fruitful of children, the husband may grow to acquire such rights over his wife's property as will lead to the emergence of an individual smaller family estate within the larger estate of the family as a whole. From this flows trouble while the family is intact; and when the time comes for partition the husband will lay claim to have the conjugal estate removed from the total pool which is to be divided up among the brothers.[1]

Once married a woman has no further economic claims on her natal family (although she may well receive gifts from it) and her economic interests are concentrated on what she has brought with her and the rights of her husband. It is from these that her children will ultimately benefit. She defends the property rights of herself, her husband, and her children, and in doing so earns that Chinese reputation for her sex so well expressed in the words

[1] Pratt, *op. cit.*, p. 153, says that the girl going out in marriage 'should be given jewellery which remains her personal property to be bequeathed to her daughters or disposed of as she wishes. The girls approaching marriageable age form a "sisters' society" and when one of their number is married they too give her a piece of jewellery.'

of one of the 'clan' genealogies quoted by Mrs Liu: 'Women are by nature ignorant, narrow-minded, sly, and jealous.'[1]

The threat which every woman posed to the family that received her in marriage resulted from the completeness with which she was received. Once married she transferred her allegiances; and the rights to her services and her physical presence were handed over from the family which gave her birth to that where she was expected to pass the remainder of her life, except for licensed visits to her own male agnates and their wives. Having formerly been a jural minor as a daughter she was now a jural minor as wife and daughter-in-law, and although, as we know very well from many descriptions of Chinese family life, she might come, especially as a widow, effectively to control the affairs of a large household, the rules of society placed her in subjection to men. The widow was technically subordinate to her eldest son.

Some fresh light is cast by Yang's book on Nanching on the important question of the degree to which married women are incorporated into the families of their husbands. In this village (which had a total population of some 1,100 people) there were four 'old maid houses', as Yang calls them, with a total membership of about sixty women, made up of 'separated wives, widows and a few unmarried women'. Since it may be inferred from the rough population data that there were some 350 women over the age of 15 in the village, approximately one adult woman in every six was a member of an 'old maid house'. 'Separated wives and widows belonged there on the theory that once a woman was married to another family, she belonged body and spirit to a family other than the parents' and after her death her spirit could not return to the parents' home. In case of alienation from her husband's home, her spirit must have another home to attach itself to in order to avoid the tragedy of becoming a homeless wandering spirit. An "old maid" house represented a home for the spirits of such women. Should death draw near a member who was living in her own parents' home, she was moved to the "old maid" house to die, so that her spirit would know where to return.' Wooden tablets for dead members were set up in the 'old maid house' altars, sacrifices being made to them on the anniversaries of their death.[2]

[1] Liu, *op. cit.*, p. 84.   [2] Yang, *op. cit.*, pp. 15, 85 f.

The implications of this fascinating fragment of ethnography are important. On going out in marriage a woman ceased to belong ritually to her natal family. As a widow or runaway or abandoned wife she might in fact spend her days in that family, but she could not die in it, and her soul tablet must find another altar. It was not simply that marriage gave a woman a new home. (It might in fact fail to provide her with a permanent new home.) It cut her off ritually from the family which had sent her out. Yang's account of marriage in Nanching will take us a little further than this, however. Not only might a married woman seek shelter in her original home; in some circumstances she could look to her natal family for protection if she was maltreated as a wife. And indeed her lineage might intervene and the issue be taken up by the two lineages involved. 'In the Wong's printed copy of their clan genealogy there was a rule forbidding male clan members from marrying any girl of a Chen clan in a village about three miles away, the result of a conflict between the two clans caused by the mistreatment of a Wong girl married into the Chen clan.'[1]

The distancing of a married woman from her original family is also brought out in Miss Pratt's brief account of a Hakka village in the New Territories. On the third day following her marriage, a girl goes home to her parents if they do not live too far away, 'but she should not stay the night and thereafter she should in theory ask her husband's and mother-in-law's permission before going back. Visiting, which must be actively discouraged at first, becomes less frequent by a natural process as the girl becomes more and more absorbed into her new home, although the affective bonds may remain very strong.'[2]

Chinese marriage conveyed to the man's family rights in the bride and her prospective children. Those who received the woman counted on acquiring her domestic and certain agricultural (and sometimes handicraft) services, her children, and her loyalty. To begin with, the new bride was ceremonially obliged to visit her parental home; it was accepted that during the early phase

---

[1] *Ibid.*, p. 90. 'A wife's parents might visit the husband and his family members to demand that they cease the mistreatment or to seek redress for a wrong. If the wife's family was poorer or weaker than the husband's and such action would be ineffective, and the wife's cause was an obviously just one, the wife's clan might intercede and the issue would become a point of contention between the two clans.' [2] Pratt, *op. cit.*, p. 154.

of the marriage she would pay fairly frequent visits there (but not sleep under the parental roof); but as time went on and the marriage, so to say, matured, the woman was more and more pulled away from her ties with those who had brought her into the world and reared her. The birth of her first child (especially if it were a boy) gave her an anchor in her new family. As she grew older, finally perhaps to become a widow living with her married son or sons, not only were her interests totally focused on the group into which she was now fully integrated, but the people among whom she had grown up in her natal family had either died or were so old as to be members of families none of which could be said to be the family in which the woman herself had been reared.[1]

The bride-receivers took rights in a wife and a potential mother. They assumed responsibility for her against the world. If she misbehaved they could punish her, but at this point it becomes clear that her natal family retained the right to protest and, if possible, interfere if the woman was grossly abused. And we may well suspect that this right was likely to be exercised only during the early phase of the marriage, both because it was then that it would probably be needed and because, even if later on the woman did in fact suffer greatly, her original family had ceased to be sufficiently interested in her. The natural development of the family cycle had carried her further into her second family and further away from her first.

On the other hand, the interest maintained in a married woman by her original family and by her own agnates more generally appears to have depended in some measure on social status. A family of high standing was less likely to tolerate the maltreatment of one of its married-out women at any stage of her life because their own status vis-à-vis the bride-receivers and the world was involved. And the fact that they were particularly concerned to ensure that she would be given a fitting burial suggests that it was less the interests of the woman herself than their own pride that prompted them to make representations to their affines. De Groot, whose work on the Amoy area is an almost inexhaustible storehouse of information, illustrates this point very clearly. He is

[1] Note the significance of the fact that two of the 'clan' genealogies studied by Mrs Liu state specifically that a married woman is not to visit her natal family after the death of her parents: Liu, *op. cit.*, p. 95.

discussing the lavishness of grave clothes and jewellery, and says that very often a dead woman's agnates interfere at her funeral to force her husband and children 'to fit out her body with a large quantity of ornaments and precious clothes'. Interventions of this kind led to fierce and even violent quarrels. And he adds: 'Such things occur more especially when the bereaved family is less numerous or less influential than the clan in which the deceased woman was born, in which case the quarrel always ends in their having to acquiesce in the demands of the stronger party.'[1] Similarly, if a married woman committed suicide (not a rare occurrence, to judge by the general statements in the literature),[2] the rage of her own agnates was stimulated by the affront to their dignity, and they would seek some redress for the wrong done them. Mrs Liu translates the following passage from a 'clan' genealogy of the Republican period: 'When a married woman, after the discovery of her disreputable misconduct, commits suicide by hanging herself, taking poison or drowning herself, her own family should not come with their fellow clan members like a mob, make trouble for her husband's family, or demand money as a compensation for her death. Only when a married woman has done no wrong and yet has been driven into suicide by intolerable mistreatment can her father, her brother, or her close relatives appeal to the government in order to correct a grave injustice.'[3]

There is a final point to be made on the control exercised over a married woman by her natal family. In Lineage Organization[4] I summarized data which indicated that, while in general her family of marriage had the right to dispose of a widow and to receive the second bride-price for her, as we should expect, there were certainly some areas (one county in Fukien province being among them) in which the natal family retained this right. It has become more obvious to me now than when I wrote Lineage Organization that while valid generalizations may be made about the social institutions of Fukien and Kwangtung – and indeed of China as a whole – there are some very important sociological problems arising from local variations in custom, a matter to which I shall

---

[1] De Groot, op. cit., pp. 701 f. And cf. ibid., p. 705.

[2] See especially P. M. Yap, Suicide in Hong Kong, with Special Reference to Attempted Suicide, Hong Kong, 1958.

[3] Liu, op. cit., pp. 88 f.   [4] Pp. 31 f.

return in a later context.[1] If in some places (villages? vicinages? –
surely not purely administrative areas such as counties) a widow
could be disposed of in second marriage by her original family,
then we must expect this departure from the general rule to be
linked with other significant variations in kinship structure.
Crucial customs will not have varied randomly.

It may be that we have been given some clue to a puzzling
feature of the evidence on divorce. That evidence on Fukien and
Kwangtung seems to suggest that in respect of primary marriage,
divorce was practically non-existent, or at any rate extremely rare.
Certainly, marriages were disrupted and wives were sometimes
thrown back on their natal families for support. Consider the
situation in Nanching. Yang tells us that divorce was unknown
there, but a wife who had been ill-treated 'by her husband or his
family often returned to her own parents for varying periods of
from a few months to many years, sometimes for life'. Long-term
separation usually led to the woman becoming a member of one
of the 'old maid houses',[2] for, as we have seen, she might pass
her last years back in her natal home but she could not be allowed
to die there. It is my impression that the same conditions (except
in respect of the 'old maid houses') hold for mainland southeastern China in general. But there is no statistical evidence worth
talking about,[3] and in the one relevant part of China for which
such statistical evidence exists, Taiwan, it points a contrary way.

Barclay's data on Taiwan indicate a far higher rate of divorce
than is usually allowed for in discussions of Chinese marriage. It is
true that his figures for the proportion of people counted as
divorced at any given time do not at first sight suggest a very high
rate, but a computation of the proportion of marriages in any one
year which were dissolved within a period of five years brings out
some surprisingly large figures. For the percentage of people
divorced at any one time we may take the data on 1905, the earliest
year quoted. (Taiwan was then only ten years away from having
been part of China.)

[1] See below, pp. 93 ff.
[2] Yang, *op. cit.*, p. 85.
[3] Of the two main genealogies studied by Eberhard in *Social Mobility*, one
contains no data whatever on divorce, while the other mentions only 6 cases
between 1803 and 1890. In three of these cases 'it is indicated that the main wife
"re-married" before the death of her husband; in one case it is said that she was
"expelled".' – *op. cit.*, p. 135.

Age	Percentages counted as divorced from a previous marriage, 1905[1]	
	males	females
15–19	0·3	0·7
20–24	1·2	1·2
25–29	1·9	0·9
30–34	2·1	0·8
35–39	1·8	0·7
40 and over	1·3	0·4

The Japanese authorities in Taiwan registered divorces occurring each year according to the time elapsed since marriage. The data have provided Barclay with the opportunity to calculate that for the year 1906 (again, the earliest year he deals with) 14·4 per cent of the marriages registered ended in divorce within five years. This percentage is based on the assumption that all marriages, first and subsequent, were being dissolved. If we assume instead that the marriage figures are for first marriages only, then the percentage rises to 22·3.[2] But if, in the interests of realism, we take a percentage intermediate between the two we arrive at something like 18 or 19. (The intermediate percentages for the years 1910 and 1915 are roughly 11 and 12.) Even if we stand by the lowest percentages for each of the three years (14·4, 9·4, and 10·5) we have some formidable figures to account for.

Barclay himself discusses the matter very informatively and interestingly within the Taiwanese context. It is true, as he points out, that the sex ratio favoured women in the marriage market; in 1905, for example, there were 119 males for every 100 females in the age-range 15–49.[3] But there are good grounds for believing that on the mainland the sex ratio was of the same rough order of magnitude. There are several other factors that need to be considered. First, we should not forget that we are dealing in the case of Taiwan with an area where the registration of persons and of their changes in civil status was efficient and enforced. It may be that precisely because these changes had to be recorded, what in pre-Japanese times would have been simply conjugal separations have later turned into divorces because of the exigencies of registration.

Second, as Barclay himself shows, a very high proportion of

[1] Adapted from George W. Barclay, *Colonial Development and Population in Taiwan*, Princeton, N.J., 1954, Table 63, p. 219.
[2] *Ibid.*, p. 221.   [3] *Ibid.*, p. 212.

Taiwan Chinese marriages were matrilocal; in 1906 and 1910 the percentages of matrilocal marriages in all registered marriages were 21·8 and 20·4 respectively.[1] We may reasonably assume that, because of the strains imposed on men by this kind of marriage, it will promote a high rate of divorce.[2] Now, matrilocal marriage was certainly not confined to Taiwan, and in one or other of its forms was to be found in mainland southeastern China.[3] But it may well be, as I am very much inclined to assume, that for reasons we do not yet know, this collection of institutions was much more highly developed across the Formosa Strait.

Third, the marriages in Barclay's data must include some secondary (as distinct from second) unions. If they are in fact present in any considerable number, then they may well have pushed up the divorce rates calculated, since the permanence of the Chinese marriage bond that we (and the Chinese) uncritically take for granted is never thought to be a property of secondary unions, which are recognized to be subject to the risk of disruption.

Fourth, we may just possibly be seeing through the medium of the figures for Taiwan as a whole (its Chinese population in 1905 was three million) some of the consequences of local variations in kinship structure, present too in the mainland but more prominent here. Perhaps in some parts of Taiwan women are subject to less control in their families of marriage; perhaps with the support of their natal families (who even in some places may be able to collect a second bride-price) they are freer, during the early years of marriage, to keep an eye open for better alternatives. We know that in 1906, of the divorced women remarrying, 49 per cent remarried previously unmarried men. The percentages in 1910 and 1915 were 53 and 48 respectively.[4] A breakdown of these general Taiwan statistics by small areas of the island would

---

[1] *Ibid.*, p. 229.

[2] Wolf reports of his Taiwan village that while patrilocal marriage is stable (even though, especially in the case of 'little daughter-in-law' marriage, it may not be harmonious or conjugally stable), matrilocal marriage may not be. 'We do not know of a single case of a daughter-in-law's deserting her husband's family. . . . By comparison we know of at least 8 cases in which matrilocal marriages failed in their original purpose.' But in 3 of these 8 cases the married-in son-in-law's wife left her parental home with him.

[3] Cf. the evidence on emigrants from Fukien in Singapore: see my *Chinese Family and Marriage in Singapore*, London, 1957, pp. 122 f.

[4] Barclay, *op. cit.*, p. 227.

be able to show us whether there were in reality such systematic local variations as I suspect. And armed with this new information we should be in a much better position to approach the mainland data again.

But even though there are few facts to go on, we may speculate on the possible variations in the stability of marriage in Fukien and Kwangtung. Once the questions are posed the answers may be found. Was marriage more stable where lineage organization was in some sense stronger? It might be argued that to cast out a woman or allow her to depart must have been more difficult when the lineage units which were in effect parties to the marriage were well organized and of high social status. A marriage among people of standing was a political transaction, and political consequences might flow from its attempted disruption. Secondary marriages would have been less affected by such considerations, and it is possible that the marriages contracted by the members of one lineage were of greater or lesser stability, other things being equal, according to whether the families immediately involved were stronger or weaker on the local scene. That is to say, a family of high social status probably showed a greater concern to prevent a divorce both because of its need to aim at the ideals of society in order to maintain its standing and because of the breach that would be entailed in its carefully worked out system of marriage alliances.

Was marriage less stable where women had more opportunities for making an independent living? We know that, despite the tendency to universal marriage for women in Chinese society[1] and the ritual importance of the married state in the after-life,[2] girls in some parts of Kwangtung chose to make their own living as spinsters (sometimes in fact literally) rather than suffer what seemed to be the worse hardships of matrimony.[3] The evidence from Shun-tê, to which we have already referred,[4] shows a high

[1] In 1905, 92·5 per cent of Chinese women in the age-group 25–29 in Taiwan were 'currently married'. See Barclay, *op. cit.*, p. 231.

[2] See Marjorie Topley, 'Ghost Marriages among the Singapore Chinese', *Man*, Article 35, February 1955, and 'Ghost Marriages among the Singapore Chinese: A Further Note', *Man*, Article 63, May 1956. Cf. Eberhard, *op. cit.*, p. 172 n.

[3] They were 'women who put their own hair up'. See Marjorie Topley, 'Chinese Women's Vegetarian Houses in Singapore', *Journal of the Malayan Branch of the Royal Asiatic Society*, vol. XXVII, pt. 1 (no. 165), May 1954, pp. 53 f.

[4] See above, p. 32.

degree of independence of action among married women where they could earn their own livelihood; girls did not usually refuse to marry, but some of them married only in order to emancipate themselves from their natal families and then live away from the husbands with whom they never shared a bed. Their unions were *mariages blancs* but they did not end in divorce. Yet perhaps where this special provision for married virgins did not exist (which is to say everywhere in southeastern China except Shun-tê, as far as I know) poor married women given the opportunity to make their living on their own were more likely to change husbands than were better-off women kept at home.

Of course, in considering the stability of Chinese marriage we need to be alert to the possibility that a new union, amounting in its social consequences to a marriage but without the benefit of ceremony or public approbation, could take place without a previous marriage by the woman being dissolved. The possibility is suggested by the behaviour of overseas Chinese of low social status.[1] Given a sex ratio in her favour, a young and poor village woman running away from her husband might not always have found it difficult to enter into another union even though technically she was still a married woman. Children born to her in the second union would be the fully legitimate offspring of the new 'husband' provided he recognized them as his own, and it is unlikely that the first husband would have wished to claim for himself the children borne by his delinquent wife to a stranger.

Before leaving the subject of the family I should like to augment the statistics on family composition I cited from Buck in *Lineage Organization*.[2] The wide ranges of household size given in the various sets of figures show how, on the one hand, domestic units could be reduced below the size of an elementary family, and on the other hand, how the households of the rich could expand to great numbers. One study[3] makes use of data on a Fukien village and on a village in Ch'ao-chou, Kwangtung, both sets of material having been collected in 1934. The Fukien sample contains 1,833 families; the range of family size is 1 to 27; the average family size

[1] See my *Chinese Family . . . in Singapore*, pp. 102, 173; and William H. Newell, *Treacherous River, A Study of Rural Chinese in North Malaya*, Kuala Lumpur, 1962, pp. 59, 62 f.

[2] P. 20.

[3] Chao Ch'eng-hsin, 'Familism as a Factor in the Chinese Population Balance', *Yenching Journal of Social Studies*, vol. III, no. 1, October 1940.

is 5·27; 85·6 per cent of the families are of 2 to 8 persons and 61·9 per cent of 3 to 6.[1] The corresponding figures for the Ch'ao-chou village are 361 families; 1 to 25; 5·6; 83 and 47·1 per cent. 'Family' here must mean 'household', and the 'family' of 27 people is presumably not as big as it seems, for it must include some servants. Yet these and similar statistics show how, in the richer village households, at the peak of its development a family could reach large numbers.

Another statistical study of the same period[2] includes data on a sample drawn from Kwangtung. The sample consists of 403 families in Kityang, near Swatow, the information having been taken from Buck's material on land utilization. Unfortunately for our present purposes, the Kityang figures in this article are generally amalgamated with those from other parts of China, but here and there Smythe makes some separate remarks on the Kwangtung sample.[3] We may note first that in Kityang (to a far greater degree than in the other places studied in the article) the headship has often been turned over to a son (usually the eldest) during the lifetime of his father. 27 per cent of the Kityang sample families show this transfer of authority.[4] In 36 per cent of the families the head has one or more married brothers living with him.[5] Now, this latter figure taken by itself seems to suggest that fraternal 'joint' families are common; but in most cases the head of such a family must have taken over his position from a living father; so that what we have here is a high proportion of families

---

[1] *Ibid.*, p. 12. But perhaps the most interesting feature of these figures is that they relate to a village (or complex of villages) with which any student of south-eastern China must be concerned. Chao has taken the data on a Fukien village from Lin Yueh-hwa's M.A. thesis (Yenching, 1935) on I-hsü, a community which, as I tried to show in *Lineage Organization* (pp. 34 ff.), is somewhat elusive. When at pp. 37 f. I raised the question of the relationship between I-hsü and the community described in Lin's *The Golden Wing*, I was not aware of Chao's article. Had I then known that the population of I-hsü was getting on for 10,000, I should have been less willing to make a case for the identity of this village with the Hwang village of *The Golden Wing* (whose inhabitants numbered 'several hundred'). But I remain puzzled. I have tried to find a copy of Lin's thesis, but none appears to be available outside China.

[2] Lewis S. C. Smythe, 'The Composition of the Chinese Family', *Nanking Journal (Chin-ling hsüeh-pao)*, vol. 5, no. 2, November 1935. I knew of the existence of this paper when I was writing *Lineage Organization* but did not succeed until much later in finding a copy of it.

[3] There seems to be no possibility of seeing the original records, except perhaps in China itself.

[4] Smythe, *op. cit.*, p. 373.   [5] *Ibid.*, p. 379.

in which married brothers are waiting for the parental generation to die before dividing the family.

Only 9 per cent of the families have generations higher than that of the head as well as married sons of the head, and only the same percentage have both married sons and married brothers of the head. Smythe comments: 'The *Kityang* area ... presents very interesting family types. Amongst the 403 families studied there, 42 per cent had relatives from generations higher than the head living in them, 38 per cent had married sons, and 36 per cent had married brothers. It would look as though here could be found many "typically Chinese families".... But only 12 families (3 per cent) had all three relationships in the family. If you add grandchildren, it shrinks to eight cases (2 per cent) and if you extend the higher generations to grandparents, it is reduced to our one rural five-generation family!'[1]

Finally, it is worth referring, however briefly, to the data contained in Barclay's general study of population in Taiwan, a source I omitted to use in 1957 by a culpable oversight. Again we can see how the households of the well-to-do may reach very large numbers; in 1905, Chinese households on the island spanned the range from 1 person to 26 plus,[2] and the correlation to be found throughout China between household size and social status appears to be confirmed in the Taiwan material, despite the difficulty in interpreting the Japanese census categories for occupations.[3] It is interesting to find that over ten per cent of households had women as their heads; the evidence bearing on this figure suggests, according to Barclay, that 'it is not always looked upon as out of the way for women to attain this position'.[4] As we know, at one point in the family cycle a widow might find herself the most senior member alive and in reality (as well as for the purposes

---

[1] *Ibid.*, pp. 380 f.   [2] Barclay, *op. cit.*, p. 179 (see graph).   [3] *Ibid.*, pp. 200 ff.

[4] *Ibid.*, p. 182. As for non-statistical matters, perhaps the most instructive passage in Barclay's chapter on family life is the one in which he discusses the factors inhibiting the expansion of families. He writes: 'Collateral ties are known to be relatively weak among Chinese – sons do not have bonds of the same strength with each other that they have with their fathers. These ties are especially difficult to maintain after the death of a father, for sons may exercise individual claims to shares in the family property. These claims sometimes lead to division of the family and its property even before the father dies; they are intensified as soon as the brothers are married.' – *ibid.*, p. 185. Tuan Chi-hsien, 'Reproductive Histories of Chinese Women in Taiwan', *Population Studies*, vol. xii, pt. 1, July 1958, has some important data bearing on family size.

of government registration) assume control of the family's estate and affairs in general. Indeed, widowhood was paradoxically a great opportunity afforded to some women in Chinese society. Unless they chose to live in sisterhoods (of which the 'old maid houses' in Nanching were a secular example), widowhood was their only chance of exercising supreme authority over adults. In the nature of things, the period of this uncharacteristic mastery was not likely to last long, but while it endured the perpetual jural minor of her society could in fact enjoy the fruits of domestic power.

3

Social Status, Power, and Government

I turn now to certain matters discussed in Chapters 7, 8, and 9 of *Lineage Organization*. So much has been published in recent years on both social mobility and local government in the Ch'ing dynasty that my earlier statements ideally require a thorough overhaul. But I must limit myself here to a few topics that bear most directly on the problem of the organization of lineages and the manner in which they interlocked with other groupings in Chinese society. To begin with, it will be convenient to approach the matter of social status through modern studies of social mobility. The lead made by Chang Chung-li and others in the systematic study of this topic has been followed by several other historians and sociologists, principally Ping-ti Ho,[1] Robert M. Marsh,[2] and Wolfram Eberhard.[3] The literature has become bulky[4] and the issues, although not in proportion, clearer.

[1] 'The Examination System and Social Mobility in China, 1368–1911', in Verne F. Ray, ed., *Intermediate Societies, Social Mobility, and Communication*, American Ethnological Society, Seattle, 1959; 'Aspects of Social Mobility in China, 1368–1911', *Comparative Studies in Society and History*, vol. 1, no. 4, June 1959; and *The Ladder of Success in Imperial China, Aspects of Social Mobility, 1368–1911*, N.Y. and London, 1962.

[2] *The Mandarins, The Circulation of Elites in China, 1600–1900*, Glencoe, Ill., 1961; 'Formal Organization and Promotion in a Pre-Industrial Society', *American Sociological Review*, vol. 26, no. 4, August 1961; and 'The Venality of Provincial Office in China and in Comparative Perspective', *Comparative Studies in Society and History*, vol. 4, no. 4, July 1962.

[3] *Social Mobility, op. cit.*, and 'Mobility in South Chinese Families', *Sinologica*, vol. VI, no. 1, 1959.

[4] A further part of Chang Chung-li's researches has been published in his *Income of the Chinese Gentry*, Seattle, 1962. Johanna M. Menzel, ed., *The Chinese Civil Service, Career Open to Talent?*, Boston, 1963, reprints many important historical and sociological papers on the subject, including a translation of P'an Kuang-tan (Quentin Pan) and Fei Hsiao-tung, 'City and Village: The Inequality of Opportunity', the substance of which was referred to at pp. 59 f. of *Lineage Organization*. There is a very useful discussion of social mobility in Bodde, *op. cit.*, pp. 68 ff. Otto B. van der Sprenkel's paper, 'The Geographical Background of

It is now obvious to me that I should have earlier made a sharper distinction between grades of literati as these were created by the official system of examinations and ranks. The holders of the lowest qualifications were not simply men of lesser attainments; there was a disjunction between their status-cum-political effectiveness and that of the 'graduates'. The first step on the ladder of success was taken by men who passed the county and prefectural examinations to acquire the status of *sheng-yüan* (a term which may be translated as 'government student'[1] or 'undergraduate'[2]) or bought the title of *chien-sheng* (Student of the Imperial Academy[3]). In the older Western view these men were the lowest graduates, the Bachelors of Arts as they were often dubbed. In fact, they were not graduates; they were men merely qualified to compete for graduate status. Until *sheng-yüan* and *chien-sheng* achieved a higher qualification (*kung-sheng* or *chü-jen*) they were privileged literati without direct access to power. (Ho calls them 'scholar-commoners'; they were not members of the official class and therefore not, in a common sinological use of the term, gentry. At most, Ho will allow the 'scholar-commoners' the status of a transitional category.)[4] 'Undergraduates' and 'Students of the Imperial Academy' were exempt from labour service and, entitled to wear scholar's garb, they enjoyed the prestige attaching to officially recognized learning. Consequently, they were able to lord it over their fellow-villagers. But since each individual among them had only a slim chance of reaching office, the 'scholar-commoners'' influence was limited and their power curbed. At least, this is the light in which they are to be seen when they are viewed from an official standpoint; if, however, we put ourselves in the position of a peasant, the restraints to which the junior scholars were subject may well seem less significant than the evident fact of their belonging to a clearly marked out and prestige-laden section of society.

the Ming Civil Service' has already been cited. See also Ch'ü T'ung-tsu, 'Chinese Class Structure and its Ideology', in John K. Fairbank, ed., *Chinese Thought and Institutions*, Chicago, 1957, the same author's *Law and Society*, op. cit., and Wolfgang Franke, *The Reform and Abolition of the Traditional Chinese Examination System*, Center for East Asian Studies, Harvard Univ., Cambridge, Mass., 1960.

[1] Chang Chung-li, *The Chinese Gentry, Studies on their Role in Nineteenth-Century Chinese Society*, Seattle, 1955, p. 4.
[2] Ho, *The Ladder of Success*, p. 28.
[3] Chang, *op. cit.*, p. 5; Ho, *op. cit.*, p. 32.   [4] *Ibid.*, pp. 35 ff.

When we consider what these men did for a living we can be sure that the classically literate part of Chinese society was not clearly divided between those who engaged in commerce and those who did not. Many even 'forsook their métier to become small tradesmen'.[1] And if this lower literate group was in trade, its superiors, from *kung-sheng* upwards, were, especially in the nineteenth century, heavily involved in business of one sort and another, whatever the theory that gentleman and business man were mutually exclusive statuses.[2] In order to pursue an official career a man may have needed to abandon his commercial activities, wholly or in part, but a family could easily specialize the economic functions of its members so that both its civil service and business interests might be maintained – one group of interests perhaps reinforcing the other.

When we study lineages, therefore, we need to be alert for, first of all, the differences between communities producing only *sheng-yüan* and those whose members included *kung-sheng* and perhaps still higher graduates. A lineage which could boast only 'scholar-commoners' had certainly raised itself above the level of the great majority of its neighbours, but it had not yet succeeded in forging a firm direct link with official power. In a similar fashion we need to discriminate carefully between the different kinds of scholars produced by different segments of any one lineage. A segment which could put a man into the bureaucracy was in a very much more important position than one whose members had not got beyond the first qualifying stage. A further lesson to be learned from the discussion is that political and commercial power might be so tightly interrelated as greatly to increase the distance between lineages (and between segments of one lineage) superficially marked only by differences in scholarly attainments. Certainly, it is still possible in the New Territories to trace an old relationship between the high standing in literacy and title-hunting of certain lineages and their control of commercial activity in local markets, a relationship I shall presently illustrate.

How uneven was the distribution of literati among lineages? To what extent were the lineages which enjoyed a scholarly reputation in reality composed of one or two scholarly families and a mass of common people? Chang has estimated that the

[1] *Ibid.*, p. 37.   [2] Chang, *Income*, chap. 6, and Ho, *op. cit.*, pp. 81 f.

literati ('gentry') formed 0·2 per cent of the population of Fukien and 0·36 per cent of the population of Kwangtung in the pre-T'ai-p'ing period of the nineteenth century; the corresponding percentages for the period following the T'ai-p'ing revolution were 0·32 and 0·36.[1] To come down to a much smaller scale of observation, we may note that Lockhart, the British official responsible for investigating conditions in the part of Kwangtung province about to be turned into the New Territories at the end of the nineteenth century, estimated that the county of Hsin-an (from which the New Territories were excised) held 150 *sau choi* (the Cantonese version of *hsui-ts'ai*, the colloquial term for the 'scholar-commoners').[2] If we assume that Hsin-an had then a population of some 200,000, as seems likely, the literati probably formed roughly 0·1 per cent of it. Hayes says, correctly in my opinion, that the literati of Hsin-an 'came generally from the larger, richer villages of the plains which had one or more village schools where the elements of a classical education could be obtained'.[3]

In fact a great many villages in the area had schools of some sort; there the rudiments of reading and writing were taught; but only the villages enjoying a tradition of scholarly achievement supported the kind of school where education could be carried to the point at which a man might begin effectively to equip himself to compete in a state examination. In a handful of New Territories villages the physical remains of such schools can be seen at the present; they might perhaps be better called 'studies'.

---

[1] Chang, *The Chinese Gentry*, Table 32, p. 164. The percentages given above are one-fifth of those shown in the table, for Chang has added four people to every literatus in an attempt to compute the size of the 'gentry' population in the population at large.

[2] Cf. Hayes, 'The Pattern of Life in the New Territories', p. 85.

[3] *Ibid.*, p. 84. According to the 1819 edition of the Hsin-an gazetteer there was a quota at that time of 8 passes at the periodical examinations for *hsiu-ts'ai*, and an additional quota of 2 passes for Hakka candidates. I am indebted for material contained in the Hsin-an gazetteer to Peter Y. L. Ng, *The 1819 Edition of the Hsin-an Hsien-chih, A Critical Examination with Translation and Notes*, unpublished M.A. thesis in history, Univ. of Hong Kong, 1961. (Only as this book goes to press have I managed to lay hands on a copy – photographic – of the gazetteer itself.) Krone, *op. cit.*, p. 95, writing about Hsin-an in the 1850s, also estimates the number of *hsiu-ts'ai* at 150 and gives the examination quotas as 8 Punti and 2 Hakka. As for holders of the provincial and metropolitan degrees, he says there were 4 *chü-jen* and 1 *chin-shih* (*loc. cit.*). In addition, Hsin-an had quotas of 8 Punti and 2 Hakka in the prefectural examinations for military *hsiu-ts'ai*; and at the time Krone wrote there were 12 military *chü-jen* and 1 military *chin-shih* in the county (*ibid.*, p. 96).

It seems to me highly unlikely that any but the sons of the well-to-do and influential families would have had access to them, and I assume that scholarship in scholarly lineages was in fact confined to certain segments of them. As far as I know, there has been only one attempt to survey the academic activity of the inhabitants of the pre-British New Territories.[1] This, because it is based on a restricted number of written genealogies and a few histories,[2] cannot be taken as a sure guide to how scholarship and scholars were distributed over the area, but it is nonetheless a very interesting indication of the way in which certain communities stand out as traditional suppliers of state graduates and 'undergraduates'.

Lo Hsiang-lin begins his account with the establishment of the famous Li-ying 'College' at Kam Tin in the late eleventh century. This 'study', as I should prefer to call it, was the first in the area, and it gave the Tang local lineage which founded it a position of eminence which, politically, economically, and scholastically, it retained until the British entered the scene. As Lo moves on from this earliest academic event to record the scholarly attainments of local men, we can see that Kam Tin and Tai Po are constantly recurring place-names and that Tang is by far the commonest surname. In Ch'ing times there appear to have been a considerable number of *chin-shih* and *chü-jen* (metropolitan and provincial graduates, respectively), although it is noteworthy that none of them seems to have held high office.[3] The various Tang local lineages, especially that of Kam Tin, were, by Hsin-an standards, highly educated and successful; but they had a very limited part to play on the greater Chinese scene.

A view of education in Hsin-an in the middle of the nineteenth century is to be got from Krone's paper. There was a 'school' in the county seat 'for pupils intending to take a degree at Canton

---

[1] Lo Hsiang-lin et al., *Hong Kong and its External Communications before 1842, The History of Hong Kong prior to British Arrival*, Hong Kong, 1963, chapter IX. (The Chinese original of this book was published in Hong Kong in 1959.)

[2] *Ibid.*, p. 143: '. . . only those scholars whose names survive in genealogical tables or in local histories are included in our list. All of them were of the native stock (Cantonese) and their native village can be specified.' It will be seen that no account has been taken of the considerable Hakka population. I was lucky enough to be able to interview a Hakka *hsiu-ts'ai* in 1963, but alas, all I got from him was a lecture on the importance of filial piety – the ideological lesson had stuck in a memory from which more interesting things had apparently departed.

[3] *Ibid.*, pp. 133–44.

[which for Hsin-an was the prefectural as well as the provincial capital]; one teacher of this school receives his salary from government. Essays are sent in and examined by the teachers, and those whose essays are the best, are admitted members of the college, and receive a small allowance of money for the purchase of oil and firewood as a stimulant to more zealous studies These, being the most distinguished scholars, have more hope of obtaining a degree at the public examinations than the rest have. It is reckoned a distinction to receive this allowance, and many of its recipients are well off. Many persons are only connected with this institution by having sent in essays, and have never studied there. This, like all other government establishments, is subject to many abuses, and successful essays are often not written by their pretended authors, but by some literary character who thus obtains a livelihood.'[1]

There was no lack of schools in the more ordinary sense of the word: 'In the first place there are numerous elementary schools, in which boys in bodies of from ten to thirty, are taught to read and write the characters.'[2] These schools were generally to be found in ancestral halls.[3] 'All the boys however do not devote so much time to study; such as afterwards engage in trade or learn a handicraft usually only remain at school from two to four years, during which time they acquire sufficient knowledge of the characters to carry on business, write letters and make out accounts, etc. If a boy intends to devote himself entirely to study, he enters a higher school in which graduates train young men for the examination. Such schools exist at Namtow [the county seat], Sai-heong, Kap-shui-hau, San-keaou and many other places. Kap-shui-hau . . . is famous for these schools, and, as the Chinese say, "diffuses the fragrance of pen and ink". Many youths repair there to study; many inhabitants of the village itself have succeeded in obtaining a degree; and several flagstaffs in it bear witness to the rank of the person over against whose dwelling they are erected.'[4] San-keaou 'boasts of having produced the largest number' of *hsiu-ts'ai*.[5] (Alas for students of the New Territories, the places mentioned by Krone are in the area of Hsin-an not taken over by the British in 1898; they now lie north of the international frontier, forming part of the horizon gazed at by tourists and frustrated anthropologists.)

[1] Krone, *op. cit.*, pp. 88 f.   [2] *Ibid.*, p. 93.   [3] *Ibid.*, p. 94.
[4] *Ibid.*, *loc. cit.*   [5] *Ibid.*, p. 95.

But scholarship and the titles to which it led were not simply concentrated within particular local lineages. They tended to be the prerogatives of segments of these favoured local lineages, a fact concealed by statements and figures which merely locate *hsiu-ts'ai*, *chü-jen*, and *chin-shih* in particular settlements. Now Marsh has called in question my earlier formulation of the view that opportunities for scholarly advancement were likely to be restricted to certain segments of a lineage. The lineage, according to him, 'was characterized by a feeling of mutual responsibility. To share one's wealth with one's kinsmen, immediate and remote, was highly sanctioned.' And he goes on to argue that in differentiated lineages there were economic mechanisms for the pooling of resources. 'Indeed, providing funds for the education of impecunious younger members of the lineage was one of the primary uses' of the income from lineage property.[1]

The last statement is correct but its interpretation, in my opinion, is not. In a large local lineage there was not one lineage estate; there were several, corresponding to the hierarchy of segments. The chances were that the estate of the local lineage as a whole was smaller than those of some of its constituent units; it had come into existence first, was less likely to have been added to, and might indeed have been depleted, whereas the estates of segments had been built up precisely to assert the separate identity and superior social status of their members. These greater estates, belonging to units lower in the segmentary hierarchy, were the property which served to promote scholarship and ensure a differential access to titles among members of the local lineage as a whole. From my experience in the New Territories I should hazard the guess that the great majority of titled scholars in one of the favoured local lineages were in fact drawn from no more than, say, a tenth of the total lineage population.

Marsh says that the question of the degree to which lineage income and amenities were in fact made available to the poor is an empirical one, 'and only further research can determine the actual extent to which the sons of the poorer branches of a lineage were aided in their mobility-striving by contributions from wealthier branches of the lineage'.[2] (I of course agree with him on this point.) In support of his own view he cites Chang Chung-li,

---

[1] Marsh, *The Mandarins*, pp. 177 f.

[2] *Ibid.*, p. 179 f.

Ping-ti Ho, 'and some other Chinese scholars'.[1] (I note, however, that Ho in his latest statement on the subject, while stressing the importance of 'clan' assistance to poor students, qualifies his argument with the remark that 'educational facilities and examination subsidies instituted by clans were not always adequate but were likely to benefit those whose families' economic standing was above average'.[2]) I am inclined to put my view of the matter in the following way. Lineage income was often applied to setting up and maintaining schools to which all lineage children had access, but these were not the schools where training for the examinations was carried out. Lineage members with literary ambitions were trained in 'studies' and by tutors sometimes financed out of common estates.[3] The subsidies paid to students out of common money (for meals at regular essay-contests and for travelling expenses in connexion with examination-taking, for example)[4] were a 'public' investment in the few men likely, because of their family advantages, to succeed. Indeed, it seems to me to be significant that Mrs Liu, after discussing the financial aid given to candidates in the examinations, comments that it was 'far less generous than the awards for the degree holders'.[5] This, I think, puts the matter in a proper perspective. The emphasis in investment was on the chosen few. So that not only were the rich segments in a specially fortunate position, but they in fact discriminated among their members in favour of a small number of 'families' of high standing.

Social status was regulated by scholarly attainments and by riches, a formula which applies both to groups and individuals. A local lineage taken as a whole enjoyed a position which rested on the sum total of its titled men and the wealth at its disposal, so that even the humbler members of the community shared significantly in its social status vis-à-vis the greater world. Inside a local lineage of high standing men were sharply differentiated from one another according to the particular social status of their families and segments. Some segments and families were indeed so rich and caught up in the preoccupations of politically inspired scholarship that, living in villages and spending their days among

---

[1] *Ibid.*, p. 179.   [2] *The Ladder of Success*, p. 211.
[3] The whole matter of 'academies' (*shu-yüan*) and schools is discussed in Hsiao, *Rural China*, pp. 235 ff.
[4] Liu, *The Traditional Chinese Clan Rules*, p. 129.   [5] *Ibid., loc. cit.*

farmers, their members were in fact strangers to the peasant's way of life. They were landlords (individual or collective), business men, gentlemen of cultivation and leisure. It is for this reason that the Chinese countryside cannot be seen simply as the home of the peasantry. Chinese civilization was agrarian, but its rural society was not uniformly peasant. In my opinion, it is wrong to stress the high proportion of the Chinese population made up by farmers and their dependants; in fact, the proportion is significantly low. Even if we exclude the cities and towns, we find a sizeable fraction of the Chinese population engaged in occupations clearly not those of peasants. Chen Han-seng reports of a survey in the 1930s covering 152 Kwangtung villages (in 38 *hsien*) that 85 per cent of the total population was made up by peasant families, the balance of 15 per cent being composed 'in the main, of merchants and officials, both active and retired, only to a small extent of artisans and other types of workers'.[1] If one out of every ten village families was that of a merchant or official, the countryside was far from being a homogeneous peasant sector of Chinese society.

To understand how power was distributed in the lineage I attempted in *Lineage Organization*[2] to discuss the bearing on it of the governmental system. On this subject too the recent literature has been eloquent,[3] and I shall try briefly to comment on a few points in it, beginning with the relationship between the county magistrate and the people for whom he was responsible.

The material set out in Ch'ü's book is very informative on this question, furnishing us with a clearer picture of local government than has hitherto been available. Fukien and Kwangtung had, at the end of the last century, a total of 136 *hsien* (counties, or 'districts', as Ch'ü calls them),[4] each with a magistrate personally responsible for its government, although in the discharge of his duties he was likely to be helped, both generally and in the carrying out of particular tasks, by a number of subordinate officials, among whom in some counties there were assistant magistrates.[5]

---

[1] Chen Han-seng, *op. cit.*, p. 2.   [2] Pp. 63 ff.

[3] See Hsiao, *op. cit.*; Ho, *Studies on the Population of China*; and Ch'ü T'ung-tsu, *Local Government in China under the Ch'ing*, Cambridge, Mass., 1962. Mrs Sybille van der Sprenkel's thesis, referred to in *Lineage Organization*, has since been published in a revised version as *Legal Institutions in Manchu China, A Sociological Analysis*, London, 1962.

[4] Ch'ü, *op. cit.*, p. 3 (Table 2).   [5] *Ibid.*, pp. 8 ff.

By the rule of 'avoidance' a magistrate was prevented from serving in his own or a neighbouring province and in a province in which certain of his agnates or matrilateral kinsmen were already in office.[1] (The language difficulty to which this rule could give rise[2] is well illustrated by an imperial edict issued in 1728 which is quoted in the 1819 edition of the Hsin-an gazetteer. The Emperor complains of the unintelligibility of officials who are natives of Fukien and Kwangtung, and stresses the plight of the ordinary people of these two provinces in their relations with officials; when an interpreter is interposed between official and subject, truth may well be a casualty.[3])

In Hsin-an at the time the New Territories were created, the county magistrate, whose *yamen* was on the western coast of the *hsien*, had immediately below him an assistant magistrate, posted to the eastern coast, and two deputy magistrates, one of them stationed in the walled city of Kowloon. In addition, there was a number of military officers in the county.[4] Describing Hsin-an some forty years earlier, Krone gives a fairly detailed account of the formal administration. There were several civil mandarins in the county: the county magistrate; three officers stationed at different points in the *hsien* (one of them in Kowloon); a 'director of police' residing with the magistrate; and two 'Inspectors of Education'. The three officers, each stationed at a different place, and the 'director of police' in the county capital were each responsible for a fixed number of villages, and it would appear from Krone's account that together they had the whole county within their co-ordinate jurisdiction under the general supervision and control of the magistrate.[5] There was an establishment of about one thousand soldiers in the *hsien*, commanded by a hierarchy of officers, but Krone makes it clear that their garrison and guard duties were largely neglected.[6] The activity of the civil mandarins appears to have been minimal. The subordinate mandarin at Fuk-wing, whose jurisdiction extended over 200 villages, 'confided to me, in a conversation that I had with him, that he had nothing to do but to eat, to drink and to smoke'.[7] The people usually paid their taxes, but some resistance 'occurred a few years ago, when a village, for what reasons I do not remember, refused

[1] *Ibid.*, pp. 21 f.   [2] Cf. *Lineage Organization*, pp. 63 f.
[3] Quoted Ng, *op. cit.*   [4] Hayes, *op. cit.*, pp. 82 f.
[5] Krone, *op. cit.*, pp. 82 f.   [6] *Ibid.*, pp. 84 f.   [7] *Ibid.*, p. 73.

to pay the amount due to government. The Mandarin however had sufficient force to compel them to comply with their [*sic*] demands, and in order to teach them a lesson for the future, he closed and partially defaced their ancestral hall.'[1] But the 'mandarins in the Sanon [Hsin-an] district have very little power. The people pay the taxes, but do not allow the mandarins to interfere with their own local government. Law suits, differences and offences are very seldom brought before the mandarins. The mandarin from whom I learnt the preceding facts had not, as far [as] I know, during a period of several years, more than one case brought before him for decision; in this instance he was both plaintiff and judge – the criminal being a youth caught stealing fruit in his garden.' The prisoner was brutally treated. 'This solitary act of justice was much laughed at by the people.'[2]

A magistrate's *yamen* was heavily staffed with private secretaries, clerks, runners, and personal servants. The clerks were locally recruited and, embedded as they were in a network of social ties, they could further the interests of those to whom they were obliged by kinship or friendship.[3] Although the tenure of a clerkship was nominally five years, the incumbents often managed to prolong their service, and in default contrived to hand their positions over to kinsmen.[4] Even a small county seems to have had more than a hundred clerks, while a big one might employ ten times that number, the paper work of the *yamen* being very heavy. But in fact a few of the clerkships were nominal offices, sold to rich locals who sought, both for reasons of prestige and because of the need for protection, to gain some kind of official status.[5] At a lower social level the government runners (who acted as messengers, guards, policemen, and so on) formed another large locally recruited and self-perpetuating class of *yamen* servants.[6] As a counterweight to the local and official staff the magistrate had with him a collection of servants and assistants for whose pay he was himself responsible and who were tied to him by bonds of personal loyalty. Finally, the *yamen* held a corps of private secretaries, administrative experts recruited and paid by the magistrate himself to help with the many technical tasks he was called upon to perform (in law, taxation, the examining of aspirant bureaucrats, and so on). These men were them-

[1] *Ibid.*, p. 85.
[4] *Ibid.*, *loc. cit.*
[2] *Ibid.*, p. 92.
[5] *Ibid.*, pp. 38 f.
[3] Ch'ü, *op. cit.*, p. 36.
[6] *Ibid.*, pp. 74 ff.

selves literati or literati-in-the-making; most of them were *sheng-yüan*, some even *chü-jen*.[1]

Through some of his staff, therefore, the magistrate was willy-nilly caught up in the local society, and his *yamen* could be brought under pressure to serve the interests of the most powerful groups in the county. When these groups included literati in their ranks their influence was enhanced. 'An important feature' of the elite formed by the local literati 'was that it was the only group that could legitimately represent the local community in discussing local affairs with the officials and in participating in the governing process.'[2] The many aspects of the status of the literati and of their influence on local government are clearly and fully discussed by Ch'ü.[3] In the context of the present argument it is necessary only to stress the advantage accruing to a group of kinsmen from their numbering literati among them. 'Other relatives of any gentry member – brothers, uncles, nephews, sons and grandsons – because of their connection with this one gentry member were also often very influential in their community. The higher the gentry member's position, the greater the influence of his relatives.'[4] 'In this environment, one's ability to protect one's self and one's family depended primarily on one's position in the bureaucratic hierarchy. It followed that each family or clan looked upon the gentry member within it as its protector.'[5]

We come now to a third regular link between the magistrate's *yamen* and the village or local lineage: the system of local administration. In *Lineage Organization*[6] I concluded that, while the *ti-pao* (as a kind of constable) was certainly a common feature of the rural landscape in southeastern China, the *pao-chia* system may have existed only in name. Since then Ho, Hsiao, and Ch'ü have between them written extensively on the subject[7] and, to pass quickly from their grand surveys to a much smaller scale of

---

[1] *Ibid.*, pp. 93 ff.
[2] *Ibid.*, p. 168. Ch'ü is here speaking of the 'gentry', and he distinguishes, p. 171, between them and the literati on the grounds that some literati never became gentry (because they failed or did not take the examinations) and some gentry (having bought their ranks) were not literati. But, in the attempt to get away from the deceptive English word 'gentry', I have here preferred 'literati', even though it may need to be used sometimes in other than its literal sense.
[3] *Ibid.*, pp. 168 ff.   [4] *Ibid.*, p. 178.   [5] *Ibid.*, p. 180.   [6] Pp. 64 ff.
[7] And cf. Mary Clabaugh Wright, *The Last Stand of Chinese Conservatism: The T'ung-chih Restoration 1862–1874*, Stanford, Calif., 1957, pp. 136 ff. and chap. VII (on local control) generally.

observation, I have managed to form some impression of the standing of the system in the county of Hsin-an in Kwangtung. It has certainly become apparent to me that the *pao-chia* system, in conjunction with a wide array of other forms of local grouping, both official and unofficial, is a matter of vast complexity. And it is by no means yet clear to me how lineages fitted into the total network of local groupings.

Hsiao, of the three writers just mentioned, deals most thoroughly with *pao-chia*, treating it alongside *li-chia*, a system 'originally intended as a help in the collection of the land and corvée imposts'. *Pao-chia* was a system 'to facilitate what may be described as police control'. Both were systems 'of subadministrative divisions, which were superimposed upon but did not replace the natural divisions' of villages, towns, and *hsiang* (major segments of a county, not official administrative divisions in the Ch'ing dynasty).[1] As *pao-chia* was planned, it was to group 10 *hu* (households) in one *p'ai*, 10 *p'ai* in one *chia*, and 10 *chia* in one *pao*; while in the *li-chia* system 10 *hu* were to form one *chia*, and 10 *chia*, along with an extra 10 *hu* (being those households which had the largest number of tax-paying adult men) one *li*.[2] But while these systems were designed in the early years of the Ch'ing dynasty to be quite separate in both grouping and function, by the eighteenth century *li-chia* seems to have been merged into *pao-chia* and the joint system to have declined in effectiveness.

Two purposes were to be served by *pao-chia*: the registration of individuals and households,[3] and the reporting to authority of crimes and criminals. The latter function was apparently the more important. The aim, it seems, was to produce a cheap system of political control without calling upon or stimulating local self-government. In the period when the state seriously attempted to get the system to work, an effort was made to draw all subjects of the Empire within its scope, and it is interesting to us that local lineages 'were also integrated into the control system by turning them into supplementary units of the *pao-chia*'. Hsiao goes on to quote from an imperial order issued in 1726: 'In

[1] Hsiao, *op. cit.*, p. 12.

[2] *Ibid.*, p. 32. To complicate matters, a third kind of unit, the *she*, was recognized as an official division, grouping villages together in some cases, but apparently being intended primarily as a small unit of households. The *she* seems often to have been merged in the *li-chia* system: *ibid.*, pp. 36 ff.

[3] For this reason Ho, *Studies on the Population of China*, draws on *pao-chia* data.

villages and walled rural communities where clans with one hundred or more members dwell together, and where the regular *pao-chia* cannot make thorough inspections, a *tsu-cheng* [clan head] is established in each clan. . . .'[1] *Rural China* contains a detailed survey of the fate of the system, as reflected in official writings, and it appears that after the first quarter of the nineteenth century *pao-chia* became 'a mere *ku-shih* (an antiquated formality)' having generally failed of its purpose.[2] The *ti-pao* (or *ti-fang*), however, did not disappear. In fact, he does not seem to have been created at the beginning of the dynasty, but in the mid-eighteenth century he is defined as the head of a group of villages with both police and tax duties, being then distinct from any office-holder in the *pao-chia* system; yet by the latter part of the nineteenth century he had in effect come to stand for all that was effectively left of the *pao-chia* and *li-chia* systems, except perhaps for the units of local militia which were organized as a military version of the old system of police control.[3] 'Before the nineteenth century drew to an end, some observers had come to the conclusion that the *pao-chia* as an instrument of police control had "disappeared in reality as well as in name".'[4]

The 1819 edition of the Hsin-an gazetteer seems to imply that *pao-chia* was in full force,[5] but by the end of the century, when British administrators came to take over the greater part of the county, other forms of local administration appear to have caught their attention. They found *ti-pao*, whom they regarded as a superior sort of constable,[6] but government below the level of the county magistrate seemed to them to be a matter of *self*-government within divisions known as *tung* ('cave') and *hsiang*.[7] In my opinion Lockhart took a somewhat romantic view of local self-government as he saw it in Hsin-an; he makes it appear to be

---

[1] Hsiao, *op. cit.*, p. 47. The same passage is quoted *ibid.*, p. 69, but in a slightly different translation.   [2] *Ibid.*, p. 55.   [3] *Ibid.*, pp. 63 ff.
[4] *Ibid.*, p. 67. See also Ho, *op. cit.*, especially pp. 36 ff., 48 ff., 67 ff. Ch'ü, *Local Government*, discusses *pao-chia* at pp. 150 ff.
[5] See Ng, *op. cit.*
[6] See *Lineage Organization*, p. 66 n.
[7] See Hayes, *op. cit.*, p. 83. On *hsiang* cf. pp. 22 f. above. I have not yet been able to convince myself that I know what *tung* were. As my remarks below on another form of grouping in the New Territories will make evident, a great deal of research has yet to be done on local government and structure in the area. I have begun to examine the British records on the early New Territories in an attempt to answer some of the problems raised by Lockhart's terminology.

democratic;[1] but I imagine that he was right in seeing the hand of the state play only very lightly over the countryside. By this time, at any rate, imperial control was weak.[2]

One other form of local grouping is mentioned in the first British writings on the New Territories: *yeuk* (the Cantonese form of *yüeh*, 'pact'). I propose to discuss it at some length because it leads on to some interesting questions of inter-lineage relationships. The discussion can most conveniently be opened by a reference to the history of one of the New Territories market towns, Tai Po.[3] There for long stood a market town at Tai Po: Tai Po Kau Hui. It was (and physically remains) just by the Tang lineage settlement of Tai Po Tau, although it seems to have come under the control of Tang people further north in the settlement of Lung Yeuk Tau. As Masters of the Market the Tang people taxed sellers and, if the stories now told are to be taken as history and not as retrospective justifications of revolt, they harassed buyers by their exercise of the privilege of claiming choice goods. From time to time their monopoly of the right to hold a market in the area was challenged by their neighbours, and in the early 1890s, the matter having been brought to the *hsien* court at Nam Tau, a ruling was given by the magistrate that only the Tang had the right to build shops in the vicinity of the market. This decision (which was inscribed on a stone slab and placed in the Heavenly Queen Temple in Tai Po Kau Hui) appears to have been the

[1] Hayes, *op. cit.*, pp. 83 f., quotes his account of how disputes were first dealt with in village councils, and could be taken to a *tung* council and still higher to a general council consisting of the representatives of the various *tung*.

[2] It is a matter of some interest that when the British first administered Hong Kong island they began by imitating or adapting the *pao-chia* system, whereas the administrative arrangements made for the New Territories half a century later were of a different kind. Ordinance no. 13 of 1844 was enacted 'for the appointment of and regulation of native Chinese Peace Officers Paouchung and Paoukea within the Colony of Hong Kong'. In 1848 the Governor described the system in town and country as 'consisting precisely of Tithings and Hundreds superintended by Tithing men and Hundreders' and commended it as being 'most grateful to the people as well as being most efficient in its results' – and it would cost nothing, since the officers were to be elected and honorary. But in fact, although the system lasted for some time, it was not very effective, and the 'Chinese Peace Officers (commonly called *tippos*) . . . were discontinued' – Charles Collins, *Public Administration in Hong Kong*, London and N.Y., 1952, pp. 65, 128. And cf. G. B. Endacott, *Government and People in Hong Kong*, Hong Kong, 1964, pp. 37 f.

[3] As I have already said, place names in Hong Kong have official spellings. Surnames are also given in the official (Cantonese) romanization.

culmination of a series of challenges to Tang power by a local lineage surnamed Man in the nearby village of Tai Hang. In response to the unfavourable outcome of the lawsuit, the Man and their allies almost at once rallied local support to found a new market some half a mile from the old one. This was the beginning (about five years before the entry of the British) of the modern market town of Tai Po[1] and the origin of the alliance known as the Ts'at Yeuk (the Seven Yüeh). The new market flourished and in a short time consigned its rival to decrepitude. The founders of the new Tai Po market built a Civil and Military Temple as its centre, housing there the public weighing scales from which they and their successors have derived a steady income.

The story goes that the member of the Man local lineage who led the successful revolt against the Tang monopoly started the new market by calling a meeting of the leaders of seven *yeuk* around Tai Po, each *yeuk* taking up a share in the market in the form of shops. The land on which the market was built appears to have been for the most part the property of the Man. Now it is probable that the Ts'at Yeuk dates from this event in the early 1890s, as my informants assert,[2] but the *yeuk* of which it was composed were presumably much older. A *yeuk* was a collection of neighbouring villages (but not necessarily all the villages in one area) operating as a unit and sometimes holding a common estate. *Yeuk* and complexes of *yeuk*, such as the Ts'at Yeuk, can be shown to have been common in what was to become the New Territories (although the Ts'at Yeuk is the only complex to have survived intact to the present day, as far as I have discovered). The Ts'at Yeuk embraced over seventy villages of a great variety of surnames, but the individual *yeuk* were of unequal

[1] Most of the story up to this point is told in Sung Hok-p'ang, 'Legends and Stories of the New Territories, I, Tai Po', *The Hong Kong Naturalist*, vol. VI, no. I, May 1935. I followed up the clues given in this article and collected a number of accounts of the founding of the new market and of the Ts'at Yeuk associated with it. Mr R. G. Groves was until the spring of this year (1965) in the field carrying out a detailed study of Tai Po and its ties with the surrounding villages. The stone slab recording the magistrate's decision no longer stands in the temple. When the temple was recently rebuilt the stone was cast into the yard where I found it encumbered with rubbish, a neglected minor monument of late Ch'ing history. Now see Mr Groves's paper, 'The Origins of Two Market Towns in the New Territories' in Royal Asiatic Society, Hong Kong Branch, *Aspects of Social Organization in the New Territories*, Hong Kong [1965].

[2] Apart from the inscribed stone slab I have discovered no contemporary document on the subject.

size, so that while, for example, the Man settlement at Tai Hang constituted a *yeuk* on its own, Lam Tsuen *yeuk* consisted of twenty-six villages. When the villages making up the whole complex are plotted on a map they can be seen to form a more or less continuous arc round Tai Po (on one side the town faces the sea), but there are two striking irregularities in the physical distribution of component villages. First, the three villages making up the *yeuk* of Fan Leng (Fanling) stand away to the north, being in fact so much out of the immediate Tai Po area that today they fall administratively into a different sub-district. Second, about twenty villages within the range of the arc are not members of any *yeuk*.[1] Some of them are settlements which have come into being since the 1890s, but a few certainly existed at the time the new market was planned and were deliberately excluded or excluded themselves from the union. Naturally, the Tang settlement at Tai Po Tau is one of them; they were the general enemy. Others were probably clients of the Tang and unable or unwilling to participate in the revolutionary move.

The Tang and the Man are both Punti local lineages (that is, they are 'Cantonese'). The former are members of the most powerful higher-order lineage in the New Territories, the chief local lineages of which are situated on the Yuen Long plain. They have a long history of moderately successful scholarship and undeniable mastery of a large part of the county from which the New Territories were cut out. The Man local lineage belongs to a clan of which the most important settlement is at San Tin. The Tai Hang Man had for long intermarried with the Tang (their written genealogy shows that the Tang gave them many women), were rich, and had produced some scholars. Their rivalry with the Tang at Tai Po Tau and Lung Yeuk Tau was not new in the 1890s. As the story of the market demonstrates, the competition was in part commercial, and the Tang at Tai Po Tau tell of a leading Tang and his Man counterpart competing to see which of them could lay the longer line of silver dollars along the path leading north from their settlement. But the area in which the Tang and the Man lineages were settled was predominantly Hakka territory, and it was necessary for the Man, if they were to succeed in their contest with the Tang over the market, to enlist Hakka support.

[1] It is perhaps worth noting that the Hakka village described by Miss Pratt was a member of one of the *yeuk*.

Second in importance to the Man in the story of the market were the Hakka Ma of Wun Yiu. They appear to have formed a small but well-to-do settlement. The last flickers to be seen today of the hostility to the Tang in Ts'at Yeuk circles fail to suggest that the fight over the market was a quarrel between Hakka and Punti as such, and my impression is that, whatever may have been in earlier times the state of feeling between communities speaking the two Chinese languages, by the end of the nineteenth century local alignments by no means depended solely on ethnic solidarity.[1]

It is possible to piece together rough accounts of *yeuk*-complexes in other areas of the New Territories. I shall not go over all the evidence here, but to introduce a contrast with the purely rural character of the Ts'at Yeuk, let me consider the Four (Sz) Yeuk of Tsuen Wan, the Six (Luk) Yeuk of Sai Kung, and the Nine (Kau) Yeuk of Sha Tin. These three *yeuk*-complexes were to be found in the neighbourhood of the walled city of Kowloon, which was the only centre of government in that part of the county to be taken over by the British. It held the *yamen* of a deputy magistrate and certain military officials, no doubt acquiring some of its importance as a seat of government in the second half of the nineteenth century from the proximity of the British Colony of Hong Kong. The Six Yeuk and the Nine Yeuk were certainly of mixed Punti and Hakka villages. The three complexes were in some fashion tied in with a council, formal or informal, in Kowloon City; and it appears likely that the local deputy magistrate used this organization to make and keep contact with villages in his neighbourhood. In 1879, according to its own records (for the organization still exists, although in a different form and with other functions) there came into being in Kowloon City a body known as the Lok Sin Tong; members of the three *yeuk*-complexes of Tsuen Wan, Sai Kung, and Sha Tin were represented on it. Its primary object seems to have been to promote charity, public works, and education. In general character it would appear to have been an association of local notables.

The network of *yeuk*, while certainly not covering the whole of

[1] It should be noted that Hsin-an does not appear to have been much affected by the Hakka-Punti fighting of the mid-nineteenth century. Cf. Laai Yi-faai, Franz Michael, and John C. Sherman, 'The Use of Maps in Social Research: A Case Study in South China', *The Geographical Review*, vol. LII, January 1962, map at p. 94, where no area shown for 'feuds . . . between Hakkas and the Puntis' lies east of the Canton delta.

what is now the New Territories, was nevertheless widespread. From such evidence as I have been able to collect, I am inclined to argue that complexes of *yeuk*, if not individual *yeuk* themselves, were formed to protect the interests of the weak against the strong. I suspect that strong lineages did not join in such alliances. The Tang of Lung Yeuk[1] Tau and Tai Po Tau stood aloof from *yeuk*, as did, I think, nearly all the influential lineages in the New Territories. And it is probably significant that the Man of Tai Hang came to form a *yeuk* on their own when they assumed leadership in the struggle over the market; for up to that point I assume that they were important enough to be independent of such formal alliances, becoming a *yeuk* (and so assimilating themselves to the pattern of their humbler neighbours) in response to the needs of a new situation in which they were forced to seek allies. The villages in the Luk Yeuk of Sai Kung were subject to Tang landlords or taxlords (it would not be possible to decide which they were without a longish debate on the relation between the rents collected and taxes exacted, officially or otherwise, by strong lineages),[2] and they may have used their contacts with the Kowloon organization to ward off the direct penalties for their being weak. In a part of the Empire where the state could not be relied on to redress wrongs and protect property and lives, the weaker communities were forced to seek among themselves (and sometimes, as the case of the Ts'at Yeuk illustrates, with the aid of a stronger community) protection against being molested by local powers.

We must examine the term *yeuk* before attempting to push the argument any further. It can be taken to mean a pact or agreement, and several of my informants interpreted *yeuk* and *yeuk*-complexes as contracts or joint enterprises freely entered into. (It is, as one man explained to me, like a business partnership in which people take shares.) But in fact it is possible to argue that what we have caught a glimpse of at the end of the Ch'ing dynasty may have been less a spontaneous and popular form of grouping than a development of an official and imposed form of control. *Yeuk*, in the context we have been discussing, may be taken to be an abbreviation of *heung yeuk* (Mandarin: *hsiang-yüeh*), a term with a long history in Chinese local government and

---

[1] The character for this part of the name is different from that for 'pact'.
[2] Cf. *Lineage Organization*, pp. 75 f.

administration. It appears first in Northern Sung, when a Confucian scholar set out a scheme for a kind of village self-government in which country people were to promote among themselves (as good Chinese should) morality, education, social solidarity, and mutual aid. The plan seems to have enjoyed some vogue in Ming times, but the early Ch'ing rulers took over the term to give it a new meaning: *hsiang-yüeh* became a public lecture system by means of which the masses were to be indoctrinated with the political ethics of Confucianism in a kind of adult education. Yet by the nineteenth century *hsiang-yüeh* had once again undergone a transformation, a lecture system having developed into a framework of state control to the point where (to increase the complexity of administrative groupings we have already examined) *hsiang-yüeh* was sometimes taken to be synonymous with *pao-chia* and *li-chia*. On the other hand, a contrary process was also at work, moving *hsiang-yüeh* back some distance towards the kind of self-government which had originally been conceived under its name. It is on record that in places in Kwangtung province the heads of *hsiang-yüeh* assumed roles of leadership in such a way as to take command of local affairs. Moreover, *hsiang-yüeh* were used as a framework for organizing militia (*t'uan-lien*) for local defence. (During the troubles of the nineteenth century *t'uan-lien* and *pao-chia* came often to be closely associated, even to the point of merging;[1] so that in the last phase of Ch'ing rule *hsiang-yüeh*, *pao-chia*, and *t'uan-lien* may perhaps be regarded as three forms of state control so weakened as to promote local initiative and encourage local self-government.) And it is an interesting speculation that, if we manage to find the evidence, we may discover that, just as the *ke yüeh hsiang-yung* (the village braves of the several *yüeh*) rallied to the defence of Canton against the British in 1842, so some of the armed resistance to the British when they first arrived in the New Territories was bound up with the Ts'at Yeuk and other *yeuk*-complexes.[2]

[1] See Hsiao, *op. cit.*, p. 66. Ch'ü, *op. cit.*, p. 151, on the other hand, insists they were kept separate.

[2] I should have been even more lost in the complicated historical question of *hsiang-yüeh* had it not been for Hsiao's exposition in *Rural China*, pp. 184–205. See also Ch'ü, *op. cit.*, pp. 162, 203, 321, and Liu, 'An Analysis of Chinese Clan Rules', pp. 69 f. Sidney D. Gamble, *North China Villages, Social, Political and Economic Activities before 1933*, Berkeley and Los Angeles, 1963, makes at pp. 118 f. a brief historical reference to *hsiang-yüeh*, saying that by the end of the Ch'ing dynasty it had practically disappeared. He concludes, p. 119: 'The hsiang-

My tentative conclusion – there is more evidence, both documentary and oral, to be collected before firmer views can be expressed – is that, while early Ch'ing policy may have popularized the term *hsiang-yüeh* in the course of spreading the system of public lectures, yet at the time we are concerned with, at least in coastal Kwangtung, *yüeh* were looked upon by the people who engaged in them as instruments of local control independent of state supervision. They might be used for treating with the state, as seems especially to have been the case with the three *yüeh*-complexes oriented to Kowloon City, and might have allied themselves with officialdom in the face of banditry or attack by rebels and foreigners, but they were far removed from being mere tools in the hands of the government. From the point of view of the people, the *yüeh* were *their* organizations; in the early British writings on the New Territories and in the statements made to me by men separated from the heyday of the system by only one or two generations, the autonomy of local groupings seems to be fairly clearly indicated. Again, Liang Ch'i-ch'ao (1873–1929), the reforming literatus, whose home village lay in another part of coastal Kwangtung, seems to see some historical link between *hsiang-yüeh* and the existence of a high degree of local autonomy in his own ancestral region.[1] In short, whatever

yüeh, village officer, appointed by village heads in Shansi for a one-year term of unpaid service, may be a remnant of the earlier system.' And cf. *ibid.*, p. 344. Martin C. Yang, *A Chinese Village, Taitou, Shantung Province*, London, 1948, p. 173, calls the *hsiang-yüeh* a tax collector although originally, he says, the man's chief duty 'was to convey to the villagers the Emperor's instructions as to how to be a filial son' and so on. It will be seen, then, that the term *hsiang-yüeh* can, according to context, mean a system, a grouping, an office, or an office-holder.

[1] See his *History of Chinese Culture* (in Chinese), modern reprint by Taiwan Chinese Book Co., 1956, pp. 56–60. I was lucky enough to have my attention directed to this passage when I was discussing my puzzlement over *yeuk* with Mr Lo Hsiang-lin and Mr P. K. Yu of the University of Hong Kong. Hsiao, *op. cit.*, pp. 345 ff., translates a large part of this very same passage of Liang's book, but does not indicate that Liang deals historically with *hsiang-yüeh*. Besides documenting Kwangtung lineage organization in a most interesting way, Liang's account says something important about the interweaving of *pao-chia*, local militia, and village self-government. The settlement described (on an island off the coast of Hsin-hui) was divided into three *pao*, one of which was constituted by the Liang lineage of 3,000 souls. 'Matters that only concerned one *pao* were decided locally, but those that affected all the three *pao*, were dealt with by a sort of federated organization known as the *San-pao-Miao* [Temple of the Three *Pao*]'. The seat of the government of the *pao* made up by the Liang lineage was their ancestral hall, where the highest authority was vested in the 'council of elders'. 'There was

Ch'ing policy may have planned in the way of measures of local control came, at least when dynastic power was at a low ebb, to be used by the country people as modes of self-government in an autocratic state.

But it is important – and the point brings us back to the distribution of power within the lineage – to remember that local self-government, whatever form it took, was not democratic. Liang's account of his own local lineage recalls a common form of internal control (and is the more significant because the facts he presents speak against an interpretation of his account as being romanticized). The council of elders was composed of lineage members over the age of 51,[1] but younger men who 'possessed *kung-ming* above the *sheng-yüan* or *chien-sheng* . . . were eligible to participate in the deliberations of the council. . . .' The decisions of the council were carried out by four to six managers (*chih-li*), appointed from among the younger lineage members. The council met more than twenty times a year, two of the meetings, at spring and autumn, being fixed. 'The total number of the elders exceeded sixty. Only a minority of them, however, attended the meetings. Decisions were occasionally made with a "quorum" of only a few elders.'[2] In dealing with the state, collecting taxes owed to the government, preserving the peace, righting wrongs, organizing defence forces, and in a score of

a *pao-chang* whose duty was to deal with the local government. His social position was very low. Unless he was an elderly person, he could not attend the meetings of the council.' In each of the three *pao* there was a *hsiang t'uan*, a rural corps of militia. The militia in the Liang lineage were under the direction of the council of elders. Those who volunteered for service and were accepted received double shares of 'the sacrificial meat'. – Hsiao, *op. cit.*, pp. 345 f.

[1] By Chinese reckoning; roughly equivalent to 50.

[2] *Ibid.*, p. 345. At p. 346 we find Liang's account of how the lineage worked as a legal institution. If a dispute arose, a settlement was attempted by 'elderly relatives' of the parties. The disputing parties might then appeal to the ancestral hall of the lineage-segment to which they belonged. From here they could go to the council of elders. (Cf. the account given by Lin Yueh-hwa of a similar process in I-hsü in Fukien: *Lineage Organization*, p. 36.) Litigation beyond this level (i.e., in an official court) was rare, because 'it was considered highly improper for any clansman to disobey the elders'. The council could also punish offenders. Men who 'violated laws of the imperial government, such as those against gambling and feuds, were punished by being whipped in front of the ancestral tablets, or by *t'ing-tso* . . . for a stated period.' *T'ing-tso* was the penalty of being barred from receiving a share of the sacrificial meat. Defaulting tenants of lineage land were subject to this punishment. Again, lineage members who stole were tied up and paraded through the streets to be jeered at and insulted (*yu-hsing*).

other matters, the local lineage, either on its own or in combination with others, managed its affairs by dint of placing them effectively in the hand of those of its members who, by virtue of their standing in the greater world and their resources of power within the lineage itself, were capable of formulating policy and acting in what they considered to be the interests of the community. The lineage elite was certainly subject to the control of public opinion and, in the extreme, it might run the risk of so alienating the ordinary members that they might withdraw their support; but whatever these checks on the abuse of power, the lineage was not (as it has been imagined to be by some people) a little republic where elders in the literal sense were the leaders and all voices were to be heard.

The material on *hsiang-yüeh* helps to correct a bias in my earlier treatment of the position of weak lineages. For, although I gave a place to the groupings of weak lineages of different surnames,[1] I had overlooked the possibility that there might be a regular pattern of local alliances between lineages such that hostilities between them could be kept in check and an effective balance be maintained between a few dominant lineages on one side and a mass of weaker lineages on the other. The small lineages in the Ts'at Yeuk of Tai Po found a champion in the Man lineage; it needed their support, but at the same time was their buffer against the Tang. And because it had connexions in the wider society[2] it could at once both dominate and shield its allies.

The question of local alliances takes us back to a problem raised in Chapter 1: the relationship between what Skinner has defined as standard marketing communities and what I have called 'vicinages', the latter being areas within which local lineages tend to be grouped to form higher-order lineages.[3] It will be remembered that according to Skinner's argument, 'composite lineages' are likely to be confined to the communities centred on the lowest level of market town. In the model which Skinner constructs, there are eighteen villages in a standard marketing area

[1] *Lineage Organization*, p. 113.
[2] When the new Tai Po market was set up and the government had to be convinced that it did not infringe the rights of the Tang – or rather, prevented from taking official cognizance of the fact that the new market did indeed infringe these rights – the Man of Tai Hang, according to one of my informants (not himself a Man), used their ties with an official whose surname was Man.
[3] See above, p. 23.

with a total population of 1,500 households (say, 7,000 people).[1] The Hsin-an gazetteer of 1819 lists 41 market towns (*hsü-shih*) and 854 villages and hamlets (*ts'un-chuang*).[2] On these figures a standard marketing area included, on the average, some twenty villages or hamlets and about 5,000 people. (The assumption here is that there was a total population of 200,000; the gazetteer itself gives an 1815 population figure of a quarter of a million.) It will be seen, therefore, that the nineteenth-century numerical data on Hsin-an support Skinner's general analysis of traditional China as a whole.[3]

There is a further respect in which the analysis appears to be confirmed by the Hsin-an material. Basing himself on an example drawn from Fukien province, Skinner suggests that a dominant local lineage within the 'composite lineage' of the community may have control of the market itself.[4] The Tang at Lung Yeuk Tau seem to have been in this position with regard to the old Tai Po market, although the Tang local lineage at Tai Po Tau itself were the only other Tang in the area. A clearer example is to be found in the control of the predecessor of the modern Yuen Long market, in the western part of the New Territories, for here, in the heart of the Tang country, one segment of a local Tang lineage were the owners of the market. Again, the old market at Sheung Shui was the property of the powerful Liu local lineage. It would seem, therefore, that control of the lowest level market town characteristically gave the controllers the dominant voice in the area served by the market, and that where there were two

[1] Skinner, 'Marketing and Social Structure. . . . Pt. I', pp. 18, 33. On the general subject cf. Martin M. C. Yang, 'The Traditional Market-Town Area as a Modern Rural Community in China', in Chinese with English abstract, *Journal of Sociology*, National Taiwan Univ., no. 1, December 1963.

[2] Ng, *op. cit.* Krone *op. cit.*, p. 80, cites this information from the gazetteer and comments: 'Many of the villages mentioned in this list are now deserted or destroyed, but many new ones have also appeared, and we may fairly say that their numbers have rather increased than diminished.' He goes on to say that there 'are in the district [i.e. *hsien*] forty places where markets are held . . . generally built in a rectangular square . . . [and] visited every third or fifth day by hundreds and sometimes thousands of people, who assemble from the whole neighbourhood, and frequently from great distances'.—*ibid.*, *loc. cit.* Krone is evidently describing not only 'standard' but also higher level markets. 'Those who frequent these markets are usually joined in league for mutual protection against robbers.'—*ibid.*, p. 81. This last remark may possibly be a reference to *yeuk*.

[3] Kato Shigeru (cited by Eberhard, *Social Mobility*, p. 241 n.) finds that in the late nineteenth century a market served 8,149 people in Kwangtung and 5,849 in Fukien. [4] See pp. 24 f. above.

or more local lineages of the same higher-order lineage in this area, the ownership of the market by one of them (or by one of its segments) gave it undisputed precedence. How significant the control of the market was for local domination is brought out dramatically by the story of the creation of the new market at Tai Po: commercial and political mastery were wrested from the local Tang at one blow.

Where the local lineages of a dominant higher-order lineage were distributed over a restricted area it is clear that they provided the framework for local organization above the level of the village. The Tang local lineages in the Yuen Long area, many of the local lineages in Hui-an *hsien* in Fukien (according to Amyot's material),[1] and the Ong local lineages in Chi-chou 'district' in Taiwan[2] assumed this role. The area, so to say, took its character from the dominant group, while divisions of the area in turn took theirs from the local representatives of this group.

But it does not follow that a local community so constituted on the framework of a dominant higher-order lineage or a local community formed by a *yeuk*-complex was necessarily, in Skinner's language, a marketing community. True, the Ts'at Yeuk was centred on a market; the market was indeed its *raison d'être*; but it remains to be discovered whether the other *yeuk*-complexes were. (I think, on the other hand, that we should not attach too much importance to the fact that the Ts'at Yeuk alliance did not include all the villages in its area. What we see to have taken place in the 1890s was the beginning of an organization which soon passed under British rule; if the traditional conditions of the Chinese Empire had persisted, the excluded members might have eventually been brought in. And my impression of the other evidence on *yeuk*-complexes is that it indicates each of them to have embraced all the villages in its respective area.) The 'district' of Chi-chou, as described by Wolf, does not appear to have been connected significantly with a market; it was on a much smaller scale than that implied in the term 'marketing community'.[3] That there were significant local units above the level of the village, not defined in the official administrative system, is beyond dispute, and we cannot possibly refuse our assent to Skinner's proposition that 'Anthropological work on Chinese society, by focusing attention almost exclusively on the village,

[1] See pp. 22 f. above.   [2] See pp. 23 f. above.   [3] But see above, p. 25 n. 3.

has with few exceptions distorted the reality of rural social structure'.[1] But we are evidently only at the beginning of an understanding of the forms the local units took.

There is a final point to be made arising out of the discussion of *yeuk*. By introducing the subject of the relationship between Punti and Hakka, the data suggest a criticism which could be (and indeed has been) made of my earlier treatment of ethnic diversity in southeastern China. (In reviewing *Lineage Organization*, my friend Professor Skinner castigated me thus: 'The anthropologist is taken aback to find no open acknowledgement or description of the ethnographic distinctions among the major peoples of the region – Hokkiens, Cantonese, Hakkas, etc.'[2] I must apologize for having shocked him.) In writing my earlier book I worked on the assumption that since I was concerned with a few general principles of social structure rather than the cultural apparatus in which these principles were expressed, I could justifiably ignore the differences in custom between, say, Hokkien and Tiuchiu or Cantonese and Hakka. Of course the provinces of Fukien and Kwangtung are very heterogeneous in their spoken languages, and of course there is a strong presumption (let alone good evidence collected among Overseas Chinese from these two provinces) that other cultural differences are correlated with those of language. But I chose to assume that these differences would not be relevant at the level of generality at which I was trying to write. Having now seen something of Hakka and Punti lineages in the New Territories, I think I was justified in the procedure I adopted; but the time has come, the general framework having been established, to pay more attention to the particular cultural differences between Punti and Hakka that might conceivably have a bearing on variations in lineage forms and modes of action in the realm of kinship. It is a reasonable question to ask, and may be one well worth trying to answer, whether, for example, Hakka lineages tend to be small and genealogically simple only because they are poor, or also because of some special elements in the Hakka tradition which inhibit genealogical elaboration. It would be prejudice to dismiss the question out of hand (as I confess my impulse would have me do). The more striking cultural gap between the Hakka and the Punti taken together and the Tanka

---

[1] Skinner, *op. cit.*, p. 32.
[2] *Pacific Affairs*, vol. XXXII, no. 2, June 1959, p. 208.

and Hoklo boat people (these four ethnic groups encompassing the total range which can be studied in the traditional New Territories) is not at first sight relevant to problems of lineage organization: the boat people do not have lineages. But in fact it may be useful to ask whether it is only a way of life, considered primarily in its economic and residential aspects, or a cultural background which prevents deep patrilineages from being formed. What happens to boat people when they settle on land?[1]

On the other hand, it might be argued that, even within the schematic framework of my earlier essay, there was an immediately relevant organizational aspect of ethnic divisions which was overlooked: perhaps 'Hakka' and 'Punti' were bases of social action as well as being the names of cultural entities. In other words, there may have been situations in which communities were united by, or on the basis of, their consciousness of a common cultural identity. In fact, Myron Cohen, a young American anthropologist, has, in so far as the Hakka are concerned, tackled this question very ably and interestingly in a dissertation which, because it is unpublished, I can do no more than refer to.[2] Of course, the Hakka-Punti fighting of the nineteenth century[3] is evidence enough of ethnic solidarity, but I am not yet convinced from my knowledge of the New Territories that there has been a consistent pattern in which being Hakka or Punti has been a basis for social organization. The material on *yeuk* suggests that ethnic divisions were irrelevant to alignment, although one might also argue that ethnic solidarity, by being one of several bases of extra-village organization (along with patrilineal descent, secret society, and territorial alliance), contributed to that very complexity of social ties which made it possible for some sort of order to be maintained in a part of China that one might have superficially supposed was well on the road to anarchy.

It seems fairly clear, however, that having once started to investigate the significance of the cultural differences between Hakka and Punti (or any set of spoken-language groupings), we shall not be able to stop there, for we may well discover that these are not the units within which variations important to our

[1] The only close study of the boat people in Hong Kong has been that by Miss Ward, whose papers are cited above', p. 17 n.

[2] *The Hakka or 'Guest People': Dialect as a Sociocultural Variable in Southeastern China*, M.A. thesis, Columbia Univ. [1962?].

[3] See *Lineage Organization*, p. 116.

enquiry occur. In an earlier context I referred to local differences in the extent to which a woman's natal family exercise control over her second marriage.[1] It seems almost certain that this structurally crucial variation does not follow language lines; as with other important differences, it may need to be pinpointed in marketing communities[2] or whatever other unit of local organization we fix on. Indeed, I should be inclined to look first to small-scale local variation, for I think there is a great danger in the study of southeastern China that people will assume for all Hakka or Hokkien or Cantonese or Tiuchiu that what some of them do in one place is characteristic of the behaviour of all of them.

The one subject I attempted to deal with in *Lineage Organization*[3] about which I am scarcely any better informed now is secret societies. We can hardly expect field work in the New Territories to add greatly to our knowledge of this topic (at least in respect of its significance in pre-British times), but we may not be altogether unrealistic in hoping that future historical research will help to explain the role of the secret societies in the social organization of southeastern China.[4] I shall confine myself now to a single point. Skinner has pointed out that in Szechwan the lodges of the Ko-lao Hui were organized within standard marketing communities, their headquarters being in the market town.[5] I think there is an indication in the early British records of the New Territories that some market towns were in fact the centres of Triad Society activity, and the question arises whether we should consider the secret society in southeastern China as an arm of the power by which the group that controlled the market town (often a local lineage or a segment of one) maintained, or sought to maintain, its dominance of the local scene.

The power generally accruing to dominant lineages – to hold their neighbours in subjection, to extract rents in the form of 'taxes', to seize land, to fend off government interference – rested in the last analysis on the acts and abstentions of the state. Lineages resisted government and relied on that very government for their ability to resist. From the state flowed the honours and privileges

---

[1] See p. 59 above.
[2] Cf. Skinner, 'Marketing and Social Structure . . . Pt. I', p. 39.
[3] Pp. 117–25.
[4] An informative study of secret societies in modern Hong Kong has appeared, but it does not touch upon questions I am concerned with here: W. P. Morgan, *Triad Societies in Hong Kong*, Hong Kong, 1960.   [5] Skinner, *op. cit.*, p. 37.

which were the basis of every dominant lineage's power. If it pushed too hard against the government, miscalculating the distance to which a particular official was prepared to retreat and its own ability to exert influence on him from above, it ran the risk of suffering the only sanction (apart from brute force, which the government was rarely in a position to apply) that would make it smart: the refusal by the magistrate to allow its men to take the periodical examinations. For without titled scholars and the power built up by them, a lineage lacked the foundation for dominating its neighbours and holding the government in check. By encouraging the men within his jurisdiction to take and succeed in the examinations and by making relatively few demands on the people he governed – he was usually content to collect his taxes and ensure a semblance of order – the magistrate was in fact creating that power to resist which, when the balance between government and the governed was very delicate, might be a terrible danger to him. State and people were locked together in a system; the state promoted centres of local power to which it looked for support and from which it could expect defiance. For most of the time, lineage organization was in the eyes of the state a good thing. In its best form it was eminently Confucian; it fostered scholarship; it taught obedience. But let it go a shade beyond high utility and the good thing was a very bad thing indeed. Suddenly local power was a menace, virtue became vice.

4

Relations Between Lineages

In this chapter I take up afresh two problems discussed in *Lineage Organization*: the significance of the marriage links between lineages, and the system of violence within which lineages stood opposed and allied.

My earlier discussion of the first problem started from the question of matrilateral cross-cousin marriage. The ethnography of it has been somewhat added to since 1957. Newell, having worked among southern Tiuchiu living in Malaya, has emphatically asserted that they practise cross-cousin marriage neither overseas nor at home in China,[1] not even to the limited extent suggested for northern Tiuchiu by Kulp.[2] A recent brief survey of cousin marriage in China as a whole (reinforced by the author's work on a village in Taiwan) concludes *inter alia* that 'cross-cousin marriage is usually merely allowed rather than preferred, even with the MoBrDa [mother's brother's daughter]; that FaSiDa [father's sister's daughter] marriage tends to be disapproved rather than allowed; and that MoBrDa marriage, though actually preferential in some regions, is in general merely permissible'.[3]

From my limited experience in the New Territories I cannot make any more definite contribution to the southeastern Chinese

---

[1] *Treacherous River*, pp. 50, 216 f.　　[2] See *Lineage Organization*, pp. 97 f.

[3] Gallin, 'Cousin Marriage in China', p. 108. At p. 107 Gallin cites a local estimate of the extent of cousin marriage in the village he studied in Taiwan: c. 1.5 per cent of all males marry a mother's brother's daughter, c. 0.5 per cent a father's sister's daughter, and c. 2 per cent a mother's sister's daughter. 'In other words, in this informant's opinion, "only about 4 per cent of all marriages are with *ch'in ch'i* (cousins), and the remainder . . . are marriages with strangers or friends".' But we may suspect that the informant has said more than Gallin allows for – or rather, less than Gallin thinks: the 4 per cent of cousin marriages appear from the way the informant speaks (contrasting *ch'in ch'i* with strangers and friends) to be in reality the proportion of marriages with all non-agnatic cousins, of whatever degree of collaterality.

data than to say that in general matrilateral cross-cousin marriage seems to be of little significance, while Miss Pratt's ethnography shows that the people of the Hakka village she studied in the New Territories 'quite firmly denied the practice of cross-cousin marriage, although they had heard of it in other parts of China'.[1] As for evidence on other regions of China, we have, in addition to Gallin's survey, a little information from Mrs Liu's study of written genealogies and Cornelius Osgood's recently published work on a pre-war study of a village in Yunnan. Mrs Liu finds that among the rules against undesirable (that is to say, not prohibited but reprehensible) marriages set out by sixty-three 'clans', the rules of three 'clans' are against 'cross-cousin marriage'.[2] The term 'cross-cousin' is not defined, but I suspect from what Mrs Liu writes at p. 82 that what is in fact discouraged by these rules is marriage with the father's sister's daughter. On the other hand, no rule in this collection seems to recommend or approve any form of cross-cousin marriage. Osgood says of the Yunnanese village he studied that 'the ideal choice' was the mother's brother's daughter, but there was no accompanying prohibition of marriage with the father's sister's daughter since she was in fact a 'desirable' mate.[3]

This is scrappy evidence for southeastern China, let alone the country as a whole, and it is certain that we have not yet got far enough to pinpointing the particular areas in which matrilateral cross-cousin marriage is stated to be preferred; for this would be the necessary first step towards establishing the demographic and social causes and consequences of a form of marriage that has so uneven a distribution over the country. Clearly, to use a term of art that has been created in the heated anthropological debates of recent years, there is no 'prescriptive' system of cross-cousin marriage in China such that lineages 'intermarry systematically and asymmetrically on a regular "wife-giving/wife-receiving"

---

[1] Pratt, *op. cit.*, p. 151.

[2] *The Traditional Chinese Clan Rules*, pp. 80 f.

[3] *Village Life in Old China, A Community Study of Kao Yao, Yünnan*, N.Y., 1963, pp. 276 f., 360. W. R. Geddes, *Peasant Life in Communist China*, Monograph no. 6, Society for Applied Anthropology, Cornell Univ., Ithaca, N.Y., 1963, reports on a very brief study in 1956 of the village described by Fei Hsiao-tung in *Peasant Life in China*; at pp. 28 f. Geddes goes over what Fei said on cross-cousin marriage in the village, amplifying the analysis at one point, but not treating the matter more generally. The implication appears to be that cross-cousin marriage no longer takes place in Kaihsienkung.

basis'.[1] But in those parts of the country where mother's brother's daughter marriage is 'preferred', are we to assume that a man marries the daughter of the brother of his mother in the literal meaning of those nouns? It would seem so, and the model for explaining this 'preference' will presumably need to rest, not on the total configuration of ties between the descent groups involved, but on the structure of the relations between closely linked kinsmen.[2]

Having put this question aside, we can try to gain a clearer understanding of the network of marriages of which each local lineage was a centre. How far afield did people go in their search for brides? Were marriages, so to say, repeated to lead to continuous alliances between local lineages? Gallin has supplied some data for his Taiwanese village: the 154 married women living in it came from a total of 52 different places, and no pattern 'was discernible in the places of origin of those women nor in the many villages and cities into which women [from the village under study] married. The people of the village have established *ch'in ch'i* [matrilateral and affinal] relationships with a very large number of new families in many other villages and districts, reflecting the belief that the extension of the circle of one's relationships is desirable and beneficial.'[3] But of course we are not here dealing with the 'classical' form of the southeastern Chinese lineage, but rather with the kind of local community whose marriage network reflects its agnatic heterogeneity and, probably, its involvement in a modern system of economic life and communications.

Miss Pratt's Hakka village in the New Territories brings us closer to the kind of community we are primarily interested in. We find there a much more regular pattern of recruiting brides. Of 67 married women in the village 28 had at least one other female agnate as a fellow-villager, 12 of these relationships

---

[1] E. R. Leach, *Rethinking Anthropology*, London, 1961, p. 54.

[2] Cf. *Lineage Organization*, p. 100, fn. 1, and for later work on the general problem see Rodney Needham, *Structure and Sentiment, A Test Case in Social Anthropology*, Chicago, 1962. The Chinese case having been removed from the arena of this particular debate, we can see more clearly now that the job to be done for China is to determine what local demographic and family circumstances promote the choice of a cousin as a bride. This kind of approach to the study of marriage is well exemplified in Wolf, *op. cit.*

[3] Gallin, *op. cit.*, p. 107.

involving ties within the agnatic *wu fu*.[1] Miss Pratt goes on: 'When it is remembered in addition that thirteen of the total number of wives came from villages on mainland China with which marriages were not now so easily arranged, these figures seem more significant.' The 'normal radius' of the marriage area is four to five miles, but within this circle there are several villages with which women are not exchanged, although some of these places are easily accessible. Since this is hilly country, some of the villages from which the brides come (and presumably to which they go) are in fact a long walking distance away, even when as the crow flies they are quite close. Miss Pratt points out that the practice of arranging marriages though matchmakers will tend to lead to the recruitment of women from the same villages, and that in view of the severance of jural connexions between the married woman and her natal family, 'it appears that, without actual formulation, the preferred distance should be just too far for a woman to run home after disputes in her husband's family'.[2]

We find further statistical material on the geographical spread of marriages in Okada's work on Amoy Island in 1940. It provides data in respect of 37 households, drawn from a total of four villages. Okada analyses the local origins of 48 spouses who married into the households studied, and the destinations of 13 villagers moving out of their households on marriage.[3] (These villages formed, like Miss Pratt's village, 'emigrant' communities; consequently, many marriages by villagers were contracted overseas.) Okada comments, although the data he presents will not by themselves establish his point, that Amoy Island made up a marriage area.[4] However incomplete the figures may be, they give us a rough idea of the dimensions of a marriage network.[5]

[1] See *Lineage Organization*, pp. 41 ff.

[2] Pratt, *op. cit.*, pp. 151 f.

[3] Okada, *op. cit.*, p. 58.

[4] This must mean that people on the island do not normally go beyond it for their marriage partners; it is unlikely that the island as a whole forms a single undifferentiated marriage area; it is a small island (roughly 12 km. by 10 km.) but it includes a large port city.

[5] Statistical data of this sort are hard to come by for China. A set of figures for a village near Peking can be found in Jean Dickinson, *Observations on the Social Life of a North China Village*, Peking, 1924, p. 42. (I am indebted to Professor Wolf for the opportunity of seeing this rare publication.) Yang, *A Chinese Village*, p. 84 says of Nanching that people usually had to go to neighbouring lineages within a radius of five or ten miles for their brides.

Distance	Spouses marrying in	Spouses marrying out
same village	8	2
within 1 km	3	0
„ 2 km	4	1
„ 3 km	11	0
„ 4 km	2	2
„ 5 km	2	2
„ 6 km	7	4
„ 7 km	5	0
„ 8 km	2	0
„ 9 km	4	1
„ 10 km	0	1
totals	48.	13

It is of course obvious that if we start from a given community and ask which other communities it exchanges women with, we shall always finish up by establishing a 'marriage area' in one sense; and there is less interest in this kind of exercise than in enquiring into the possibility of there being discrete areas within each of which the marriages of its component communities are contained. Now Skinner has argued that standard marketing areas form just such entities,[1] and on the very first day I spent at work in the New Territories I was told by Professor Potter, who was then still living in Ping Shan, that he had come to the conclusion that the marriage area was centred on the market town; all marriages (at least those involving major wives) were traditionally between villages oriented to a common market town. The argument, in both theory and fact, is therefore very strong. Since the market town is the node of a communications network, villages come to know of the availability of women through it. Because villages oriented to different market towns (even though they are physically close) will have few dealings, the likelihood of marriage between their several members is very low. Indeed, the matchmakers themselves may be operating from the market town.[2]

An important qualification, inherent in the theory itself, needs to be made. The higher the standing of a lineage or family,

---

[1] 'Marketing and Social Structure . . . Pt. I', p. 36.
[2] Skinner, *ibid., loc. cit.*: in the village studied by Miss Pratt the most successful matchmaker was a widow who made a habit of frequenting Tai Po town, where she acquired information on the availability of marriageable girls.

the less likely will its social and economic relationships be bounded by the unit defined in terms of the lowest level of market town. The horizons of the literatus and the substantial merchant are wider than those of the common man; the strong and the prominent have higher centres of communication and range more widely in their search for brides for their sons and husbands for their daughters. A second qualification must be made in the light of the kind of ethnic heterogeneity to be found in the New Territories. Traditionally, the boat people did not marry among the land people; their networks of communication were different. Again traditionally, some Hakka women moved on marriage into Punti communities without the reverse flow being possible; and in their search for brides I suspect that Hakka families had sometimes to exceed the limits of any area defined by their local market.

Although the further evidence on marriage now being collected in the New Territories will certainly reflect the greater dispersion of networks made possible by modern systems of economic relationships and communications, it will be interesting to see how far it can be made to confirm general theory and Potter's findings in the western part of the region. There could be another source of information on the subject: written genealogies – that is, such of them as offer adequate data, for most written genealogies seem to be very deficient in this regard. Eberhard deals with the matter in his recent book, drawing almost all his data from one of the two southern genealogies under scrutiny – for the other does not contain enough material.[1] From the data in the Jung genealogy Eberhard works out a pattern of marriage between this clan and certain others. For example, he shows that there was a consistent trend of marriage between several of the Jung 'houses' and men and women of the Yang surname, and between one Jung 'house' and members of the Cheng surname. But, despite the general interest of the information, it is not in fact as eloquent as it appears at first sight to be. It is not possible to determine from this material how particular lineages formed patterns of marriage alliances. A surname taken by itself is an index of limited power, and to know of such large agnatic units as clans and 'houses' that they formed 'alliances' with other such units does not lead us very far along the road to understanding how corporate units (lineages and their segments) sought out and maintained links

[1] *Social Mobility*, pp. 121 ff., 177 ff., 193 f.

with other corporate units. In other words, because the giant genealogy is the charter of a merely potential descent group, it is limited in what it can tell us about structurally significant relationships. (Eberhard uses the word 'family' too generously, and reading his book one needs to be alert to the ambiguity it contains.) But *Social Mobility* points the way to other studies which could tackle the problems we are concerned with. It seems unlikely from what I have seen of written genealogies that any of them will be found to supply all the data necessary for working out patterns of marriage between lineages – for even when the surnames of brides and sons-in-law are given, they do not consistently identify particular lineages. But a written genealogy studied in the field, in the full social context of the lineage to which it pertains, should be able to produce a much clearer account of how marriage links have been formed over time.

Of course, written genealogies, or detailed ones at any rate, are themselves indices of high social standing, from which it follows that conclusions drawn from them have a limited application. From the material now available I hazard the guess that the marriage network of a poor and humble lineage is at once both wider and narrower than that of a rich and powerful one: wider in the sense that the lineage is likely to be tied to a greater number of other lineages, and narrower in that its geographical range will probably be more restricted. The lineage of high standing will cast its net much further afield geographically – apart from anything else, it will, as we have seen, have a wider system of communications to keep it informed of possible matches – but it will have fewer lineages of its own status with which to ally itself and it will show a greater tendency to keep a political marriage link alive by repetition. On the other hand, precisely because lineages of high status are linked in marriage to few others, more dramatic changes can take place in the patterns of their alliances. If two lineages tied by multiple marriages quarrel, they may well withdraw from the alliance and severally cast about for new lineages with which to link themselves.

A question arises. Is it inevitable that all the marriages made by the members of one lineage will form a single system? Is it not possible that in a highly differentiated lineage the marriages of the humbler families or segments will take a different direction from those of the more powerful and ambitious families or segments?

In such a fashion a lineage as a whole may be politically differentiated by the independent marriage alliances of its component units. An answer to the question posed would bear on the extent to which families may freely choose with whom to ally themselves. How far, in selecting their brides and husbands for their daughters, are the men in a family actively influenced by the men of other families of their lineage? Is there – can there be – a marriage strategy for a lineage as a whole?[1]

The best known of all proverbs in the Taiwanese village studied by Wolf runs: 'Marriage is the means by which the worst of enemies become the closest of relatives.'[2] Like most proverbs, it can probably be interpreted in different ways, but we may borrow it as a bridge between the two themes of this chapter: marriage patterns and hostile relations between lineages. Marriages and acts of violence were each the basis of a series of relationships between units; they were both crucial elements in local systems of relations; brides and blows might be exchanged between the same lineages.

At pp. 105–13 of *Lineage Organization* I discussed what evidence I had managed to find on hostile relations between lineages in Fukien and Kwangtung. It seemed to me then, and now seems even more certain, that fighting between lineages, governed by rules, was an important characteristic of social life in southeastern China. Hsiao Kung-chuan, in his survey of the Chinese countryside in the nineteenth century, has produced more evidence to strengthen my conclusions,[3] while I have myself been able to turn up some fresh facts.

Let me first of all cite Krone's comments on violence in mid-nineteenth century Hsin-an. 'From the foregoing, it may be understood how troubled and insecure the normal condition of this district is, and for a very long period has been. Not only are robbers and pirates to be feared, but internecine wars are almost always raging between some or other of the villages; and these wars, though often arising from trivial causes, are not mere temporary quarrels, but are often long-continued and sanguinary.'[4] The mandarins taking but little part in social control, the 'disputes between villages and clans are settled by the gentry. If they cannot come to an agreement, all connection is broken off, and

---

[1] See *Lineage Organization*, pp. 99 f.   [2] Wolf, *op. cit.*
[3] *Op. cit.*, pp. 361 ff., 419 ff.   [4] Krone, *op. cit.*, p. 81.

without any declaration of hostilities, the disputants commence a predatory war on each other; in these quarrels, many a bloody battle is fought, hundreds of men perish, and whole villages are destroyed. Men of neutral villages or clans are generally well distinguished, and their rights respected; but it often happens, when a league of several powerful villages or clans are in arms against their enemies, they are not so particular, and will attack and plunder any man who falls in their way, except he belongs to a clan whose strength they fear. If, for instance, the clan Tang is at war with the clan Mân, any person of a different surname may safely pass through the theatre of war.

'Missionaries also are considered neutrals; even if they dwell in the country of one of the belligerents, they may safely pass through the villages of the hostile clan, provided only they take care that the coolies with them are also neutrals.

'The following is an example of these feuds: There are two villages respectively named Sha-tsing . . . and Pak-tau-king . . ., which carried on a war for five years; with each of these villages smaller hamlets were in league. The mandarins tried in vain to restore peace. At last the district magistrate himself repaired to Sha-tsing with a force of 1,000 men, but the inhabitants threatened to take up arms against him also, if he should show himself inimical to their party. The mandarin was at a loss what to do, till the people of San-keaou, who were not engaged in the quarrel, offered themselves as mediators between the mandarin and the inhabitants of Sha-tsing. Through their influence the magistrate was allowed to enter Sha-tsing with an unarmed body of his followers, and to pull down two old houses which belonged to the ringleaders in the quarrel. This was only to save the dignity of the mandarin, and had no influence at all upon the dispute, fighting being carried on afterwards just as before. The only way in which the government endeavours to put a stop to these disturbances, is by not allowing the fighting clans to send up their graduates for examination at Canton – a severe punishment, which not only deprives the graduates of titles and honours they might gain, but hurts the pride of the clans who are wont to boast of the number of successful candidates for literary honours which they have produced.'[1]

As a second example I may quote a missionary's report for

[1] *Ibid.*, pp. 92 f.

1885 on an area near Amoy: 'In addition to the general characteristics of the people there are bitter and long-standing feuds between the principal clans, and not unfrequently this region is the
scene of open and wasteful strife. This year has been marked by an
unusually severe outbreak of hostilities involving hundreds of
towns and villages. These clan fights sometimes place our church
members in a most difficult position. All the able-bodied men in a
village are called upon to take up arms in the common cause, and
all, save a few Christians in the place respond to the call. . . . The
native authorities are indifferent till the fighting has assumed
alarming proportions. Then ruinous fines are exacted quite in-
discriminately, whole villages are burned to the ground by a
lawless soldiery, and thus order is restored and justice vindicated!
For a time we were naturally anxious, but our churches have been
strictly neutral and few of the members have suffered more than
their share of the common loss. It is not easy for friends at home
to realize the barbarism of these *vendettas*.'[1] The same man reported
the next year of a district in the Amoy area that, at the beginning
of the year, 'village after village in this region was involved in a
clan fight of unusual fierceness'. He had visited one place where
'all the approaches to the villages were guarded by armed men,
watch towers were manned and agricultural operations almost
completely suspended'.[2]

In the first passage quoted, Bonfield speaks of 'bitter and
long-standing feuds between the principal clans'. Yet it was not
only the chief lineages in an area that took up arms, for in a bad
time all the lineages round about might get caught up in the
fighting. But it seems pretty clear that it was especially characteristic of the more powerful lineages to resort to arms. They could
call upon great resources of weapons and men (some of them
perhaps drawn from among the families dependent on them),
but, more important, they had a constant motive to fight: either
to maintain their dominance of their weaker neighbours (who

---

[1] London Missionary Society Archives, Fukien Reports, Report for 1885 from
C. H. Bondfield, Amoy, no. 8126, arrival no. 4872. I shall be drawing again on
the Archives in a later chapter, and I should like to say that I am very grateful for
access to them. I have not, however, combed them systematically (lacking the
time for so great an enterprise), but I have seen enough in them to realize that
they are an excellent source of material on society in southeastern China for
someone seeking to round out an account based in the first place on other data.

[2] Report for 1886, no. 8674, arrival no. 5902.

might also be their tenants), or to assert themselves against their rivals.

In attempting to coerce a smaller community, a strong lineage might have to reckon with the possibility that it combine with other weaker groups to make a stand; but in the plains where the great lineages were for the most part sited, they could usually have their way with the lesser groups around them and hold them firmly in check. The *yeuk* combinations which we have seen to have existed in Hsin-an[1] were probably one aspect of the attempt by smaller communities, away from the plains, to protect themselves against the power of the few great lineages in their midst or the great lineages situated at a distance. (It will be recalled that in the case of the Tai Po Ts'at Yeuk the lesser communities were able to ally themselves with one great neighbouring lineage, the Man, to protect themselves against another, the Tang.[2])

As for the struggles between lineages of more or less equal strength, it seems likely that in any one area – but how precisely to define that area I am not certain – a few of them were competing for dominance. Of course, the strength they could bring to the struggle was not simply to be reckoned in man- and fire-power; the command of economic resources (in land and other forms of capital and perhaps the control of a market) and the call on political influence (through 'scholarly' ties with the bureaucracy) were more basic and constant sources of superiority. But these lineages, proud of their high standing and jealous of their privileges, were tempted to add the argument of arms to that of economic and political power. They were the communities most likely to resort to the use of violence. An encroachment upon their geomantic sites, interference with a watercourse, the maltreatment of a bride, a casual insult – provocations to fight, great and small, were inherently numerous; and they were effective in evoking a violent response because they rested on more or less permanent relationships of hostility.

Krone and Bondfield use the word 'feud' for the conflicts they describe, and I have myself in the past used this term for the characteristic mode of violence in southeastern China. But it would probably be more in line with current anthropological usage to replace 'feud' by 'vendetta' (as indeed Bondfield does at one point) in the discussion of violence between more or less matched parties. 'Feud' suggests 'blood feud', an institution in which there are precise rules for avenging a wrong by retaliating or by accepting compensation. When a person is killed, *lex talionis* prescribes that the killer or someone related to him be killed, or payment is made,[1] after which the matter is, at least in theory, closed. In fact, the tit-for-tat element was not completely absent from Chinese fighting and killing, and compensation was sometimes made for homicide. Macgowan tells us, for example, that if an equal number of people fall on each side, the two parties to a fight can settle their accounts and come to terms. If, on the other hand, there is a preponderance of dead on one side, 'it is in nearly every case necessary to appeal to the mandarin to use his authority to settle the matter'. (The magistrate then grows fat on the fines he exacts.) 'Murder, for example, is a crime that in nine cases out of ten is always settled by the families concerned, by payment of blood-money.'[2] But even though Chinese disputants might hope for a balancing up of casualties and be prepared in certain circumstances to pay compensation for an act of violence, the rules governing the exercise of force were never of the precise kind usually discussed under the name of blood feud. Killing was a crime;[3] the state might intervene to punish the wrongdoer; and although in practice the agents of the state might often allow a fight to run its course, no system of rules could develop whereby the redress of wrongs could be made to depend on the straightforward formula of a life for a life.

But this is not to say that there were no rules. They were never

---

[1] Cf. John Beattie, *Other Cultures: Aims, Methods and Achievements in Social Anthropology*, London, 1964, pp. 150, 175, and 'Feud' in J. Gould and W. L. Kolb, eds., *A Dictionary of the Social Sciences*, London, 1964, pp. 267 f.

[2] J. Macgowan, *Sidelights on Chinese Life*, London, 1907, pp. 284 f. In the context of his discussion of judicial enquiries into homicide, De Groot, *op. cit.*, vol. I, p. 138, says that if 'there is no question of premeditated or wilful murder, but only of manslaughter, and the culprit has been sentenced to pay an indemnification to the family of the slain, the coffin is kept unburied until the fine has been paid in full and therewith the whole affair settled. When villages have been in bloody encounter with one another, which in many parts of the empire is a matter of almost daily occurrence, the same line of conduct is followed with regard to the slain outnumbering those who have fallen on the other side, because, should peace and mutual understanding be afterwards restored, a retribution will have to be paid for the surplus.' And cf. B. C. Henry, *The Cross and the Dragon; Or, Light in the Broad East*, London [1885?], p. 70. ('Broad East': Kwangtung.)

[3] In Ming and Ch'ing written law, vengeance killing was condoned only to the limited extent that a son might kill the murderer of his parent or grandparent *immediately* after the murder. See Ch'ü, *Law and Society*, p. 82.

formulated, but it is clear that when communities fought they were not intending to exterminate[1] or enslave each other, even when they aimed to kill and take prisoners; and there appears to have been some expectation on the part of the belligerents that, after a certain number of casualties had been suffered on each side, the fight would be called off. The state was not the only third party to a clash; there were neighbours; all-out war was impossible. Perhaps, then, we had better call the intermittent quarrelling of southeastern China a system of vendetta. Communities often stood in traditional hostility against other communities, ready to take up arms and kill, but prepared after an affray to accept mediation – or to retreat from the battlefield when the government troops appeared.

The role of the local elite in organized violence is of course an important and interesting one. Hsiao seems to be right in asserting that the 'gentry dominated the scene in clan feuds . . ., but they did not always take the leadership in these ventures'.[2] The rights and honour of the gentry (however we define this group) were especially likely to be at stake when the lineages to which they belonged were in competition. Consequently, while not themselves engaging in violence, they probably often promoted it, by financing, organizing, and encouraging the 'troops' sent out to battle. (And in some cases mercenaries were hired.[3]) A fight backed by the gentry was less likely to attract the active attention of the local magistrate; and if he did eventually decide to intervene – when perhaps the carnage was greater than he could tolerate – his reprisals could be moderated by the intercession of men whom he was inclined to respect. Lineage fights appear to have been a source of income to magistrates in Fukien and Kwangtung;[4] they could be bribed to stay away and, once on the spot, they could be paid for their lenience. (The ruinous fines of which Bondfield wrote may perhaps be attributed to the fight having drawn the attention of higher authority by its unusual

[1] Except when a stronger unit was intent on chasing a weaker one from village land – perhaps to procure that local homogeneity in lineage referred to at p. 8 above.   [2] *Op. cit.*, p. 365.

[3] *Ibid.*, p. 364. D. R. De Glopper, *Origins and Resolution of Conflict in Chinese Society*, unpublished M.A. thesis, Univ. of London, 1965, makes the additional point that lineage leaders were perhaps restrained in their encouragement of violence by the fear that the toughs who did the fighting might acquire too much power.   [4] Hsiao, *op. cit., loc. cit.*

ferocity.) After long years of British rule, the New Territories are no longer the scene of lineage battles, but it is perhaps significant that the one area (the Yuen Long plain) where inter-lineage violence or the threat of it does sporadically break out is precisely the area where the traditionally most powerful and longest-established lineages are concentrated.[1] A lineage's resort to arms was in part an assertion of its right to be among the elite of the local lineages.

Poorer communities which got into a fight could expect little mercy from officialdom. Dukes tells a story of the Amoy area in which thirty-two villages were involved in an affray that started when two religious processions came into collision. 'A tax was levied upon them by the elders of the villages for the purchase of firearms and ammunition. Sentries were placed at the top of square towers to shoot at any of the hostile party that might

[1] For example, in March 1960 a serious fight broke out between groups of men and women from the villages of Muk Kiu Tau and Tin Liu in the Yuen Long District. Some 20 to 30 villagers took part in the affray, which lasted about 20 minutes, the combatants being armed with bamboo poles, hoes, iron bars, and farm implements. The immediate cause of the trouble was a minor accident involving a cyclist and a pedestrian from the opposing villages. 'The villages, which are descended from a common ancestor, have been at loggerheads since 1937 when a District Officer's award on a dispute over ancestral property went against Muk Kiu Tau and was sustained on appeal to the Supreme Court. More recently, in 1959, the Muk Kiu Tau villagers opposed a scheme by Government to resite and reconstruct an irrigation dam for the benefit of Tin Liu since they were afraid that the dam would cause flooding to their own village. Due to this opposition work had been suspended at the time of the fight but feeling was still running high. As the result of this fight three persons were detained in hospital . . .; eight other persons were treated for minor injuries.' – D. R. Holmes, *Hong Kong Annual Departmental Report by the District Commissioner, New Territories for the Financial Year 1959–60*, p. 259. In October 1955 a serious dispute arose between villagers of Nam Pin Wai and Shan Pui in the Yuen Long District. 'Shan Pui is hemmed in between a hill, a marsh and a deep river and its only access is through and round Nam Pin Wai. Nam Pin Wai is surrounded on three sides by fishponds belonging to Shan Pui. These two villages have been at loggerheads for so long (at least 300 years) that both have forgotten how it all started. But the feud has been kept alive and the physical location of the villages . . . has meant that tempers are short and violence never far round the corner. . . . The dangerous time is in the autumn; the harvest is in and hands are idle and pockets full.' The row started when a Nam Pin Wai child picked up a dead fish from a Shan Pui pond and set off a chain of 'words, blows, ambushes, arrests'. The chief representative of Shan Pui went to hospital gravely injured; there was further violence and 'by 1st November both villages were prepared for war'. The police went in and there were various attempts at reconciliation which bore fruit in December, when a treaty of peace was drafted and signed by every male over the age of 16 in both villages. – K. M. A. Barnett, *Hong Kong Annual Departmental Report by the District Commissioner, New Territories for the Financial Year 1955–56*, pp. 77 ff.

venture into the fields. The seeds could not be sown. The standing crops could not be reaped. Two small cannon were bought in Amoy, and with these they amused themselves occasionally in battering a wall or a roof. Great damage was done. The whole neighbourhood was reduced to distress. Where were the mandarins? Calmly waiting till someone was killed. When that event occurred, and was multiplied by twenty-two, the district mandarin became indignant, sent three thousand troops to take possession, levied blackmail on all the villages involved, and retreated with the spoil.'[1]

Another case of state intervention is documented by Adele M. Fielde, a missionary who spent many years in the Tiuchui region of Kwangtung. A woman named 'Tapestry' is telling the story of her life. She says that within three miles of her native village there were about fifty villages. They 'were continually engaged in feuds . . . until General Pang came into power, and he reduced the country to subjection and order. . . . Ten years ago . . . General Pang subdued the clans, burned the houses of those who would not desist from feuds, and severely punished many as a warning to the rest. As my husband had been engaged in supplying the combatants with powder and shot, and as his neighbors chose to put him forward to receive the punishment that must be dealt out to some one in our village, and as he had not the money with which to pay the fine, he fled to Singapore, whereupon General Pang banished him for twelve years.'[2] It is of interest that 'Tapestry' opens her account of the fighting with the remark that 'Sometimes the feud was between clan and clan, sometimes between village and village, and sometimes between different families in the same village. The weak gave their adherence to the more powerful, and depended on them for protection. When the feud was between clan and clan it was less disastrous, for then there was a greater number on one side, and some could safely engage in peaceful occupations. But when it was between village and village it was very distressing to all concerned.' The crops would be cut down 'and nothing was safe'. People feared to go out of the village at night, and the roads were unsafe for 'travellers and for goods. My grandfather had owned

[1] E. J. Dukes, *Along River and Road in Fuh-Kien, China*, N.Y., n.d., pp. 132 f.
[2] *Pagoda Shadows, Studies from Life in China*, 4th edn., Boston, 1885, pp. 204, 210 f.

much land, but he had to sell it to ransom my father, who had been kidnapped and taken to a powerful village of another clan.'[1] On this reasoning, the larger-scale fights were paradoxically less disruptive than the smaller-scale. It follows, no doubt, that the latter were more quickly settled, in order that ordinary life might go on.

It was inevitable that many of the lineages engaged in fighting one another were related by marriage or agnatic descent. (The mere fact of agnation itself did not prevent lineages coming to blows; within a lineage, on the other hand, it was a simpler matter to keep violence in check.)[2] In extreme cases, hostile

---

[1] *Ibid.*, pp. 204 ff. The firm and, for a time at any rate, effective action taken by General Pang to put down local fighting emphasizes the significance of the more normal state of affairs in which people killed one another with a minimum of interference from the state. The Ch'ao-chou area was particularly unruly. Jui-lin, the Governor-General of Kwangtung and Kwangsi, 'restored order in the distracted district near Chao-chow-fu, and rendered life and property secure there, successfully suppressing the village clans which for many years previously had set all authority at defiance.' – J. Thomson, *The Straits of Malacca, Indo-China and China*, London, 1875, p. 258; and see *Lineage Organization*, p. 8. About 1870, by which time the extortion of money from emigrants had been added to the more traditional reasons for fighting, Jui-lin sent 'a military mandarin with a force of 2,000 men' into the area (Thomson, *op. cit.*, p. 286). 'This officer, at the time of my visit, was in the district known as Chao-Yang. His task was approaching completion, and there was consequently more of peace and prosperity in the country than had been its lot for many previous years. Fang-Yao ['Tapestry's' General Pang] . . . pursued a rough and ready sort of system in the conduct of his operations. . . . Thus, at the village of Go-swa . . . he seized a man named Kwin-Kong . . . and required him to surrender 200 of the chief rebels of his village. Kwin-Kong produced 100, many of them, poor wretches, innocent substitutes for the true offenders. Under pressure and threats a few more victims were ultimately given up, and the whole were then beheaded, Kwin-Kong's skull being tossed into the pile to swell the number of the sufferers. It must have been bloody work; more than 1,000 are said to have been decapitated during Fang-yao's memorable march.' – *ibid.*, pp. 286 f. Cf. Herbert A. Giles. *A Chinese Biographical Dictionary*, London and Shanghai, 1898, p. 223, and G. William Skinner, *Chinese Society in Thailand, An Analytical History*, Ithaca, N.Y., 1957, pp. 54, 57.

[2] Chen Ta, *op. cit.*, p. 129, mentions a fight threatened between 'two branches of the same clan' in the 1930s. After warlike preparations had been made, the dispute (which had begun as a result of a children's squabble) was settled. In the discussion of the valuable evidence he collected on Fukien from informants in Manila, Amyot several times refers to 'feuds'; he instances fights between members of the same descent groups. Of a *hsiang* in Chin-chiang county he says: 'There has always been much internecine strife in this area. . . . Two main sets of factions divided the population. The first ran along lineage lines and set the Strong *fang* [of the Ting lineage] against the Weak. The second set ran across lineage lines: an East faction and a West faction. It was much more extensive as neighboring lineages also became involved. Fighting was about everything and nothing: the use of a water passage or a harbor, field boundaries, personal

lineages linked by marriage severed the connubium between them, but it seems quite possible that they resumed intermarrying during a lull in the hostilities. Affinity and uterine kinship were perhaps ties making for the quicker settlement of a fight and for clemency in the treatment of non-combatants and prisoners. There is very little evidence to go on, but I have been struck by a modern account of a lineage fight (in the Tiuchiu area of Kwang-tung province) in which the moderating role of matrilateral kinsmen is brought out very clearly. Miss Janet Lim tells us how in the 1920s, when she was a child, her village got into a fight with her mother's native village. The two communities were quarrelling over a piece of land. The men of her own village spent a whole night making hand-grenades and swords. Her parents 'were in a very difficult position because if they helped our village they would be fighting against their own relations. So they made up their minds that they would not help either side.' Her mother received a message from her brother to the effect that, if her village lost the 'war', he would protect her family. The fight lasted two days, during which Miss Lim's mother was informed that her father had been seen outside the village trying fruitlessly to stop the fighting. He had been stoned for his pains. The village elders finally made peace and each side brought its wounded within its walls. But relations between the two villages were bad; even the children of the two communities would not speak to one another. Miss Lim quarrelled with a little boy 'on the other bank of the lake which separated the two villages. I did not know then that he was a close relation. I learnt this fact, to my great shame, when I later visited his home with Mother.'[1] Speaking again of the same general area of Kwangtung, Adele M. Fielde brackets the frequency of 'clan feuds' with agnatic exogamy, saying of the latter that it prevented permanent divisions between the 'clans'.[2] (And it is a matter of interest that the author goes on to say that parents were reluctant to let their daughters

insults. A person who considered himself wronged could call upon his allies to defend him. Real fighting with firearms would ensue. Occasionally soldiers would be sent from Ch'üanchou to break things up but, according to my informants, they were never really successful under Chiang Kai-shek in pacifying this area.' – *op. cit.*, p. 48. For serious fighting within lineages, see the modern example from the New Territories given at p. 110 n. above, and for a nineteenth-century example in Kwangtung, see Hsiao, *Rural China*, p. 291.

[1] Janet Lim, *Sold for Silver, An Autobiography*, London, 1958, p. 21.
[2] *A Corner of Cathay, Studies of Life among the Chinese*, N.Y., 1894, p. 30.

go very far from them when they married. And 'sometimes official effort is made to prevent girls being married into distant families. Occasionally a magistrate issues a proclamation forbidding the betrothal of girls dwelling within his district to men who live beyond its boundaries. He thus prevents marriageable maidens, made scarce through the practice of female infanticide, from being disposed of to the highest bidders, and keeps them for the populating of the region under his jurisdiction.')

The many references to village walls and watchtowers are by themselves evidence of the important part played by violence in southeastern China. It is of course true – and a mere glance at the history and geography of the New Territories confirms the point – that fortifications and arms were necessary to protect villages against pirates from the sea and bandits on land. But for much of the time villages needed to protect themselves against other villages.[1] The failure of the state consistently to impose its control on the countryside and its inability to shield village communities from the depredations of marauders allowed military architecture and weapons to be used not only for defence but also in the cause of local political dominance and for the redress of local wrongs. Writing to the Secretary of State for the Colonies in 1899, the Governor of Hong Kong, having just visited the New Territories, reported that the Chinese Government took not the slightest interest in the people beyond what was required for the collection of taxes and 'squeezes'. The people, he said, were expected to manage their own affairs, provided the government was not troubled and there was no increase in the numbers of robbers to the point where they might form the nucleus of a rebellion. 'Clan' fights were the recognized way of settling disagreements between villages, and in such fights, which sometimes lasted weeks, many men were killed without the government interfering or making any enquiry into the disturbance.[2] The Governor was simplifying, but he seems to have been essentially right in the way in which he characterized the situation immediately preceding British rule. Government existed, but its political and legal abstentions promoted self-help. Lineages depended on one

---

[1] Cf. Krone, *op. cit.*, p. 81.

[2] Governor Blake in a letter dated 16 August 1899. See Confidential Print, Eastern no. 66, Hong Kong, *Correspondence (June 20, 1898, to August 20, 1900) Respecting the Extension of the Boundaries of the Colony*, Colonial Office, London, November 1900, p. 336.

another, especially for women, and they might make common cause in the face of a common danger. But their several interests, political and economic, might conflict; and then the communities might take up arms against one another. Some men might be killed and some prisoners sold off as coolies, but there were typically no 'wars' of extermination or outright conquest – although a series of defeats could lead to a lineage declining in prosperity and numbers and, ultimately, to its remnant moving away. The lineages at arms were part of a system in which the pre-existing ties between them, the interests of neutral neighbouring lineages, and, in the last resort, the concern of the state prevented controlled fighting breaking down into ruthless warfare.

The evidence on organized violence spans a long period. It cannot be dismissed as the sign of a particular crisis in the society of southeastern China. The data presented in Hsiao's *Rural China*, in *Lineage Organization*, and in this book refer to the eighteenth, nineteenth, and twentieth centuries, but in fact the pattern is probably very much older. Was it, so to say, a pattern of general violence, or were the fights, as I am arguing, essentially bound up with lineages and their interaction? Of course, it would be foolish to assert that only lineages took to the field and to deny that other kinds of local community ever made common cause in a battle – they clearly did. But I am suggesting that lineage alignments were the key to organized fighting and that it cannot be an accident that the part of China where local fighting was carried to a pitch unknown in the rest of the country was also the seat of Chinese lineage organization in its fullest form.

Doubtless, the extent to which the state intervened in lineage quarrels varied with its political and military power; during the major disturbances of the Chinese peace in the last century, officials must often have been incapable of acting to restrain local violence, even when they wanted to. And the shift to more effective firearms in modern times may well have promoted worse results than those formerly produced by cannon, spear, sword, and gingal. But there can be no doubt that, at the very least from the eighteenth century until the coming of the Communist regime, there existed in Fukien and Kwangtung a system of inter-lineage relations resting on the possibility of organized violence. This was the part of China where lineage organization had been carried to its fullest extent, where the Ch'ing rulers encountered the greatest local opposition, and where overseas emigration was heaviest.

The wealth created in fertile agricultural country and the capital brought back from overseas[1] made it possible for some lineages to expand both their numbers and their local political control. But this control rested not only on the ability to fend off the state but also to make use of it. The powerful lineage bred scholars; the scholars either entered the state's service, as was the case with the minority of them, or established links with and rights vis-à-vis officialdom. Scholars could make use of their position in a national system of power, influence, and prestige to control both their own humbler lineage-mates and the members of other lineages. The role of the scholar as official did not in fact greatly conflict with his role as a leader of his lineage. He was an active official in another province; when at home he needed to be circumspect in engaging in activity which as an official he would condemn in others, but precisely because he was an official he was able to further the interests of his own community, protecting it from unwanted interference by the magistrate and his staff and, in need, calling upon his ties with the bureaucracy to restrain or even perhaps remove a magistrate who was not prepared to be moderate in his demands. Riches and scholarship produced the lineage of high social status. Part of the profit accruing to this status was the ability to act independently of the central government by manipulating it. As Krone has shown us, perhaps the most effective sanction that a magistrate could apply to an obstreperous lineage with scholarly pretensions was to prevent its members sitting the examinations.[2] In the long run the ambitious

---

[1] The role of overseas trading and emigration in the economic and social life of Fukien and Kwangtung has never been adequately studied. Clearly, considerable capital has been flowing into the region since Sung times, and there may well be some connexion between the form taken by lineage organization and the availability of wealth created overseas. For a relevant account of Chinese emigration to South-East Asia, see Wang Gungwu, *A Short History of the Nanyang Chinese*, Background to Malaya Series, no. 13, Singapore, 1959.

[2] But the sanction had in turn a built-in restraint on its exercise, for in the long run no magistrate could afford to allow it to be seen that the county in his charge was failing to send men forward to be examined. Action taken by scholars to boycott the examinations could put the magistrate in a very awkward position vis-à-vis his superiors. See e.g. Hsiao, *op. cit.*, p. 247: 'In 1851 a number of *sheng-yüan* in Tung-kuan and pupils of a *shu-yüan* in Nan-hai (districts in Kwangtung) refused to take the prescribed local examinations as a protest against the magistrate's actions concerning tax and money matters.'

leaders of a powerful lineage had to strike a balance between complying with the local representatives of the state and making use of the strength they gained by this compliance to hold the state at bay. The power which the strong lineage used to defy the state was the power the state gave it.

But the state was not infinitely pliable. If rebellion, or what was thought to be rebellion, threatened, then the toleration of local independence could no longer be counted on. Too strong a gathering together of local power – evidenced by, among other things, the formal grouping of lineages into wider and wider units – aroused the fears of officialdom and might lead to its taking severe repressive measures. A condition for the lineage being left alone to enjoy the fruits of its local power was that it observe certain limits imposed on it; it was not to spread the area of its control too widely. But in fact the limits were nowhere specified and may often have been knowable only when they had been exceeded. So that, it would seem, as a strong lineage pressed forward in its ambition to dominate more neighbours and cast its network of alliances further and further, it needed, if it wished to remain immune from state interference, to proceed with caution. The reaction of the state was not in any precise way predictable.

5

Geomancy and Ancestor Worship

In Chapters 10 and 11 of *Lineage Organization* I discussed several ritual matters connected with the main themes of the book, throwing the accent on ancestor worship. It seemed very natural to me then that ancestor worship should be given pride of place, for it was clear that both the domestic and hall cults threw certain organizational principles of the lineage into relief and expressed ideas central to the competition within, and the unity of, lineage communities. I referred briefly to geomancy(*fêng-shui*), having noted its significance for relationships of competition, but it did not then occur to me that the subject could be taken very much further on the basis of the available literature. How wrong I was will be apparent in this second attempt to treat the ritual aspects of lineage organization. Having seen geomancy at work in the New Territories and formulated some wider ideas on it, I then realized that the old literature on southeastern China was well endowed with documents on *fêng-shui*. The treasure was there, but I did not find the key to it until I had begun to ask questions in the field.

Now Chinese geomancy is a vast subject, and I must say very clearly at the outset of this discussion that I am proposing to deal in any detail with only one major aspect of it. That aspect is the burial of the dead. I shall refer briefly to the geomancy of buildings, but say hardly anything about the system of metaphysical ideas underlying, and the ritual knowledge and practices associated with, *fêng-shui* as a whole. These other matters will have to be discussed in a later publication.[1]

The first point to make in revision of my earlier account of geomancy is that it is essential to realize that in many areas of southeastern China – perhaps very widely: I am still unable to be

[1] In preparation by S. D. R. Feuchtwang and myself. See Mr Feuchtwang's M.A. thesis, Univ. of London, 1965: *An Anthropological Analysis of Chinese Geomancy*.

precise about its extent – double burial was a common practice. Certainly, for the area around Amoy in Fukien Province there is ample evidence from the writings of missionaries. Speaking of the graves packed on the hillsides of Amoy, Macgowan says that 'to protect the living from the invasion of the dead, it is the custom to take up the coffin after it has lain in the ground for about fifteen years, and picking up the bones . . . to place these in large earthenware jars, which they bury in the ground, leaving the top to protrude somewhat, and plastering it over with white cement'.[1] Dukes, who knew the same area in the 1870s, writes: 'In every part of the land, but especially in the Fuh-kien province, jars about twenty inches deep are constantly seen grouped under the shadow of a rock. These jars contain bones which have been dug up from the grave because some calamity has befallen the family of the deceased, and in this way proved the Feng-Shui of the grave to be bad. The jars and their contents (disrespectfully called by foreigners "potted Chinaman", but by themselves "yellow gold") remain above ground often for a long course of years, till the professor of Feng-Shui has decided on an unexceptionable site for reinterring them.'[2] What the missionaries report is confirmed (except in regard to the motives for disinterring the remains) and amplified by the work of the sinologue De Groot. In his account of burial, as in what he says about many aspects of Chinese ritual and belief, there are conflicting statements, because he tries at once to give the correct mode of behaviour according to classical formulae and the common practice of his day; but, the two kinds of evidence having been disentangled, we can see what he actually observed towards the end of the last century in and around Amoy. Almost every village had its burial area where 'the villagers are laid down for eternal rest in separate graves'.[3] But some bodies were transferred from these graves when fortunes were waning or the *fêng-shui* was disturbed, the bones (as the only substance to which the soul adhered) being put into earthenware urns in their correct anatomical order, with the skull at the top. While a new grave was being sought the urns were stored 'in a locality to which some Fung-shui is supposed to cleave, as *e.g.* under an overhanging rock, or in a grotto or cavern . . . or in

[1] J. Macgowan, *Pictures of Southern China*, London, 1897, p. 182.
[2] Dukes, *op. cit.*, p. 233.
[3] J. J. M. De Groot, *The Religious System of China*, vol. III, Leiden, 1897, p. 1374.

Buddhist mountain temples'.[1] Once a new grave-site had been
found, the urn (or much more rarely, a new coffin containing the
bones) was buried in it.[2] Families 'seriously afflicted by the
Fung-shui craze' might dig up and rebury their bones several
times, but most men generally lost interest in the remains of their
forebears after a few generations, 'and thousands and thousands of
buried and re-buried corpses, and numberless urned skeletons
unburied, go the same way as the millions among the poor for the
Fung-shui of whose graves little or no outlay is made'.[3]

I have not yet found an equally detailed account of double
burial in Kwangtung, but Gray, whose experience of China was
gained mainly in Canton and Hong Kong, writes of exhumation
when tombs were thought unlucky, the bones being placed in
urns and the urns either put into new tombs or stored away.[4]
These various statements introduce into our picture of the southeastern Chinese landscape what was evidently a striking man-made
feature: the funerary urn. In the New Territories, at any rate, the
urn marks a stage in an ideal system of double burial. There the
first resting place of the dead is in most cases regarded as a temporary grave, which, after a few years, will be emptied of its
bones. The bones are then to be put in an urn, and the urn eventually buried in an omega-shaped tomb – the characteristic grave of
Fukien and Kwangtung. Most men and women who have had
children pass through the cycle of first burial and disinterment.
But only the urns belonging to families for whom geomantic reburial has become important and possible are in fact put into new
graves. Urns awaiting second burial are stored in the open air,
near the fields or on a hillside; and in reality most of them are
never moved from this position. They may begin by being tended
as the potential contents of a final grave, but after the lapse of a
generation they are more likely to turn into anonymous pots,
weathered until they crack and spill their irrelevant bones on the
ground.

Sometimes a rich man may build his tomb according to
geomancy and, once dead, enter it to stay there for ever. Usually,
however, the first grave is chosen hurriedly and is intended merely

---

[1] *Ibid.*, pp. 1057 f. The urn is illustrated in Plate XXVIII, facing p. 1058.
[2] *Ibid.*, pp. 1059 f.   [3] *Ibid.*, p. 1061.
[4] John Henry Gray, *China, A History of the Laws, Manners, and Customs of the
People*, ed. W. G. Gregor, London, 1878, vol. I, p. 327.

as the first step towards the final tomb to which the dead man or woman will move through disinterment and the funerary urn. The final graves are sited and constructed according to *fêng-shui* and may take years to prepare and fill, because the choice of a good site may call for a protracted search and because the correct time for entombment may be long delayed by both practical difficulties and ritual restrictions. The geomancy of burial is concentrated about this second interment, for although *fêng-shui* can certainly enter into the selection of the first grave and the siting of the urn, it is then only of secondary importance, since geomantic virtues flow essentially from that which is intended to be a permanent habitation.[1] Second burial and its geomantic concerns underline the link between *fêng-shui* and social differentiation: ambition is reflected in geomantic striving, and success is attributable to correct geomancy. The humble dead – or more aptly, the dead belonging to humble families – never reach a final grave, their bones being left to lie in the urns which, in great numbers, can be seen to dot the New Territories landscape, at the end of their career being toppled, split, and desolate.

We are now introduced to one part of Chinese geomancy: its connexion with burial. Another part is concerned with the siting and construction of habitations for the use of the living: houses, offices, shops, ancestral halls, temples, and so on. But the *fêng-shui* of burial is uppermost; a grave is often referred to simply by that very Chinese term; and we ought to ask why burial should be so deeply involved in a system of metaphysics and so tightly connected with social differentiation.

It is difficult for somebody brought up in a tradition which distinguishes sharply between man and nature to grasp at once the basic premise of *fêng-shui*. And yet (if I may generalize from my own experience in trying to understand what Chinese geomancy means to people who believe in it) the significance of the premise becomes apparent as soon as the outsider begins to examine a landscape through Chinese categories. One may stand by the side of a Chinese friend and admire the view – and in the New Territories, as elsewhere in coastal southeastern China,

---

[1] Some useful information will be found in B. D. Wilson, 'Chinese Burial Customs in Hong Kong', *Journal of the Hong Kong Branch of the Royal Asiatic Society*, vol. I, 1960–1. Now see H. Baker, 'Burial, Geomancy and Ancestor Worship' in Royal Asiatic Society, Hong Kong Branch, *Aspects of Social Organization in the New Territories*, Hong Kong [1965].

the combination of hills and sea produces splendid vistas. One's own pleasure is aesthetic and in a sense 'objective': the landscape is out there and one enjoys it. One's friend is reacting differently. His appreciation is cosmological. For him the viewer and the viewed are interacting, both being part of some greater system. The cosmos is Heaven, Earth, and Man. Man is in it and of it. So that while my characteristic reaction to a landscape may be to say that I find it beautiful, my friend's may well be to remark that he feels content or comfortable. (The Cantonese term I have heard is *shue-fuk*.) Man is in nature. The landscape affects him directly, in the ideal case making him feel relaxed and confident. (It is for this reason that English-speaking Chinese in Hong Kong often use the word 'psychological' to refer to the effect of *fêng-shui*. They do not mean, as one might at first suppose, that geomancy is an illusion. They are asserting a human response to forces working in the cosmos.) And just as landscape affects man, man may affect it. In a landscape there are mystical entities (an Azure Dragon, a White Tiger, and so on); as men we may harm them or improve them, weaken them or strengthen them; if we do, the landscape will no longer be the same, and in turn it will differently affect us. The landscape that I see and the one seen by my Chinese friend are not, therefore, exactly the same thing. . . .

Of course, the attempt to see through Chinese eyes and to think of geomancy as Chinese think of it will be successful only to the extent that my interpretation does not conflict with what Chinese say and do. Even then there is no guarantee that the interpretation is correct; I cannot decisively prove my intuition that there is a coherent system of ideas underlying *fêng-shui*, but I shall continue for the present to assume such a system.

The term *fêng-shui* can be literally translated as 'winds and waters'. The *ch'i* (Cantonese: *hei*), the Cosmic Breaths which constitute the virtue of a site, are blown about by the wind and held by the water. If the wind is high, the Breaths will disperse; if the water moves fast, the Breaths will be drawn away. A site is protected from high wind by its hills. Places from which streams and rivers flow too directly and too fast are avoided. An ideal site is one which nestles in the embrace of hills standing to its rear and on its flanks; it is then like an armchair, comfortable and protecting. The hills to the rear of the site support it; they give it strength. Those to the left, as the site faces its unshielded fourth side, are the Azure Dragon; those to the right are the White Tiger. The Azure Dragon is a beneficent force (one comes close to Chinese conceptions, as English-speaking Chinese themselves often do, in speaking of it as an electrical or magnetic force) which animates the hills and spreads itself in the approaches to the site. The White Tiger is a force of danger which protects only as long as it is in complementary relationship with the Azure Dragon. Azure Dragon and White Tiger must be present in the right proportions. The former must be the higher of the two to ensure a proper balance of forces between them. The one is *yang*, the other *yin*. The one is spring, the other autumn. The one is civil, the other military. They are opposite and complementary, co-operating, when they are in the correct ratio, to ensure the concentration of the Breaths.[1]

These last statements represent the core of geomantic ideas as I heard them expressed in Hong Kong. They are of course elaborated by geomancers, but in their simplest version they summarize the common basis of Chinese thinking about the nature of a site. And they are confirmed generally by what others have written about geomancy in China.[2] Whatever the regional variations and the differences between expert and lay opinion, all Chinese appear to be attached to the notion that sites can be found for and shaped to the good fortune of men, and that retrospectively the happy or

[1] Azure Dragon and White Tiger, standing respectively to the left and to the right of the site, are *yang* and *yin*. Where possible the site faces south, so that the Dragon and Tiger are to the east and west; and in the grammar of symbols of geomancy the eastern and western quarters of the heavens are the Dragon and Tiger respectively. As the two 'animals' are seen in the landscape, they are elevations of ground. Dragon must stand higher than Tiger. In the case of a grave, the burial spot lies at the exact point where the two forces represented by Dragon and Tiger cross each other. In general, the site will consist of a proper balance (ideally in the ratio of three to two) of 'male' ground (bold elevations) and 'female' (uneven and softly undulating). See e.g. Joseph Needham, *Science and Civilization in China*, vol. 2 (*History of Scientific Thought*), Cambridge, 1956, pp. 359 f.

[2] See especially the fascinating study by Ernest J. Eitel, *Feng-Shui: Or, The Rudiments of Natural Science in China*, London, 1873, and the almost equally elaborate account in De Groot, *op. cit.* De Groot's data, as he says himself, make it plain that what was true of Amoy was also generally true of Hong Kong and Canton, since his account is very much like that given by Eitel, who spent years studying the subject, mainly in Hong Kong. Although my own observations were necessarily very much more restricted than Eitel's, I was greatly impressed by the close correspondence between what I saw in 1963 and what he found nearly a hundred years ago, a correspondence made the more significant by my not having read Eitel's monograph until I had written the first draft of my account.

miserable lot of men may be explained by the nature of the sites with which they are linked. The linkage is particularly strong in burial: where our forefathers are buried explains how we fare. It is not at all surprising that well-intentioned foreigners in China found it particularly hard to weaken Chinese faith in *fêng-shui* and in its expert practitioners. The geomancers with their compasses and handbooks, their talk of the stars and the Five Elements, and their citation of the classical *I Ching*, represent a sophisticated skill which they offer largely outside the framework of folk religion.

The complexity of *fêng-shui* is itself a guarantee of its continued credibility. If it works, well and good. If it fails to work, a neglected principle, an ignorant geomancer, or an undetected alteration to the landscape can be held responsible. Starting from the assumption that man is a part of a universe in which his fortunes are inextricably woven, Chinese find no difficulty in maintaining their belief in the efficiency of geomantic technique. *Fêng-shui* is not like most of the rest of Chinese religion; there is no reliance on the will of a deity; there are no gods to serve or placate;[1] it is based on self-evident propositions; the principles which regulate the cosmos, however vaguely they may be formulated, are known to experts who, in the performance of their professional duties, operate with sure techniques. Two consequences follow from this view. One is that geomancers are held in an esteem not shared by other religious practitioners. They are gentlemen and attract the curiosity of gentlemen. The second consequence is that faith in geomancy may well survive a change in religion. Many Chinese Christians in the New Territories believe in and act by it; in China itself missionaries seem to have found in it an especial recalcitrance to their arguments. In a report for 1888 from Amoy, a missionary writes: 'The gigantic (geomantic) system of

[1] But there is an exception. In setting up a geomantic site, men must have regard to the presiding deities of the place, just as they rely on the earth-god to protect a grave once it is made. Gray, *op. cit.*, vol. I, pp. 297 f., tells us that the grave-diggers cannot begin their work until a letter addressed to the 'genii of the mountain' has been read aloud by the 'nearest of kin'. He gives the text of the standard 'letter' used. The invocation and worship of gods may also be thought necessary when a *fêng-shui* has been disastrously disturbed. In the New Territories rituals known as *tun fu* are performed to enlist divine help in correcting the harm done. But geomancers typically regard these rituals as falling outside their province. Cf. J. J. M. De Groot, *The Religious System of China*, vol. I, Leiden, 1892, p. 223, where we are given the text of a prayer recited by a mandarin at the burial of a man of high standing. The earth-god is appealed to for his help in ensuring that the grave will benefit the dead man's descendants.

Fengshui which causes devastating conflicts between individuals, families and villages, rises now and again where we thought it to be dead and buried, and has to be opposed with much decision. Even Abraham's careful purchase of a plot with a "cave" (a geomantic term!) is brought in as a proof that the Bible sanctions the seeking of specially lucky sites for burial!'[1]

But if *fêng-shui* presupposes a certain view of the universe, it also rests on assumptions about the nature of society. *Fêng-shui* is primarily concerned as a technique with siting graves and buildings, but not all graves and buildings are geomantically placed. *Fêng-shui* is a preoccupation with success, and since an appetite for success must be stimulated by a taste of it, those who lack hope are not involved in geomantic striving. In other words, *fêng-shui* is not for the poor and humble. It is when a man begins to think of the possibility of increased welfare for himself and his issue, some measure of prosperity having already been achieved, that he takes to a concern with geomancy. On their side, those who are established in their success cannot afford to ignore the need to ensure their continuing prosperity by taking geomantic precautions. Underlying *fêng-shui* is a fundamental notion in and about Chinese society: all men (that is, all Chinese fully accepted within society, not boat people or other marginal elements) are in principle equal and may legitimately strive to improve their station in life. The peasant in his cottage has as much right to hope for advancement as the mandarin in his *yamen*. All men are morally entitled to take steps to raise themselves and their descendants – by scholarship, by the accumulation of riches, and by the religious pursuit of good fortune.

Let us return to the system of burial. If a grave has been geomantically sited (and horoscopically suited, both generally and as to the time of burial, to the person to be interred) it will, sooner or later, bring prosperity to the descendants of the man or woman buried in it. 'Sooner or later': the geomancer is not usually prepared to tie himself down to a guarantee of quick results. People know that they must be patient for a few years, and their patience is in fact required by the belief that the lapse of time is necessary for the collection and concentration of the Breaths. They settle in

[1] London Missionary Society Archives, Fukien Reports, 1866–1891, Report for 1888 from J. Sadler, Amoy, no. 9680, arrival no. 4403. The reference is presumably to Genesis xxiii, 17–20, and xlix, 29–32.

the bones, and in a particularly successful case cause them to glow. From the bones the virtue passes to the living descendants, but not in any physical sense. Children benefit from the virtues of their parents' graves; how is a mystery. If they live close enough they must tend the graves or run the risk of not benefiting, but their separation from the graves by mere distance is no bar at all to their receiving the virtue. Of course, not all attempts at geomancy work, even if people are patient. Once they have made up their mind that something is wrong they may alter the site in some way or, in the extreme, even move the dead to another grave.

It is necessary to consider the role of the dead as vehicles of geomantic fortune. From my own enquiries in the New Territories I concluded that in this context the dead were passive agents, pawns in a kind of ritual game played by their descendants with the help of geomancers. The accumulation of Breaths followed automatically from the correct siting of the grave. The dead themselves could choose neither to confer nor to withhold the blessings that flowed through their bones. But other views have been held on this subject. Eitel writes that if the tomb is well placed and 'the animal spirit of the deceased . . . is comfortable and free of disturbing elements . . . the ancestors' spirits will feel well disposed towards their descendants, will be enabled to constantly surround them, and willing to shower upon them all the blessings within reach of the spirit world'.[1] And in the same vein De Groot says that *hsiao* (filial piety) makes the Chinese place the graves of his close kinsmen in such a way that 'he not only insures their rest and comfort, but also renders them well disposed towards himself, arousing in them feelings of gratitude which must necessarily bear fruits in the shape of various blessings to be showered down upon the offspring'.[2] Similar statements are to be found in other books,[3] ascribing some volition to the dead by means of which they may act upon the geomantic forces placed at their disposal. Now, it is quite possible that my own views have been biased by my paying more attention to geomancers than to laymen. I must leave the question of the volition of the

[1] Eitel, *op. cit.*, p. 20.   [2] De Groot, *op. cit.*, vol. III, p. 936.
[3] See e.g. S. Wells Williams, *The Middle Kingdom*, vol. II, London, 1883, p. 246; J. Macgowan, *Lights and Shadows of Chinese Life*, Shanghai, 1909, pp. 90 f.; and G. Willoughby-Meade, *Chinese Ghouls and Goblins*, London, 1928, p. 276.

geomantically sited dead to be decided finally by other field workers and by students of the Chinese manuals of *fêng-shui* – if indeed the matter can be decided in so definite a manner, for it may well be that there is a built-in vagueness on the point. But at least I think we may be fairly sure that if the dead have an independent role in geomancy then it is a minor one. When they are peevish because ill at ease, they may perhaps block off the benefits of the site; if in fact they are thought to have done so, they can then be comforted by attention to their graves in order to restore the flow of benefits. In the end the dead can do little to thwart the process set going by geomantic technique.

The dead in their graves are not in a position to dispense rewards for good conduct, because *fêng-shui* as a whole is quite explicitly conceived by Chinese as being at one level amoral. What the geomancer procures is a return on the investment of good technique. Chinese sometimes refer to geomancy as 'principles of Earth', and in that formulation there is implied an automatic good fortune which stands contrasted with the morally earned blessings to be got from the working of 'principles of Heaven'. The point was brought home to me in the field when I listened to *fêng-shui* stories. Let me give a brief account of one of them.

A poor duck breeder one day secretly observed a geomancer at work. The expert stuck a bamboo pole in a muddy duck-pond and left it there. During the night it flowered. The duck-breeder stole it, replacing it by another bamboo pole, to the disappointment of the geomancer when he came next morning to inspect the results of his test. He tried once more and was again foiled by the duck-breeder, and so was forced to abandon what he had thought to have proved a magnificent *fêng-shui*. Equipped with the stolen knowledge of the site, the duck-breeder instructed his wife to bury him in the crucial spot when he should come to die, which in good time she did, wrapping him in a mat in default of the coffin for which she was too poor to pay. Time passed and their son grew up to become a great scholar (a 'senior wrangler', for such stories require a dramatic elevation of status). Summoned by the Emperor to Peking, he made the long journey north. On the way, the boat he was travelling in ran into difficulty but was saved by the intervention of a god in a nearby temple. The scholar's travelling companions honoured the god for his favour, but he

himself refused to do so, going so far in his arrogance as to strike
the god on his head with his fan. Eventually he reached the capital,
and then returned home again. There he showed himself so over-
bearing in his triumph, especially in his humiliating treatment
of his maternal uncle, that his mother was forced to rebuke
him, reminding him that his father had died a humble death and
had been buried in a mere mat. The scholar agreed to rebury his
father in a fitting manner, but when he came to search for the
body he could not find it. While men were fruitlessly hunting
for it round the spot indicated by the widow, the god whom the
scholar had insulted appeared in the guise of a stranger and advised him to throw lime into the pond, whereupon the corpse
would rise. The advice was taken. The body came to the surface
of the pond, but along with it rose nine dead fish, only one of
which had its eyes open. . . . Nine bright possibilities had been
stored away in the *fêng-shui*. One of them had been realized in the
success of the scholar – and that from this day was ended. The other
eight were ruined.

What this story 'says' is that *fêng-shui* works – it is a technique
and men can use it to their advantage. But let no man think that
Heaven is blind to iniquity. For a time the wicked may profit by
geomancy, but in the end the principles of Heaven will be brought
in to correct the amoral working of the principles of Earth. (In
the story there are two immoral acts: the stealing of the *fêng-shui*
from the geomancer and the blasphemous conduct to the god.
But I suspect that the second act is merely an instrument for the
ultimate correction of the first, since *fêng-shui* stories seem often to
turn on the stealing of geomantic sites.[1])

Heaven may intervene to smash a *fêng-shui*. (It is sometimes
said to smite it with 'thunder'.) But there are more common
reasons why a geomancer's efforts may not come to fruition.
There may have been a fault in technique, a deficiency which a
subsequent geomancer is likely to detect. The conformation of the
site may have changed, either by itself in the course of time or as a
result of malicious action by rivals. (And it is not always easy to

---

[1] The argument may be pushed far enough to link geomantic success more
positively with moral worth, so that right conduct becomes a precondition for
this success. See e.g. Willoughby-Meade, *op. cit.*, p. 286 where he quotes a *fêng-
shui* textbook principle: ' "Do not fail to cultivate secret virtues; the accumulation of *virtuous deeds* being the foundation of the search for (auspicious) sites." '
And cf. De Groot, *op. cit.*, pp. 1013 ff. But I myself have not heard this argument.

detect such action, for it may consist of nothing more noticeable than a nail knocked into a crucial spot on the site.) Finally, it may be said that a change in the effectiveness of a *fêng-shui* has been due to the steady transformations worked throughout the cosmos by the orderly progression of cycles of time, usually expressed in the sexagenary system of 'stems and branches'.[1] With all these 'escape clauses' geomancy commends itself to the reasonable mind.

Chinese attempt to shape the future by *fêng-shui*, but they also by the same means try to explain the past and the present. Geomantic siting produces results. The existence of 'results' implies the pre-existence of *fêng-shui*. And, of course, retrospective geomancy is more convincing than its prospective counterpart. The present is certain and, given the complexity of geomantic reasoning, can be easily explained. Let me offer one illustration from the New Territories. The Tang lineages, as we have seen, dominated large areas of the county of Hsin-an, but they were aware that by national standards they were rather small beer. The point is made in the following story. A Sung princess married a Tang in the twelfth century. (This part of the story is almost certainly true. A member of the Kam Tin Tang local lineage was a county magistrate in Kiangsi. When the Sung forces were in retreat he retired to Kwangtung with a prince to whose daughter his son was later married. Naturally enough, the royal connexion plays an important part in Tang genealogy.[2]) When the princess grew old, a famous geomancer chose a *fêng-shui* for her which resembled a lion, asking her whether she preferred to be buried on the lion's head or tail. 'She asked what difference it would make, and she was told that if her grave was on the head her descendants would be very great men; but if on the tail they would be more humble people, perhaps officers of low degree, and, although prosperous, none would succeed to high rank.' The princess chose the tail because, being of high rank and having suffered much herself, she preferred her descendants to be more humble.[3]

[1] The role of time in the theory of *fêng-shui* is to be traced historically to the *I Ching*. See Richard Wilhelm, *The I Ching or Book of Changes*, trans. C. F. Baynes, 2 vols., London, 1951; Hellmut Wilhelm, *Change, Eight Lectures on the I Ching*, trans. C. F. Baynes, London, 1961; and Hellmut Wilhelm, 'The Concept of Time in the Book of Changes', in Joseph Campbell, ed., *Man and Time, Papers from the Eranos Yearbooks*, London, 1958.

[2] See Lo Hsiang-lin *et al.*, *op. cit.*, pp. 137 f.

[3] Sung Hok-p'ang, 'Legends and Stories of the New Territories, IV, Kam T'in (continued)', *The Hong Kong Naturalist*, vol. VII, no. 1, April, 1936, p. 34.

So far in this discussion of the geomancy of burial I have not dealt with the precise relationships between the dead and the people who, providing their *fêng-shui*, hope to benefit through them. On the face of it there appears to be no problem: children bury and expect to be blessed through their parents – the sons especially, and through them their own sons, for geomantic benefit flows agnatically. But in fact, a question of great interest arises at this very point, because, while it is true in a general way that a good site blesses all the agnatic descendants of the man or woman buried in it, it may not benefit them all equally. In fact, brothers may quarrel about the siting of the parental grave because what the oldest of them has chosen suits him to the detriment of the others and what another proposes similarly favours him against the rest. The competition between brothers for the favourable site is built into one of the techniques for judging the qualities of a site in relation to the eight points of the compass. The points are associated with the eight trigrams of the Book of Changes (*I Ching*) and are related with, among other things, eight family relationships: father, mother, first son, second son, third son, first daughter, second daughter, and third daughter. As De Groot puts the matter, '. . . the fortunes of all members of a family cannot be insured by the grave of their father or mother unless the forms and contours of the surroundings are perfect on six sides thereof'; and since this is a virtual impossibility, there is bound to be quarrelling, especially when those prejudiced are the children of a jealous secondary wife. To avoid this kind of dispute a rich man may fix on his grave during his lifetime; but trouble is not necessarily averted by this act of foresight, because the man may well die in a year during which the alignment of the grave is not in accordance with its would-be occupant.[1]

The story continues: the geomancer who built the grave put a tablet inside it which bore the words 'Three hundred years hence, an ignorant young man named So . . ., who knows nothing about "fung shui" will want to alter the way this grave faces. If he is allowed to alter it, not only will the Tang family have trouble, but So himself will have bad luck.' Three hundred years later the prophecy was fulfilled; the Tang were going through a bad patch and, on the advice of a man called So, they began to change the position of the princess's grave. When they found the tablet they were seized with terror, and So withdrew his advice.

[1] De Groot, *op. cit.*, vol. III, pp. 1028 ff. And cf. J. Dyer Ball, *Things Chinese, or Notes Connected with China*, 4th edn., London, 1904, p. 313. One of the German missionaries working in northern Hsin-an quotes a conversation with a geomancer in which the differences in fortune between members of one family are explained (and the explanation is attacked) in the following words: 'Unsre

1. A geomantic prospect in the New Territories, 1963. The graves in the foreground form an unofficial cemetery; the sea and small islands can be seen in the distance, on the right.

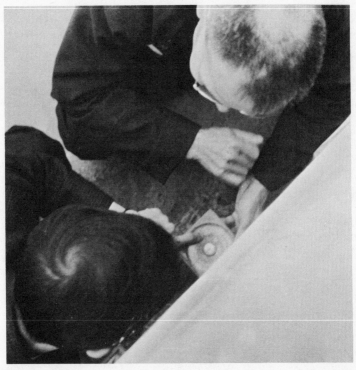

2a. A geomancer in the New Territories, 1963, explaining the use of his compass at a graveside.

2b. Main gate of a walled village in the New Territories, 1963. The two curved protecting 'arms' are additions made for reasons of geomancy.

Sons may wrangle for a long time (perhaps years) over where to bury their parent, and in doing so they demonstrate for us how in geomancy there is competition not only between rival groups of villagers or kinsmen, but also between men related in the closest possible manner. In a polygynous family, however, the sons of different mothers may seek their separate paths to fortune through their several maternal tombs. And this possibility introduces us to another interesting problem. I know of no evidence to suggest that Chinese think of women's graves as being either more or less effective in geomancy than men's, and yet during my enquiries in the New Territories I was struck by the prominence of women's graves in *fêng-shui*. To some extent we must expect women to figure more often than men because of their crucial positions in a patrilineal and polygynous society: men descended agnatically from one ancestor can nevertheless differentiate themselves in respect of the women married to him, and so escape from the inconvenience of sharing geomantic fortune with those whose success it is their very last wish to promote. (And since both polygyny and *fêng-shui* activity will traditionally have been found mainly among the better-off, it seems to follow that they will in fact have had more women's than men's graves to concern themselves with. For secondary wives must usually have been drawn from poorer families.) Patriliny linked the fortunes of agnates together; geomancy gave them the chance of individualizing their fate.

But there is another reason why the graves of women are important. Every man engaging in the hunt for geomantic fortune must try to strike a balance between two conflicting aims. On the one side, he wants to maximize his chances by making use of the greatest number of graves (since some of them may prove fruitless, and in any case particular graves may be thought to

---

Lehre gibt darüber Aufschluss. Der Einfluss der Gräber ist für die verschiedenen Familienglieder verschieden. Des Grossvaters Grab wirkt beglückend auf die ältesten Enkel, benachtheiligt aber die Nachgebornen, aber die Gräber der Eltern benachtheiligen den ältesten Sohn und sind Glück bringend für die jüngeren Kinder. Entgegnung: Da hebt ja das Fung Schui sich gegenseitig auf und Glück wird Allen zu Theil, dem widerspricht aber die tägliche Erfahrung. Merkwürdig und unerklärlich bleibt dabei, dass Eltern, die bei Lebzeiten ihre Kinder gleich lieben und für Alle gleich sorgen, nach ihrem Tode eins dem andern vorziehen. Das ist gegen die "Principien des Himmels" und gegen "die Gefühle der Menschen".' – F. Genähr, 'Ueber chinesische Geomantie', *Berichte der Rheinischen Missionsgesellschaft*, Barmen, no. 6, June 1864, p. 166.

produce particular benefits, so that a range of them may be considered necessary to procure a rounded success). To ensure a large number of chances a man can go to work on the graves of more distant lineal ascendants – and the system of double burial and the practice of moving graves make it possible for him to call on many candidates. But if he does so, he finds his conduct in conflict with an equally important aim: to reduce the number of people with whom he will need to share the geomantically induced fortune. The further back he goes in his genealogy, the greater will be the number of collateral beneficiaries. In fact, it is my impression from what I have seen that men strive to confine their attention to the graves of their fathers and paternal grandfathers and their mothers and paternal grandmothers. The women are necessary not only to discriminate among agnates but also for swelling the number of chances open to a man when he is unwilling to look to higher generations.

That geomancy implies a harsh competition between agnates probably accounts for the fact that many lineages attempted to check its effects. In her study of lineage rules Mrs Liu analyses those of thirty 'clans' which refer to *fêng-shui*. Seven rules appear to be in favour, twenty to have what Mrs Liu calls an 'ambiguous attitude', and twelve to be against. Of these last twelve rules, six express the view that geomancy is a superstition, and six, while allowing search for a good site, disapprove of the belief that fortune or misfortune follows from geomantic causes.[1] (It is not clear to me how these thirty-nine rules are distributed over the thirty 'clans'.) A further scrap of evidence comes from a village near Peking where the 'history' of a lineage condemns anyone who, believing the words of the geomancer, 'seeks to benefit his own feng-shui by breaking the burial system' prescribed – graves were to continue to be arranged in a fixed pattern in the two lineage graveyards.[2] None of this material is drawn from southeastern China,[3] where, perhaps because of the popularity of *fêng-shui*,[4]

---

[1] Liu, *The Traditional Chinese Clan Rules*, p. 169.

[2] Gamble, *North China Villages*, p. 262.

[3] Mrs Liu's total sample of genealogies is 151. None of these is from Fukien and only 2 are from Kwangtung. See *op. cit.*, pp. 211 ff. I am assuming that neither of the Kwangtung genealogies fell into the smaller sample of 30 from which rules concerning geomancy were extracted.

[4] There can be little doubt about the universality of *fêng-shui* beliefs and practices in China, but, partly perhaps because of the appropriateness of the

lineages were not generally in a position to restrain the geomantic efforts of their members; but I should be surprised if warnings against its dangers did not appear in some Fukien and Kwangtung genealogies.

A further implication of *fêng-shui* remains to be considered before I try to round off this part of the discussion. Each new 'permanent' grave entails a search for a new site. One cannot assume that a site in which an ancestor has already been successfully installed will answer for a fresh burial. Even if an old site has been fruitful, it is unlikely to suit a new candidate, and in any case the virtue to be derived from it may be confined to a tiny spot already covered by the former corpse. (In fact, it seems that in popular belief the virtue of a good gravesite can be stolen or shared by burying one's dead near it; whence the quarrels over poaching which seem to underline the jealousy of the unsuccessful; but I think the geomancer's view would be that a new grave near an old one would succeed only in spoiling the latter by altering the conformation of its surroundings and would not itself benefit in any way.) People scatter their tombs, usually but not necessarily, confining themselves to the general area within which their village has traditional burial rights. The few compact graveyards to be found in the New Territories nearly always turn out on inspection to be the resting place of immigrants or townspeople. No permanent common graveyard is required for the poor;[1] at most they are likely to finish up in funerary urns. So that when at Ch'ing Ming people go out to the hills to visit the dead in their omega-shaped tombs, the visitors are not all the time crowded together as they would be in a cemetery, but are sorted out in small groups according to the sites they tend, even if they begin by clustering around the tomb of a remote ancestor. The dead are points of differentiation.

To end this account of the *fêng-shui* of burial and to give it some reality I shall summarize and quote from a 'dialogue, written by a Chinese scholar' which vividly conveys the style of geomantic

topography and the opportunities for dispersed burial, southern China seems to have had the reputation of being especially active in geomancy. Cf. Richard Wilhelm's assertion that geomancy as a method of feeling one's way into one's surroundings must be distinguished 'from many excrescences of popular super-stition, such as the doctrines of wind and water which are met with, especially in South China.' – *The Soul of China*, trans. J. H. Reece, N.Y., 1928, p. 176.

[1] *Lineage Organization*, p. 78.

thinking.[1] It begins with the duty of a man to see to the burial of his parents.

Q. When a man's parents die, is it necessary for him to seek a propitious spot in the hills for their burial?
A. It is his duty with all his heart and strength to seek such a place.
Q. What are the best means to employ in searching for a suitable location?
A. If the deceased, in his lifetime, has already selected a spot, then a great outlay of money and strength may be avoided; otherwise it will be necessary to engage a professor of geomancy who has acquired some repute, and with him make the search.
Q. What are the tests by which a professor of ability is known?
A. He may be recommended by friends, who have tried him, or his proficiency may be tested by having him examine some old tomb and show its good points: in what way literary honour or military prosperity has come; in what particular years civil and military officers have arisen in the family; at what time, according to the indications, sons have been given; what is the present condition of the descendants; also whether white ants have penetrated and injured the bones, or water soaked and destroyed them, thus cutting off the family and name. If he answers these without mistake he is a first-class professor, and such are exceedingly rare.

The dialogue continues on the securing of the geomancer's services. He may take anything between ten days and two years or more to find a suitable site.

Q. What considerations would hasten or delay?
A. If those concerned readily agree to the methods of the professor, and are free and generous in everything, he will also do his best to please them, in the hope of being recommended to another family: and further, in the purchase of grave lots the professors get a commission of three or four per cent, so that under such circumstances everything may be settled in ten or fifteen days. If, on the other hand, those concerned think they know something of geomancy themselves, and bring up objections to the professor's statements, desiring to have all good influences centre in one spot, he will simply accept their hospitality for a short time, and after he goes, others will

[1] See Henry, *The Cross and the Dragon*, pp. 166 ff. Henry was a nineteenth-century missionary ('Ten Years a Missionary in Canton', as he announces on his title page) who was so little sympathetic to Chinese religion that he concludes his citing of the dialogue on geomancy with the comment 'All this shows it to be pure deception.' It is lucky for us that hostility was accompanied by curiosity.

be engaged with no better success, so that three or four years may pass before a suitable place for burial is decided upon.

We are now told how the geomancer 'goes to the hills to search for a site', and of the criteria by which he chooses.

A. . . . It is said that the Dragon follows the watercourse, and the meeting-place of waters is the meeting-place of the dragons, where the virtues of hill and stream are united and the grass ever green. Such a place being found, the conformation of the land on all sides is observed, and if there appear no outlet for the good influences in the air, it is pronounced an auspicious site.

Q. What outside marks are sought?

A. In the distance there should be groups of mountains with streams of water encircling them; in front a stretch of level plain, a pond, or lake. In the wider circuit, the level space should be large enough for ten thousand horses, and the watercourse be sufficient to admit a dragon boat. If the expanse be wide, children and grandchildren will multiply and be strong. If the front is towards the star of luck, some of the family will rise in office. If on the right and left the rocks assume the shapes of drums and flags, it presages military power. From the top of the hill the view should extend for miles, with mountains and streams interspersed. If the hills opposite are in the shape of moth wings, it indicates that beautiful daughters-in-law and good daughters will appear.

A distinction is made between open and covered graves, the former being excavated from the surface and the latter from the side of a hill. The open graves are the more common because less expensive to make.

Q. What is the proper method in making an open grave?

A. Choose a lucky day and an auspicious hour, and accompany the professor of geomancy to the place, taking workmen with you. Open the compass, adjust it with care, and observe the direction of the needle, that you may know where to begin. First, worship the gods of the hill and of the earth, that you may not incur their wrath. This is called making the cave, or opening. It is easier for the professor to indicate the location in general than to mark the exact spot.

Digging the grave one finds different kinds of soil, sand, and gravel.

A. . . . Those buried above the hard clay find the air warm and comfortable, and have no trouble from water or white ants. . . .

Q. Having found the proper clay, what is the manner of burial?

A. A lucky day must be chosen. The whole family must give the day, month, and year of birth of each to a fortune-teller, who will cast their horoscopes and determine the proper time to proceed.

Q. Where there are a number of brothers, may not disputes arise?

A. This is often a source of trouble. Different positions are canvassed as to their bearings upon different scions of the house, and the geomancer is at a loss to know what to do. Sometimes each brother will engage a different professor, and years will elapse before the matter is settled, the coffin meanwhile remaining in a temporary receptacle.

Q. Why are the dead sometimes left for years in these 'earth pavilions' unburied?

A. Because, as intimated above, the family may be large, and the brothers cannot agree upon a suitable place. Another reason is that after negotiations for a propitious site have been carried on some time, the family may become poor, the children and grandchildren scattered, so that the matter is dropped. Sometimes while the coffin rests in this temporary receptacle, sudden prosperity comes to the family, and believing they have found the place where the best influences centre, they are not willing to move, lest reverses come.

Q. What reasons are given for exhuming and removing the dead?

A. A more favourable site may have been found under the direction of the geomancer, who is constantly suggesting new places and pointing out defects in the old. It is too shallow perhaps, or the dew and mist do not fall and rise propitiously, or a stream sweeps past it in an unlucky manner, or the sand has moved, or the watercourse changed, so that it must be exhumed. If, in digging, water or white ants appear, the necessity for immediate removal is evident; and often it requires several changes before the final resting-place is found.

Q. How are young children treated in burial?

A. In this the pernicious effects of geomancy are seen. The care bestowed on the burial of parents is for personal advantage. When young children die they are supposed to be under the curse of Heaven, and are called unlucky: and before daylight in the morning they are given to coolies, who, receiving only thirty or forty cents, carry them out and bury them at random in some shallow grave in the waste land near the city, treating them with no more respect than if they were mere animals.

Q. It is said that quarrels and lawsuits often arise about burial-lots, breaking up families, exciting bitter hostilities, and often causing the loss of life. Whence these evils?

A. These evils are due to geomancy. Every one wants the best, but people are numerous, and lucky sites few. The rich have bought up broad tracts, so that the poor man who wishes only six feet of earth finds no place for burial. In villages, the large and influential clans often use violence to secure their ends, and the evils are multiplied. Quarrels and bloody fights ensue, boundary stones are removed, the bones of the dead are dishonoured and years are spent in litigation. Magistrates find it difficult to give judgement in such matters. Chü-fu-tsz [Chu Hsi: the story is a well-known folktale] was involved in a case of this kind, where a man, taking an old stone, cut his name upon it, and surreptitiously set it up in a rich man's burying-lot. Ten years afterwards he brought the case before the magistrate, who, seeing this proof of the peasant's right, rebuked the rich man for his oppression of the poor, and commanded him to vacate the place in favour of the poor peasant. When Chü-fu-tsz had retired from office he was accidentally strolling over the spot, and struck with the favourable surroundings of the place, exclaimed, 'I have never seen anything to equal this.' An old man, who happened to be standing near, recounted the history of the lawsuit, that had come under his own jurisdiction. The philosopher incensed at the thought of the injustice practised, cursed the place, and forthwith there came violent wind, thunder, and an earthquake, and a great chasm yawned where the beautiful site had appeared.

Q. What becomes of the poor who cannot afford lucky sites?
A. They are buried one above another in the waste places, no stone to mark the place, or anything to distinguish one from the other.

The dialogue now turns to the geomancy of ancestral halls and houses, into which subjects we need not now follow it; but the very last statements may be quoted to illustrate how the sceptic, in attempting to rebut the claims made for geomancy, may fasten on the moral interpretation of good fortune.

A. It must be confessed that geomancy is not reliable. It springs from covetousness. In their books it is said, 'The cave (the grave) is in their hearts, not in the hills'; 'The happy man finds a happy burial-place.' 'If the rich master of the house has happiness, the professor has eyes to see it.'

A *fêng-shui* disturbed gives off a baleful influence (in Cantonese, *shaat hei*, 'killing Breath'). The art of the geomancer partly consists in remedying such a defect and in protecting a grave from the dangerous Breaths emanating from certain imperfections in the natural setting. If we now turn briefly to the *fêng-shui* of buildings we shall see again that the attempts made by men to improve their fortunes by geomancy may entail harm to other people. And in certain contexts of this broader kind of *fêng-shui* the rivalries within and between lineages are plainly in evidence.

In the *fêng-shui* of buildings we see a kind of political hierarchy, the apex of which is formed by the state and the base by individual dwellings. Between these two extremes lie administrative units, cities, towns, villages, lineages, and segments of lineages. Any territorially defined entity or residential area may have its fortune promoted and attacked by geomancy, so that individuals live within what we may call a segmentary system of *fêng-shui*, their destiny being under the influence of the geomancy of a series of more and more inclusive entities. The fortunes of a lineage are affected by the siting of its ancestral hall. (And it is for this reason that the hall is rarely to be found inside a walled village; for geomantic siting requires that a construction have an unimpeded front aspect.) Each member of the lineage looks to the *fêng-shui* of his own house for his success.[1]

[1] Cf. the following extracts from Henry's dialogue on geomancy. 'Q. In a large village and powerful clan, what is of first importance? A. The ancestral hall, where the fragrant incense is ever kept burning. Q. Is it necessary that the site of this hall or temple be in a good geomantic position? A. The ancestral hall requires the best site in the village. . . . Q. What are the things that specially pertain to geomancy in the structure? A. Before the door should be an empty or lucky room; the direction in which the water from streams, or springs, or rainfall flows is important in determining the increase or dissipation of wealth; the doors must be placed so as to admit free circulation of air; and many other signs. . . . Q. Where streams meet a small pagoda is often seen; what significance has it? A. It is erected at the dictates of geomancy. The place where the water flows out being low, with no hill or high embankment to obstruct the escape of good influences, a pagoda is erected to check these influences and throw them back over the land. Sometimes two on opposite sides of the stream will combine in the work of restraining the outflow of good luck. They are usually in the shape of a scholar's pencil . . . and are supposed to be especially efficacious in bringing literary blessings to the place.' – *op. cit.*, pp. 172 ff. 'Q. When a man wishes to build a house in a village, how does he go about it? A. He first purchases a plot of ground, at a propitious distance from the ancestral hall, idol temples, and open-air altars, and engaging a professor of geomancy to choose a lucky day, encloses the lot with a wall, and prepares to lay the foundation. Q. What are the ceremonies required in this work? A. He must give public notice of his intentions, that all the village may know, and all trouble from personal offence or interference be avoided. . . . Q. In every village there are houses fronting in different directions; is this objectionable? A. The lay of the land varies in different places. . . . Q. In opening a new village, what ceremonies are required? A. This is a very difficult matter. . . . The man who founds a village should have great wisdom, ability, and the help of the gods, to enable him to combine influences that will hold the descendants together'. – *ibid*, pp. 174 f. As for the last statement quoted: geomancy aims to keep a community intact, but geomancy is one of the very reasons why it sometimes splits.

Villages, lineages, and individuals may quarrel with one another over geomantic interference. One community may damage another by putting up a structure which overlooks it or so modifies the appearance of the general setting as to suggest a noxious creature bent on the destruction of the neighbour. Within a village the height and position of a new house are watched with close attention lest it damage the fortune of other houses; and caution must be exercised in modifying an old house (by piercing a wall to make a window, for example) lest a deleterious effect be produced on the *fêng-shui* of nearby houses. At this level, action in geomancy can be seen to be a form of social control, which works as long as the individuals or communities in contact are concerned in the long run to maintain peace among themselves. The ambition of one party to get the edge on the other can be checked by an accusation which the first must ultimately accept if it wishes to stay on good terms with its neighbour. But if one party is dominant and eager to see its rival defeated, it can make use of geomancy to further its ends. And families, segments of lineages, and lineages may think themselves so much under attack by *fêng-shui* that they are forced to abandon their houses and their fields. The weakness they ascribe to their having been attacked is, from our point of view, the weakness which made it possible for them to be successfully attacked.

Interesting as is the subject of the geomancy of buildings, we must leave it here. It has been necessary to consider it briefly in order to show that not all *fêng-shui* is connected with the cult of the ancestors. But the part which is (the geomancy of burial) throws a new light on ancestor worship. Unlike the *fêng-shui* of buildings, that of graves works through a physical medium: the bones of the dead. They (or at least some substitute for them) are indispensable, and the surest way to destroy a rival for good is to tear open his ancestral tombs and pulverize the bones they contain. In the context of *fêng-shui*, bones *are* descent; without them one is cut off from the most powerful source of ancestral benefits. The bones of people who die leaving no sons are valueless; they transmit nothing. (But let it not be supposed that, because bones are anatomical, Chinese think in Western biological terms. The bones of my adoptive parents bring me fortune. The attempt to apply alien biological categories to Chinese thought leads to misunderstanding, as in the parallel case of the significance of blood. Chinese can establish the relationship of nameless bones to a living person by 'testing' their compatibility with the latter's blood: if the bones absorb the blood, the relationship is established. But it is a relationship of kinship, not of consanguinity in the literal sense. Similarly, the blood of two living people can show whether they are related to each other; if the two blobs of blood merge when put into water, then the relationship is demonstrated. But since the tie between husband and wife can be confirmed in this manner we can be sure that biology has nothing to do with it.[1])

But the ancestors as they are represented in their bones are not the ancestors worshipped in their tablets. Each dead forebear appears in two separate guises. Bones and tablets form opposite and complementary parts of the cult of the ancestors. In ancestor worship, men look to their forebears for protection and feel morally obliged to them for any benefit that accrues from the merit accumulated by the dead during their lifetime. They sing their praises and laud their virtues. The ancestors are active in caring for their descendants and will not capriciously cause them harm. In the geomancy of burial, the ancestors, so far from being active agents, are essentially passive pawns in the hands of their descendants. It is not for them to decide to help the living. If their bones have been made comfortable and the site properly adjusted, then benefits will flow. If the bones are ill at ease and the *fêng-shui* badly arranged, then disaster will inevitably fall on the living. The ancestors have become part of the 'principles of Earth', and Earth is the source of amoral fortune. The bones are tools which men use to prospect their fortune from an Earth which gives what skill can take from it. (I had formulated this view before coming upon a striking denunciation of *fêng-shui* made in 1882 by the *Tao-t'ai* – Circuit Intendant – stationed at Amoy. He was attacking the common, and to officialdom reprehensible, practice of delaying burial because of the false arguments of geomancers. 'People wish only to make use of a set of unconscious white bones of their forefathers as implements wherewith to seek fame and glory for their descendants; but they simply forget that wealth and consideration in human life are from the outset fixed by Heaven. . . .'[2])

---

[1] See De Groot, *op. cit.*, vol. III, pp. 1376 ff.
[2] De Groot, *op. cit.*, vol. I, p. 134.

True, Heaven may intervene to frustrate the undeserving in their search for Earthly fortune, but no man setting out to make his future with his ancestral bones is likely to think of his own moral condition and the hazards to which it may give rise, even if, looking back on his experience with *fêng-shui*, he may be encouraged to attribute his lack of success to some moral lapse or shortcoming. The ancestors as bones are *yin*: they are of the Earth, passive, and retiring. The ancestors in their tablets are *yang*: they have affinities with Heaven and are active and outgoing. *Fêng-shui* handles *yin*, ancestor worship *yang*.[1]

Geomancy (in its aspect of burial) and ancestor worship emerge, then, as two faces of a single religious phenomenon – let us call it the cult of the ancestors. Each face of the cult presents a distinct configuration of attitudes towards the dead and has different implications for behaviour between agnates. In the geomancy of burial what strikes us above all is that men are constantly striving to individualize their fate and better themselves at the expense of their patrilineal kinsmen. It is as though Chinese thought of fortune as a kind of fixed fund. Not only is there a quantum of material riches, such that one man's wealth is another man's poverty, but numerous offspring and great honours for some detract from the progeny and glory of others. Good *fêng-shui* sites are limited; men cannot all prosper equally; each man must seek to raise his riches and his standing by depressing those of his agnates. And we have seen that the bitterest competition may be found in the relations between brothers. The greater the honour and wealth at stake, the greater is the struggle to capture it and deny it to others.

If we now oppose ancestor worship to this view of geomancy, and simplify to make the contrast sharp, we shall see that in worshipping their ancestors the Chinese are stressing harmony and unity instead of competition and individualism. In ancestor worship men are required to come together in peace to pay their

---

[1] Geomancy in its 'Chinese' form has a wide distribution in East Asia. It would seem that where in this region societies are not organized in terms of patriliny (in Japan) only the geomancy of buildings appears. (I am indebted to Professor Robert J. Smith for advice on what to read on Japanese geomancy.) Where, as in China itself, in Vietnam, and in Korea, we find patrilineal organization, we also find the geomancy of burial alongside that of buildings. On Vietnam, see Hickey, *op. cit.*, especially p. 40; on Korea see Cornelius Osgood, *The Koreans and their Culture*, N.Y., 1951, pp. 149, 244.

devotions to common forebears and to seek solidarity in the shade of that joint religious action. The difference between the two halves of the cult of the ancestors can be further stressed by saying that whereas in ancestor worship men are under the dominance of their dead fathers (and of the dead of remoter generations), so that a hierarchy of forebears imposes a restraint upon the relations between the living descendants, in the geomancy of burial men liberate themselves from their ancestors to give themselves up to an anarchic pursuit of narrow self-interest.

This is a simple model, and we know that in reality harmony and competition are not so clearly segregated in the total cult. It is inherent in the lineage organization that segments tend to differentiate themselves out to mark their separate status; ancestral halls and estates are the material and religious means for their doing so. At every level of a complex lineage, its segments are in competition. In the admission and arrangement of ancestor tablets in the halls and in the performance of the grand rites, living men and the dead with whom they are more nearly tied are sorted and deployed to show crucial differences in social status and ambition.[1]

Similarly and inversely, the tombs of key ancestors may be used as rallying points for their descendants at the time of the spring and autumn festivals, to bring together in ritual unity greater and lesser groups within the lineage. The lineages of the New Territories have their key tombs which traditionally, and still to some extent, attract crowds of descendants at high points of the ritual year. Of the Hwang lineage in northern Fukien which he describes in *The Golden Wing*, Lin Yueh-hwa tells us that over a period of about ten days the people go out to the graves to make sacrifices. The first sacrifice is made at the founding ancestor's tomb on the first day of the eighth lunar month, the family temporarily in charge of the plot of land held in the name of the founding ancestor 'making sacrifices and preparing a feast for the whole clan for that particular year'.[2] The food having been sacrificed, it is then distributed to all the families gathered around the tomb and a grand picnic begins. 'Whenever the village elders raised their wine cups to toast one another, they added words to their toasts celebrating the merits of their forefathers. All the males of the clan, from those first able to walk, to those of old

[1] See *Lineage Organization*, pp. 79 f.   [2] *Op. cit.*, p. 60.

age, participated in the sacrificial feast.'¹ In the days following this great event 'each day the people swept only one tomb, and each day they progressed from the tomb of more remote ancestors to those of the more recent ones. Like the branches of a tree, different lineages [i.e. segments] of a clan deviate from a single ancestral trunk. So in respect to the more recent ancestors the different lineages separated to sacrifice at their proper tombs.'² And it is important to add that while the graves of key ancestors might function as ritual points of reference alternative or supplementary to ancestral halls, they were sometimes substitutes for them. Not all segments which were based on common lands also enjoyed ancestral halls. For them the tomb of the ancestor in whose name the segment's estate was held was the only ritual centre.

The overlapping functions of ancestor worship and geomancy are to be seen in two further ways. First, people pray at their ancestral tombs and by that act place themselves under the hand of their ancestors in no less a fashion than when they offer prayers at the domestic shrine or in the ancestral hall.³ Second, lineage and segment ancestral halls each have their individual geomancy and are one of the 'causes' of the superior fortunes of their congregations. But the contrast between the geomancy of burial and ancestor worship nevertheless stands: in one, the accent is put upon the paramountcy of selfish interest, the subordination of forebears, and private action; in the other, on the supremacy of the common good, the dominance of ancestors, and collective behaviour.

The distinction gives us a reason for enquiring more closely into the status of Chinese ancestors. In what sense do they dominate

---

¹ *Ibid.*, p. 62.   ² *Ibid.*, p. 63.
³ For an example of prayers offered at tombs see *Lineage Organization*, p. 90 n. And cf. the example given by Williams, *op. cit.*, p. 253: 'Taukwang, 12th year [1833], 3d moon, 1st day, I, Lin Kwang, the second son of the third generation, presume to come before the grave of my ancestor [i.e. father's father], Lin Kung. Revolving years have brought again the season of spring. Cherishing sentiments of veneration, I look up and sweep your tomb. Prostrated I pray that you will come and be present, and that you will grant to your posterity that they may be prosperous and illustrious. At this season of genial showers and gentle breezes I desire to recompense the root of my existence and exert myself sincerely. Always grant your safe protection. My trust is in your divine spirit [presumably: *shên*]. Reverently I present the five-fold sacrifice of a pig, a fowl, a duck, a goose, and a fish; also an offering of five plates of fruit, with libations of spirituous liquors, earnestly entreating that you will come and view them. With the most attentive respect this annunciation is presented on high.'

their descendants? The question cannot, in fact, be satisfactorily answered from the Chinese material alone, for the extent of the ancestral dominance will be seen to be significant only when it is contrasted with what we can find in other ancestor-worshipping societies. I propose, therefore, to undertake a brief discussion of Chinese ancestor worship within the framework of ideas and ethnography built up by anthropologists in recent years. The discussion will involve me in comparing Chinese data with 'savage', a comparison which will probably be as shocking to sinologues as it is expected by anthropologists (the latter having grown used to seeing the Chinese invoked for comparative purposes in the writings of such of their eminent colleagues as Radcliffe-Brown and Fortes).

It will be useful to begin by making a distinction between ancestor worship as a cult of immediate jural superiors and as a cult of descent groups. The two things are usually found together (which is why we need to separate them), but an example of how the first can be seen to operate by itself is given in Fortune's admirable study of the religion of the Manus in the Admiralty Islands. In this society, as the opening sentence of the book informs us vividly, each man 'worships his Father, not in Heaven, but in his house front rafters, not one Father for all, but each man his own'.[1] Ancestral lines of ghosts emerge in the *tandritanitani* cult. The dead are invoked to curse or bless their descendants, but the relationship between the cursers/blessers and those cursed/ blessed is a complicated one: the daughter's children of a married pair curse the wife of the son's son of that pair; the pair's matrilineal female descendants bless their son's daughter.[2] The ghosts invoked, being patrilineal ascendants of the husband of the pair and matrilineal ascendants of his wife, do not belong to one descent group. More important, they are not tended ghosts, cared for and cherished ancestors. The only ghost who in fact is tended is what Fortune calls Sir Ghost, a man's personal spiritual guardian. Sir Ghost is nearly always a man's own father, represented by his skull kept in the rafters. Between a man and this tended ghost there is a compact, such that the son (as he normally is) looks after the dead father and vice versa. When the son dies, then *ipso facto* Sir Ghost has failed to keep his side of the bargain and his skull is

[1] R. F. Fortune, *Manus Religion*, Philadelphia, 1935, p. 1.
[2] *Ibid.*, p. 84.

thrown out – Sir Ghost becoming mere ghost. As long as a ghost is Sir Ghost he is a stern moral figure who watches over his ward and the latter's household, punishing faults and protecting virtue.[1] We have a clear case of what I have called, certainly very clumsily, the cult of immediate jural superiors. Let us consider some examples of such cults set in the wider cults of descent groups. We shall find these examples in the Africanist literature.

An excellent one is to be got from Middleton's work on the Lugbara of Uganda and the (former Belgian) Congo. In this society the cult of the dead is the most important part of the religion, and it is moreover primarily a lineage cult. In fact, the Lugbara cult of the dead is more narrowly ancestral than most, for there is no idea of an after-life except in regard to ancestors, and no conception of a heaven or hell or punishment after death for the life lived on earth. The ancestors appear in the cult in two guises: as the collective body of the ancestors of a lineage – collectively they send sickness to the living and shrines are set up for them collectively; and as individual ancestors 'in certain situations which are significant in relation to responsible kinship behaviour and authority'.[2] Middleton calls the second category 'ghosts'. They are remembered in genealogies where they feature as 'the apical ancestors of segments and lines of descent'. By definition, ghosts are 'big' men, and even the recently dead are considered responsible and conscientious. But 'I was told that while alive a man may not be respected by his son, or at least may not be obeyed by him, because the son wishes to acquire the father's status for himself. "But this is because sons do not respect their fathers, who are 'big' men." It is also said that a man puts shrines for his dead father "because he respects him" – the contradiction is a situational one and needs no explanation for Lugbara. It follows that a ghost, who is defined by his having a shrine for himself, is a respected ancestor and so also a responsible one.'[3]

A Lugbara invokes the ghosts to bring sickness to one of his kin or dependants whose behaviour he wants to control. But in addition the ghosts are thought to bring sickness on their own initiative. In the case of invocation it is typically a man calling on

---

[1] *Ibid.*, pp. 12 ff.
[2] John Middleton, *Lugbara Religion, Ritual and Authority among an East African People*, London, 1960, pp. 33 f. [3] *Ibid.*, p. 34.

the ghosts to bring sickness on his own son, and it is to be noted that one may invoke the ghosts only if one's father is dead, for it is then that one may erect a shrine to acquire the power of invocation as part of one's new position as head of a family segment.[1]

We may next look very briefly at Goody's conclusions from his study of the LoDagaa of Ghana where once more we come upon the central importance of authority. A man has domestic authority over his son, and may punish and reward him. The son of a dead father comes under the direct control of the latter's spirit – 'indeed all men at all times are subject to the authority, sometimes capricious, of the ancestors'.[2] Again, only a man who has had a child can have a shrine built for him.[3] But part of the interest of this case lies in the fact that the LoDagaa comprise two sections of population (distinguished by Goody as LoWiili and LoDagaba), each with its own rules for the transmission of property rights. Among the LoWiili all property is inherited patrilineally, while LoDagaba transmit only immovables patrilineally and moveables matrilineally. So that while there is a broad common pattern of ancestor worship in the LoDagaa as a whole, there are in fact important differences between LoWiili and LoDagaba in the givers and receivers of sacrifice. Among the former, sacrifices are made between close agnates; among the latter the recipients include both close agnates and matrilineal kinsmen. The underlying reason for the LoWiili sacrifices, Goody tells us, 'was that the donor had accumulated wealth with the help of his agnatic ancestors and had now to make a return prestation'.[4] *Mutatis mutandis*, the same argument can be applied to the LoDagaba where, we are told, the position is best summed up in the proverb 'Father and son eat together in life but not in death.' The LoDagaba do sacrifice to their fathers, but not so commonly as the LoWiili.[5]

There is tension between the holder of an estate and the heir to it. But while in one sense the tension is resolved by the holder dying and the heir taking over, in another sense the tension remains, for 'the corporate group is seen as consisting of both living and dead, so that the superordinate position of the holders is

---

[1] *Ibid.*, p. 40.
[2] Jack Goody, *Death, Property and the Ancestors, A Study of the Mortuary Customs of the LoDagaa of West Africa*, London, 1962, p. 376.
[3] *Ibid.*, p. 383.   [4] *Ibid.*, p. 399.   [5] *Ibid.*, p. 403.

3a. Obeisance in the main ancestral hall of a New Territories lineage at the time of the chief annual rites, 1963.

3b. Firing crackers at the graves at Ch'ing Ming, 1963, in a public cemetery in the New Territories.

4. An altar in an ancestral hall, New Territories, 1963. The ancestor tablets are decorated with gold foil.

maintained, and in some ways enhanced, at death. The ancestors are not only fellow members of the corporate group, but also authority figures, who maintain the norms of social action and cause trouble if these are not obeyed.'[1] Among the LoWiili, a man, whether alive or dead, has the power of life and death over his agnatic descendants; and while alive his power is reinforced by his custodianship of his dead father's shrine.[2] But in the LoDagaba section, authority over a man is shared between his father and his mother's brother, and the mother's ancestors are accordingly thought to inflict misfortune. In both cases men are at once happy and sad, pleased and guilty, at the death of the person from whom they inherit. 'In the main, it is those from whose death one bene-fits that one fears as ancestors.'[3]

But the African ethnography which has the best claim on our attention is that on the Tallensi of Ghana, because Fortes, its compiler and analyst, has more than once drawn the analogies between certain of its religious and social features and those of China. In three studies published in recent years[4] Fortes has set out a series of reasoned observations on the subject of ancestor worship and concepts connected with it, drawing heavily on his Tallensi data and making reference in two of them to the Chinese.[5] Although the Tallensi and the Chinese stand at opposite ends of the spectrum of civilization and politically have nothing in common, their systems of lineage and ancestor worship are in limited respects comparable. Tallensi lineages are exogamous localized groups depending for their unity essentially (in Fortes's view) on the cult of the lineage ancestors. 'Just as there is a hier-archy of lineage segments of greater and greater inclusiveness, until finally the entire lineage is included, so there is a hierarchy of ancestors and ancestor shrines.'[6] (At this point we need only note the major difference from the Chinese system that among the Tallensi maternal ancestors play a great role.)

Jural and ritual authority is vested in men enjoying the status of fathers, and until a man's father has died he can have no jural independence 'and cannot directly bring a sacrifice to a lineage

---

[1] Ibid., p. 407.   [2] Ibid., p. 408.   [3] Ibid., p. 410.
[4] Oedipus and Job in West African Religion, Cambridge, 1959; 'Pietas in Ancestor Worship', Journal of the Royal Anthropological Institute, vol. 91, pt. 2, July–Decem-ber 1961; and 'Some Reflections on Ancestor Worship in Africa', in M. Fortes and G. Dieterlen, eds., African Systems of Thought, London, 1965.
[5] Especially in 'Pietas'.   [6] Oedipus and Job, pp. 26 f.

ancestor. He is, as it were, merged in his father's status.'[1] The exercise of paternal authority, even if kindly, produces 'hostility and opposition' in the sons – a fact which the Tallensi recognize and which is 'dealt with by means of a number of ritual avoidances between a man and his first-born son'.[2] As the sons grow up to manhood their father's authority seems even more intolerable, but they are bound by the duty of filial piety. 'It requires a child to honour and respect his parents, to put their wishes before his own, to support and cherish them in old age, quite irrespective of their treatment of him. The supreme act of filial piety owed by sons is the performance of the mortuary and funeral ceremonies for the parents.'[3] These ceremonies 'are the first steps in the transformation of parents into ancestor spirits, and the worship of ancestors is in essence the ritualization of filial piety'.[4] And, as Fortes puts it in another context, 'the obsequial ceremonies which reinstate a deceased father as an ancestor in his family and lineage end by spiritually releasing his eldest son from jural authority and ritual dependence and establish him as his father's heir'.[5] As for the behaviour of dead ancestors, they all 'exact ritual service, and propitiation in accordance with the same rules of unpredictable and more commonly persecutory rather than beneficent intervention in their descendants' lives'.[6]

These notes on the Tallensi, brief as they are, will, added to what we have seen of the ethnography on the Manus, the Lugbara, and the LoDagaa, help us to a perspective on the Chinese case. I think it will be clear that what is common to the Chinese and the three African examples – the function of certain ritually treated ancestors as points of reference for the determination of units of lineage structure – is important but not very interesting. In contrast, what is common to the primitive examples and absent from the Chinese – a tight relationship between the transfer of jural authority and property rights from a recently dead man to his son and the worship by that son of his father – seems not only important but of the greatest possible interest. It may lead us straight to the heart of the question with which we began the enquiry: the nature of the dominance by the Chinese father of his son.

To make my point clear, I shall need to examine how Fortes has used evidence on China to come to a conclusion which is the

[1] *Ibid.*, p. 27.   [2] *Ibid., loc. cit.*   [3] *Ibid.*, p. 29.
[4] *Ibid., loc. cit.*   [5] 'Some Reflections', p. 131.   [6] *Ibid.*, p. 135.

opposite of mine. He says, correctly, that in China 'the first-born son has a unique place in the sequence of the generations'.[1] But he then quotes a statement to the effect that in former times the eldest son had the sole right to make sacrifices to the dead parents and goes on to conclude from evidence on modern China that 'this rule still prevails'. (Here he cites what I said at p. 82 in *Lineage Organization* on ancestor tablets and what Lin Yueh-hwa writes in *The Golden Wing* about the first-born son's extra share of inheritance.[2]) He then moves on to assert: 'The emancipation of jural majority, economic independence and the ritual autonomy demonstrated in the right to perform sacrifices to the ancestors comes (as in ancient Rome) at length only after the death of the father, as Hsu specifically states. . . . This coincides with the dead father's establishment as an ancestor; and it is noteworthy that tablets dedicated to ancestors are so arranged that those of fathers and sons are on opposite sides of the ancestral hall, successive generations being thus kept apart after death, as they were divided by degree in life, and alternate generations being grouped together [the *chao-mu* order] in accordance with the well-known principle of the merging of alternate generations. . . .' (And for the last point he cites Granet.[3])

There has been a muddle of the evidence. In the first place, all that Hsu says is that under the rule of the unity of the household-family (which, incidentally, he has just *contrasted* with the primo-geniture of other societies) 'sons do not attain social maturity until the death of their father. Whatever property the father has automatically becomes the property of his sons.'[4] Second, what Granet discusses is the rule of *chao-mu* in the ancient period of Chinese history and has only limited relevance to the China of the last two thousand years.[5] Third, my own earlier discussion of ancestor tablets was an attempt to make it clear that, while the

---

[1] 'Pietas', p. 179.   [2] *Ibid.*, p. 180.   [3] *Ibid., loc. cit.*

[4] Francis L. K. Hsu, *Under the Ancestors' Shadow, Chinese Culture and Personality*, London, 1949, p. 109. (Fortes gives the page reference as 209, but this is clearly a slip.)

[5] Fortes here refers to Marcel Granet, *La religion des Chinois*, Paris, 1951, pp. 86 ff., but in fact he must be thinking of pp. 73 f. in the chapter entitled 'La religion féodale'. Of course, some of the writing on Chinese social institutions is careless about time (the continuity of Chinese history being both a fact and even more an ideological necessity for Chinese themselves), and the implication that the *chao-mu* system has persisted to the present as a full-blown institution can easily get slipped into general statements about the kinship system of China. (See e.g.

retention of the family's domestic tablets was the prerogative of
the senior son and to that extent reflected the persistence of a
primogenitory bias in modern Chinese society, it was in fact
possible for the younger sons to make substitute tablets and carry
on independent worship in their own houses.

I have already in an earlier context touched on the decline of
primogeniture in Chinese society and shown that the eldest son's
special share of the parental inheritance is a relic which in modern
times has certainly not marked out any effective seniority in
descent. All brothers are essentially equal, and the estate of their
father (defined in the broadest possible manner to include not
only his material property but also his privileges and standing)
passes to them either equally or jointly.[1] A son may well await
his father's death with impatience in order to be liberated from
paternal control and to realize his share of the property, but when
his terrible wish is fulfilled he will not then be in the position of
one who, stepping into his father's shoes, takes control of his
brothers. As we have seen, the fraternal relationship is not such
as to allow of a stable unit presided over by the eldest brother in
the absence of the parents.

Jean Escarra, *La Chine, passé et présent*, Paris, 1949, p. 94.) The *chao-mu* notion is
certainly not dead in modern China (it is, after all, inscribed in their classics for
educated men to read), but it can hardly be said to play a significant role in kinship organization and ancestor rites. A vivid example of the way in which classical
ideas of how tablets ought to be arranged in hall shrines can intrude into modern
custom is given in the autobiography of Hu Shih's father, part of which is translated as Appendix 53 in Hu Hsien-chin, *The Common Descent Group in China and
its Functions*, N.Y., 1948. There the autobiographer explains that having studied
books on ritual, he had decided to arrange the tablets in his lineage's rebuilt
ancestral hall 'on the right and left in alternate generations, beginning with the
first ancestor' (*op. cit.*, p. 173). He was opposed, because his lineage mates (and
others in the area) were used to ordering their tablets with the first ancestor in
the centre – i.e. in accordance with the general method in modern China of
keeping all the tablets of one generation on the same level, one generation below
the other; and he had finally to yield classical principle to customary practice
(*ibid.*, pp. 173 f., 177 f.). Another modern example, this time in the arrangement
of graves, is to be found in Gamble, *North China Villages*, pp. 261 f. In one of the
villages (studied in the early 1930s), a large lineage had two graveyards, where,
according to the *chao-mu* rule, the graves on the left were of even generation and
on the right of odd. It should be noted that an adherence to the *chao-mu* order is in
conflict with *fêng-shui*. The written history of the lineage says: '. . . if anyone,
believing the words of the geomancer, seeks to benefit his own feng-shui by
breaking the burial system', then he is unfilial and should be punished by the
lineage leaders (*ibid.*, p. 262). On the patterned arrangement of tombs as given
in books on ritual, see De Groot, *op. cit.*, vol. III, pp. 832 f.

[1] See p. 50 above.

In fact, to come back to the ritual side of the matter, men do not stand as intermediaries between the ancestors and their sons, and the emancipation of the sons by their father's death is not an entry into ritual majority. From this fundamental characteristic of the Chinese family flows what, in the light of the comparative ethnographic evidence, appears to be the relative ineffectiveness of Chinese ancestors, their general air of benevolence, and doubtless too the lack of strong feelings of hatred or guilt towards them on the part of their descendants. (If Chinese hate any among their kin, they hate their brothers; and by now it will have become clear why this should be so.)

A Chinese ancestor rarely applies negative sanctions to his descendants. As long as he receives the sacrifices due to him (which need consist of nothing more elaborate than simple food, drink, and incense), he will normally be content to preside as the benign protector of his offspring – and a protector, at that, whose powers to bless and succour are limited by his influence with the supernatural beings from whom these powers really stem. Ancestors do not watch over the general conduct of their descendants and are not the censors of their former housemates. They will visit punishment on their descendants only if they are neglected or are personally offended by some lapse of family conduct which reflects on them (above all, the failure to provide them with a secure line of descent). Let me cite evidence recently collected by Wolf in Taiwan. He says he found numerous examples in the village he studied of sickness and other misfortune ascribed to the neglect of ancestors. 'The various misfortunes of one village woman were attributed to her deceased father-in-law who was angry because she had failed to cook his favourite dish for the New Year's offerings; the illness of a child was ascribed to his father's deceased parents who were said to be angry because their son had made a matrilocal marriage; and the illness of another village child was interpreted as being the result of his grandfather's older brother's "coming to call him". This man had died without children of his own, and so the family was advised to give him their son in adoption as a means of placating him.'[1]

The argument so far may be summarized by our saying that a Chinese man's estate tends to be dispersed among his sons when he dies, and that as a dead ancestor he has comparatively

[1] Wolf, *op. cit.*

little to offer either generally or in the form of support to the
new heads of families who follow after him. But we have yet to
look more closely at an aspect of the relations between living
parents and children on which Fortes rightly lays stress for an
understanding of ancestor worship: filial piety.

Hsiao is poorly translated as filial piety, for englished in this
way it has, as Fortes well says, 'the flavour of unctuous conformity'.[1] *Hsiao* is a duty which children owe their parents, and
it is not for us to endow it with a sentimental halo derived from
our habit of thinking of it in the conventional English translation.
In fact, the sinologues seem to be moving towards a more appropriate rendering. Writing recently of Balazs, Arthur Wright
has said that in 'speaking of the cardinal virtue of Confucianism,
hsiao, "obedience", often mistakenly translated as "filial piety",
he stressed the effects of the inculcation of this value by indoc-
trination and punitive laws on the development of Chinese
society. . . .'[2] Very well, the Chinese owe their parents obedience,
and they owe it as a return for the gift of life. A man's loyalty
to the interests and wishes of his father is supposed to outweigh all
other loyalties and attachments. The state supports the father in
commanding obedience; a wayward son can in the extreme be
hauled into the magistrate's court. The father is sustained in
exercising his rights by the institutions of the lineage and the
village; the disobedient son lays himself open to a range of sanctions, including corporal punishment in public. And in a crowded
agrarian society there are few opportunities for the son to run off
and make his own way, unless he is willing to emigrate or become
a bandit or soldier. But when all this has been said, it is still true
that, in comparison with the control exercised by fathers in many
other patrilineally organized societies, the control at the disposal
of the Chinese father is limited. And it is limited precisely because,
in the absence of a true primogeniture (backed up by the sanctions
of disciplinary ancestors), there is a more gradual transfer of
authority from one generation to the next. As soon as a man
begins to lose his grip on the family, having become old or sick,
hsiao will not prevent his sons from claiming a larger share of
economic benefit and domestic authority. Indeed, some sons may

[1] 'Pietas', p. 177.
[2] Introduction, p. xvi, to Etienne Balazs, trans. H. M. Wright, *Chinese
Civilization and Bureaucracy*, New Haven and London, 1964.

secede from the family, taking out their share of the family estate. As we have seen, a rich man of high social standing was likely to be a 'strong' father, holding the fissiparous tendencies of his family in check;[1] but even in this most favourable of conditions he was never absolutely immune to the gradual wearing down of his authority by his ambitious and pushful sons. In ancient times the Chinese lineage system and ancestor worship may very well have had properties that Fortes has seen in their modern successors; and with the points he makes we might be able to arrive at a better interpretation of the 'feudal' society of China than has hitherto been reached; but while modern Chinese ancestor worship certainly bears some striking resemblances to that of the Tallensi and certain other primitive societies, it differs radically from them in crucial respects.

There is a further aspect of ancestor worship to be considered. In *Lineage Organization* I spoke of the element of memorialism, 'in which ancestors were cared for simply as forebears and independently of their status as ancestors of the agnates of the worshippers'.[2] What I then had in mind (although clearly I did not express the point very well) was the distinction between ancestor worship as a set of rites linking together all the agnatic descendants of a given forebear (the cult of descent groups) on the one hand, and ancestor worship as the independent tendance and commemoration of forebears as it were for their own sake, on the other. In the light of the analysis of the cult of immediate jural superiors, 'memorialism' is now due for revision.

Chinese worship their ancestors (not merely 'venerating' them, as some have asserted) in the cults we have so far examined. But there is also a sense in which, in certain contexts, they commemorate them. The importance of the distinction becomes evident when non-ancestors are included in domestic shrines and treated along with ancestors. People 'remember' them; but they also 'remember' their ancestors – and in the sceptical versions of ancestor 'worship' (in which the tenders of shrines either deny the existence of the dead as sentient beings or at least are very doubtful about it) such tablets, plaques, or pictures of the dead as are put up are intended to serve to keep their memory alive. I imagined, when I discovered that Chinese in Singapore sometimes

[1] See p. 47 above.
[2] P. 84. And cf. my *Chinese Family . . . in Singapore*, pp. 218 f.

keep on a plaque the name of some non-kinsman former member of the household,[1] that I was seeing a departure from custom dictated by special foreign conditions. I was not. Domestic shrines in China sometimes commemorate non-kinsmen and demonstrate that memorialism overlaps with ancestor worship.[2]

[1] *Ibid.*, p. 219.

[2] Memorialism as distinct from worship can, I think, be seen in a different context illustrated by an incident which occurred in Kwangtung in 1867. The county magistrate and 'gentry' of En-p'ing *hsien* raised money for the repair of the local Confucian temple by proposing to build an academy (*shu-yüan*) to serve as a shrine in honour of local men. People who contributed to the building fund were entitled to put their ancestors' tablets in the shrine, in positions of honour varying with the amounts donated. It proved a successful idea and was copied by others. See Hsiao, *Rural Control*, p. 229. True, there was a shrine and rites must have been performed in it, but in this context no ritual link could have been implied between the dead men so honoured and their descendants. The latter were worshipping their ancestors elsewhere; here they were commemorating them in a dramatic and public manner. The argument on memorialism needs to be taken much further – but not in this book. Cf. the interesting paper by David W. Plath, 'Where the Family of God is the Family: The Role of the Dead in Japanese Households', *American Anthropologist*, vol. 66, no. 2, April 1964. In thinking about Chinese ancestor worship I have been greatly helped by the following work: Daniel R. Scheinfeld, *A Comparative Study of Ancestor Worship, with Special Reference to Social Structure*, M.A. thesis, Univ. of London, 1960. For an additional source on ancestor worship in southeastern China (although less promising than its title), see Peter Wei Lin, *The Social Effects of Ancestor Worship in a South China Town*, M.A. dissertation, Faculty of Political Science, Columbia Univ., 1922. The 'town' of the title is in fact a lineage-village in northern Fukien.

6

Lineages in China

I was at some pains in my earlier book on the subject to stress not only the tentativeness of the conclusions but also the provisional nature of the facts. As to facts, I think I am now more secure; indeed, there is a great deal of merely repetitive evidence that I have not bothered to set out in detail. But the conclusions remain, as in some measure they always must, temporary. In choosing significant facts about a society and arranging them to make an argument, the anthropologist is given the freedom of the prisoner's cell. He is a captive of the ideas which come of a discipline at a given stage of its development, but within the range of those ideas he can wander at will. In this imaginary gaol the walls are constantly being reordered and broken down to be rebuilt; but there are always walls.

In another discipline, or different tradition within the same discipline, different facts will be assembled on the same topic and other conclusions drawn from them. Let me illustrate from the recent work of a well-known Chinese scholar who, for many years now, has been working within one kind of American anthropology ('culture and personality'). In *Clan, Caste, and Club*[1] Professor F. L. K. Hsu has built up an argument about the Chinese 'clan' within the framework of a comparison between the civilizations of China, Hindu India, and the United States. The picture he paints is in certain crucial respects at variance with the one I have offered in both *Lineage Organization* and this book. Starting with different ideas and asking different questions, he reaches a different goal.

In the perspective he has chosen, it is necessary for Hsu to establish in the first place that the family and the 'clan' are the central and characteristic modes of organization of Chinese society (in contrast to the caste and 'club' of the other two civilizations). The Chinese approach to the world, characterized by 'situation-centeredness or mutual dependence',[2] flows from the

---

[1] Princeton, N.J., 1963.   [2] *Ibid.*, p. vii.

key modes of social organization. The family is the 'basic school of all cultures',[1] but it is particularly potent in China, while the Chinese 'clan' extends the principle of mutual dependence out into wider society – the 'clan' is the 'immediate and direct extension' of the family.[2]

The Chinese family is in its structural ideal the joint family, ordered by patriarchal authority and filial devotion.[3] It is a family in which individuals live out their entire lives, not seeking to escape from it in old age (as in Hindu India) to renounce worldly goods and kinship ties. (Monks are a special case.) 'Throughout the lengthy Chinese history there have been some instances in which a successful official of one dynasty refused to serve another, but no such man ever renounced family or even career when he did not have to.'[4] Moreover, family relationships are not severed by death, the dead remaining as members 'of the great family', their bodies kept in the house as long as possible before burial, their 'graveyards . . . taken care of as though they were family compounds'. Every year they are welcomed home to be reunited with the living, and they are invited to be present on special family occasions.[5]

The 'Chinese interest in genealogy is universal'. Although the poor are of course 'less capable of concretizing this interest . . ., all members of the clan are included in the same kinship genealogical books financed by the rich'.[6] While Chinese desire a glorious ancestry, 'throughout China the provision for and the veneration of the departed souls do not appear or vanish, increase or decrease, with the individual's desire to ascend the social scale. . . .'[7]

In the cult of the ancestors there is kindliness, not fear. 'It can be stated unequivocally that ancestral spirits, in every part of China, are believed to be only a source of benevolence, never a source of punishment to their own descendants.' A Chinese suffering misfortune will suspect the action of deities or ghosts, never of an ancestor.[8]

By 'clan' Hsu certainly means what I have called a lineage, for among its characteristics he lists the possession of 'certain forms of property . . ., benefits for education and public welfare, . . . ancestral halls, . . . graveyards, . . . legislation on rules of behavior,

---

[1] Ibid., loc. cit.   [2] Ibid., p. 60.   [3] Ibid., pp. 28 ff.
[4] Ibid., p. 36.   [5] Ibid., pp. 37 f.   [6] Ibid., p. 38.
[7] Ibid., p. 39.   [8] Ibid., p. 45.

and . . . council of clan elders which pass judgements and settle disputes'.[1] This is the *tsu*, the divisions of which are *fang*.[2] But the *tsu* definitely dominates its divisions and establishes an overall unity which suppresses cleavages and tensions. 'It is, of course, not alleged that Chinese clans are free from internal tensions. . . . But . . . there is remarkably little intraclan tension; and when it does occur, it is not very explosive. Certainly I do not know of any clan in China which has been split, with subsequent moving away of some members of the clan to a new locality, because of an irreconcilable quarrel.'[3] The 'clan' takes its strongest form in south and central China, but its 'general and basic pattern is the same' all over the country.[4]

The 'cohesive Chinese clan' encloses the 'centripetal Chinese family'. The centripetal character of the one goes with the cohesive quality of the other,[5] which in turn allows it to flourish in a society with a strong central government.[6] The family fosters in the individual 'a centripetal outlook' which enables him to 'satisfy his need for sociability, security, and status with little difficulty in the framework of the cohesive Chinese clan and the Chinese ideal of complete harmony among men'.[7] Membership in the 'clan' being so embracing and stable, there is 'little incentive for the individual to disengage himself from his permanent moorings in search of entanglements in the wider society and

[1] *Ibid.*, p. 61.

[2] *Ibid.*, pp. 61 ff. Here Hsu makes some valuable points on the terminology of the Chinese clan and lineage. (Cf. above, pp. 25 f.) Of *tsung* he says that it is used 'when two or more clans [sc. lineages] bearing the same surname at first thought to be unrelated turn out to be linked to a common ancestor. Such a linkage is called *lien-tsung*.' But what in fact is established as a *tsung* will also later come to be known as a *tsu*. See also *ibid.*, pp. 63 f. for comment on the use of *tze*.

[3] *Ibid.*, p. 66. I may point out that in this context (*ibid.*, pp. 65 f.) Hsu criticizes some of my own formulations on the subject. In objecting to the weight I give to cleavages within the lineage Hsu says: 'In a similar vein Freedman speaks of "the tensions between the principle by which families related within the agnatic Wu Fu were ritually encouraged to come together and the principle according to which they might legitimately conduct their own domestic rites as separate units". . . . The facts, including some quoted by Freedman himself, show no tension along this line whatsoever.' Perhaps Hsu has been misled as much by his misquotation (I wrote 'a tension' not 'tensions') as by my lack of clarity. I was certainly not referring here to tensions in the sense of conflict of interests, but to conflicting ways of organizing worship.

[4] *Ibid.*, p. 71.   [5] *Ibid.*, pp. 72 f.

[6] *Ibid.*, pp. 73–8. And see *ibid.*, pp. 79 f. note 27, where the strength of the 'clan' in south China is explained by the remoteness of this region from northern centres of the major dynasties.   [7] *Ibid.*, p. 224.

world. Between the Chinese Imperial Government and the clan there was a scarcity of intermediate groupings that were not based on territory or occupation. . . . Self-advancement and advancement of one's family tended to be identified with each other. . . .'[1]

The final point I shall extract from Hsu's argument takes us back to the relations between lineages. 'Clan' fights occur in the extreme south and central parts of China, he says, but in the rest of the country they are very rare. Moreover, in south and central China when these acts of aggression occur they are 'usually rooted in concrete reasons such as disputes over water rights. . . . In the normal course of events there are neither interclan disputes over clan ranking nor interclan claims of superiority. If and when the members of one clan feel superior to another, this superiority is understood and rarely if ever expressed, least of all by members themselves. There are specific Chinese rules of custom against open expressions of superiority. Such expressions are regarded as boastful even if they are founded in fact.'[2]

It hardly needs to be said that Hsu's model of the Chinese lineage and mine are so different that they almost appear to mock each other. The difference between them cannot be due simply to the fact that Hsu is generalizing for China while I have largely confined myself to the south-east, for Hsu explicitly builds facts from that area into his account. The divergence springs from the use of evidence and the interpretation of it. I have shown, for example, that serious quarrels break out in lineages and may lead to fighting. Hsu denies it. As for the relations between lineages, I have produced evidence that hostility is based on the claim to superiority; so far from that superiority being unstated, it is constantly and ceremonially asserted. I have argued that ancestors can in certain conditions be hostile; Hsu makes them utterly benign.

But it is not so much the separate facts as the total pictures which are in conflict. For Hsu the lineage and the family look like relatively closed and comfortable worlds beyond the frontiers of which individuals are nervous to tread. Peace, harmony, and security prevail within; outside there is danger. In fact, on my showing, competition and conflict are inherent at all levels of the social system; brother contends with brother, segment with seg-

[1] *Ibid.*, p. 225.   [2] *Ibid.*, pp. 125 f.

ment, lineage with lineage, the lineage with the state. But there is also harmony because each contender must be united against its opponents – war without and peace within. I hate my brother but I am united with him against other families. The members of a lineage struggle among themselves for scarce resources of land and honour, but they stand shoulder to shoulder when they are confronted by another lineage. Harmony and conflict are not mutually exclusive; on the contrary, they imply each other.

Paradoxically, my studies centred on the lineage in southeastern China, having been forced to consider the relationship between lineage and other groupings and institutions, have brought out the dependence of kinship on a complex web of solidarities; whereas Hsu, trying to interpret Chinese culture as a whole, has ended by bringing 'clan' to a dominating position within it. In fact, there is no simple key to Chinese society; its lineage organization is one important feature of it; and the significance of that feature cannot be understood in isolation from the other institutional and ideological bases of the society. There can be no satisfactory study of the Chinese lineage which does not rest four-square on the study of China as a whole.

Of course, this latter study does not exist. The new sinology of history and the social sciences is literally new and cannot yet produce its great synthesis.[1] While we await it, we must manage as best we can with the fragments at our disposal. I should like now to seize on one of these fragments to broaden out my subject.

In one paragraph of the 'Discussion' in *Lineage Organization*, I touched on the problem of the uneven distribution of large local-ized lineages in China,[2] saying that it may be that the cultivation of rice was one of the conditions predisposing local communities of agnates to build themselves into large settlements. It is generally agreed by writers on China (although it does not follow from this that it is true – the point needs to be more carefully checked than I have been able to do) that the kind of extensive lineage system we have been examining is above all characteristic of the south-eastern and parts of the central regions of the country. These are irrigated rice-growing areas, and it is clear from both the evidence

[1] See the eloquent exposition of some of the major difficulties in the way of bringing this synthesis to birth, written by a leader of the leading sinology: Arthur F. Wright, 'Chinese Studies Today', *Newsletter of the Association for Asian Studies*, vol. x, no. 3, February 1965.

[2] *Op. cit.*, pp. 129 f.

on other parts of Asia and the data on China that this form of agriculture allows dense populations to build up on small surfaces of land.[1] Moreover, and more to the point, I suspect that there is a positive correlation between extent of irrigation and the degree to which land is held in joint estates (the corporate lands of lineages and their segments). Tucked away in Chen Han-seng's *Agrarian Problems in Southernmost China*, there is a statement that while no less than 35 per cent of the total cultivated land of Kwangtung province is 'owned by clans and other corporate bodies', 60 per cent of all the land is irrigated, and 'among the irrigated lands, the percentage of collective lands is even higher'.[2] We know that the percentage of corporate estates varies widely within Fukien and Kwangtung, and that it varies widely enough within small areas of these provinces.[3] Is it because mature and productive irrigation works have a corresponding distribution?[4]

The logic behind the question is this. Intensively irrigated and worked rice paddies have initially required a great investment of labour (in the making of channels, dams, terraces, and so on) but the rewards to this investment are extremely high, and it allows the system of cultivation to be intensified in response to growth in the number of people living off it.[5] To produce such a system, groups of men have had to co-operate;[6] it has been built up piecemeal over time, but co-ordinated labour has been required at most stages of its evolution. It is perhaps in the productivity and co-operative nature of the enterprise that we can see a key to common estates. In some cases a joint investment of labour may have led to the establishment as an undivided estate of the land on which the labour had been expended. It is important to remember that the present limits of cultivation in Fukien and Kwangtung were certainly not reached before the end of the eighteenth

[1] The question is well treated in a recent study of agriculture in Indonesia. See Clifford Geertz, *Agricultural Involution, The Process of Ecological Change in Indonesia*, Berkeley and Los Angeles, 1963, especially pp. 28 ff.

[2] *Op. cit.*, p. 35. John Lossing Buck, *Land Utilization in China*, Nanking, 1937, p. 186, arrives at 69 as the percentage of crop area irrigated in what he calls the Rice Region of China, as compared with 15 per cent in the Wheat Region. The high density of irrigation in Fukien and Kwangtung can be seen at a glance in Map 2, *ibid.*, p. 187.

[3] See e.g. the table at p. 32 of Chen's book where the range of percentages of 'clan land' of 10 villages in P'an-yü *hsien* is from 6 to 75. The range in the present-day New Territories is from near zero to 90 per cent.

[4] Cf. Eberhard, *op. cit.*, p. 40.   [5] Cf. Geertz, *op. cit.*, p. 32.

[6] Hsiao, *Rural China*, pp. 283 ff., has some useful data on local irrigation works.

century. For hundreds of years new land was being gradually brought into use by the extension of irrigation works, drainage, and reclamation of coastal strips, and some of this 'new' land, as it came into being, was (I am suggesting) entailed to be the permanent property of a group, and not divided up among families by the normal mode of inheritance.

There is, in fact, some contemporary evidence which bears on the historical point. In *A Chinese Village in Early Communist Transition*, where he is describing a community near Canton, C. K. Yang tells us that many of the fields of the alluvial plain had been created by means of dykes from the shallow mud flats along the river bank, one third of the village's cultivated land having been enclosed in this manner. Among the reclamations was a recent one known as the 'new enclosure', some fifteen acres of highly fertile land. It had been made in 1936 when, as a result of the slump, people had come crowding home to the village and wanted land to cultivate. A number of families of the Wong lineage owned sections of the mud flat on which one crop of rice a year could be precariously grown. 'Now that the need for more land had become urgent, the Wong clan finally decided to use its public funds and mobilize the manpower of the entire clan to build the dike, the land thus reclaimed to be rented at a nominal rate to each family in the clan on the basis of so much land per male for a period of fifteen years, after which the disposal of the land would revert to the full authority of the owners.'[1] (History of course overtook the plan for the reversion, for by the end of the fifteen years the village was under Communist rule.) If we ignore the provision for the delayed return to private family ownership, we have an example of how the massing and co-ordinating of resources could lead to a lineage estate.[2]

I do not yet know enough about the geographical sources on China to be able to take the argument further. Presumably, it would be possible to correlate, at least in Taiwan and the New Territories, the incidence of high productivity, mature and elaborate irrigation works, large-scale lineages, and high proportions of 'indivisible' estates. Certainly, a casual inspection of

[1] *Op. cit.*, pp. 9, 24, 26 f.
[2] And cf. Chen Han-seng, *op. cit.*, pp. 28 f. Eberhard, *Social Mobility*, p. 220, quotes a report on Taiwan (1959) which appears to attribute joint estates to, among other things, 'reclamation of land through common efforts in the early history of Taiwan'. See below p. 188.

the data on productivity in the New Territories today[1] suggests clearly enough that the powerful lineages were situated where the land yielded most.

Of course, the argument has assumed that joint estates lie at the heart of lineage organization. They are not its simple cause; they are also one of its effects; but we know that a lineage does not grow and differentiate itself internally without an elaborate hierarchical series of land-holding segments. Poor lineages can exist with the most exiguous of common property – perhaps with none at all; but they will never grow in numbers or strength to become a force on the local scene without bringing into being, first, a lineage estate and later, estates for the segments into which they divide themselves. Land tenure and segmentation are almost inevitably associated.[2]

But there is another side to the question of the special position of the southeast on the lineage map. Has it anything to do with pioneering on the frontiers of China? We know that lineages are not given once for all. Over long stretches of time new lineages come into being, the nuclei from which they start having differentiated themselves from their parent groups. Established lineages shed members or segments and perhaps go into decline. Villages composed of several agnatic groups see the rise of one of these groups at the expense of the others. A lineage occupying a site on its own admits strangers and finds later on that it is now a member of a multilineage community.[3] But in general in Fukien and Kwangtung, certain lineages entrenched themselves early on and survived into our own day as the masters of those around them, rich, proud, and powerful.[4]

Many of the Chinese ancestors of the people we study today in

[1] See Grant, *The Soils and Agriculture of Hong Kong*, chap. VI.
[2] See pp. 33 ff. above   [3] See p. 8 above.
[4] The Tang local lineages of Hsin-an (Pao-an) county are a case in point. Establishing themselves in late Sung times in what were then (and now as a result of their labours are even more) fertile valleys, they spread a network of control over agricultural land in a large part of what was to become the Colony of Hong Kong during the nineteenth century, and were the landlords/taxlords of numerous minor communities. The British land system greatly reduced their rights to land outside the boundaries of their own villages. For useful notes on the history of some of the Tang local lineages, see Balfour, *op. cit.*, pp. 446 ff. and Sung Hok-p'ang's two articles already cited and others in the same series: *The Hong Kong Naturalist*, vol. VI, nos. 3 and 4, December 1935; vol. VII, no. 2, June 1936; vol. VII, nos. 3 and 4, December 1936; and vol. VIII, nos. 3 and 4, March 1938.

southeastern China moved down into the region in T'ang and Sung times. They found barbarian societies which for the most part they gradually eliminated (to some extent by marrying their women),[1] seizing their land and bringing empty land into cultivation. From the beginning of the eleventh century, as Ho Ping-ti puts it, there was an 'almost incessant construction of irrigation works and the expansion of the frontier of rice culture in southern China'.[2] It was to begin with wild country, and large areas of it remained so, to attract the pioneers of later times – up to about the end of the eighteenth century.[3] Defence was a necessary part of community life, for there were brigands on land and pirates from the sea. It may be that these were the conditions which, acting upon patrilineally organized pioneers (or at least on pioneers bearing a patrilineal ideology), stimulated the growth of relatively independent and tightly settled local lineages which, precisely because they were so organized, built up a system in which interlineage relations were characterized by violence. A successful lineage could stay where it was; less fortunate lineages and the disfavoured families and segments of fortunate ones moved on again to better their luck. Along such lines, we may surmise, there developed a network of settlements made up of a large number of single lineages, a number of villages dominated by a single lineage, and a smaller number of multilineage communities.[4] Although the pattern could never be fixed, for changes

[1] Cf. *Lineage Organization*, p. 7, and see Hisayuki Miyakawa, 'The Confucianization of South China', in Arthur F. Wright, ed., *The Confucian Persuasion*, Stanford, Calif., 1960 (although some of Miyakawa's views of the barbarian societies of the south must strike an anthropologist as being a bit odd).

[2] Ho Ping-ti, *Studies on the Population of China*, p. 191. Rice cultivation was made much more productive by the introduction into Fukien at the beginning of the eleventh century of an early-ripening variety from Champa. Thereafter, other early-ripening varieties were developed. By the twelfth century new strains of rice were in use which matured in 60 days after being transplanted. – Ho, *ibid.*, pp. 170 f.

[3] Ho, *ibid.*, p. 183, says that rice culture in China Proper seems to have reached saturation point by about the middle of the nineteenth century. Eberhard, *Social Mobility*, p. 169, says that no more land was available in Kwangtung after 1800.

[4] The attempt made by Eberhard, *op. cit.*, to trace the movement of 'clan' units in southern China from written genealogies (cf. p. 27 above) is relevant to this point. But the method is limited both because we can never be sure of all the historical 'facts' and because, even if we can trace the links between settlements, we can rarely discover whether or not they are settlements occupied only by the members of the 'clan' in question.

were likely to take place in all but the most powerful lineages, this was perhaps the situation at the time the modern frontiers of cultivable land were reached. Then, from about the beginning of the nineteenth century, pioneering having become impossible in the region itself, movement was likely to reduce the proportion of single lineage settlements. But the disturbance of the general pre-nineteenth-century pattern was not as great as it might have been, for emigration to Taiwan had already become very important and overseas emigration was to build up during the century. (People from Fukien and Kwangtung sometimes moved inland, notably to depopulated Szechwan in the first two centuries of the Ch'ing dynasty.)

If there is any merit in this general argument, it will lead us to the conclusion that when settlement took place in rough frontier conditions, single lineage communities were likely to develop fairly quickly, and that when, in contrast, people moved into areas under firm government control, any initial agnatic heterogeneity in the incoming groups was probably perpetuated. It seems to me, from what little I have grasped of the situation in Taiwan, that the hypothesis can be tested there in the limited sense that the history of settlement of those areas where lineage organization is now (or at least was until recently) strong can be compared with that of those where it is weak. Naturally, the hypothesis must be more widely set within the framework of the spread of Han-Chinese civilization as a whole, and it will be seen to have some use only if the mode of settlement on the other frontiers of expansion (to the west and south-west) can be shown to fall into the same pattern. It is, however, not essential to the argument that single lineage communities will always emerge; what is at stake is the development of organized and internally segmented lineages, endowed with common property, and capable of concerted action to defend themselves, by force if necessary, against both the state and their non-lineage neighbours. And such lineages may be grouped so that two or more occupy the same village.[1]

[1] A few data on Yunnan relevant to this matter are to be found in Fei Hsiao-tung and Chang Chih-i, *Earthbound China, A Study of Rural Economy in Yunnan*, London, 1949, but unfortunately the authors offer very little on the social organization of the communities whose economies they study. But note what they say at p. 11: 'Clan organization is stronger in Yunnan than in other parts of China. Here the clan possesses common property.' Hsu's *Under the Ancestors' Shadow*,

We may be led on by this line of thought to consider the social organization of the people from Fukien and Kwangtung who, especially after the middle of the nineteenth century, in a sense carried the frontier of Han civilization overseas – to South-East Asia, the Americas, and Oceania. (In Britain we have in the last few years been witnessing – and to some extent gastronomically benefiting from – a latter-day manifestation of the movement in the shape of a flourishing Chinese restaurant 'culture' established mainly by men from the Hong Kong New Territories.) Now, in the pioneering phases of the overseas migration, when Chinese had to group and defend themselves in wild territory, it would seem likely that some version of lineage organization appeared. Perhaps, for example, we should look for it in the so-called *kongsi* set up in Borneo in the eighteenth century.[1] But for the most part, urban conditions, non-agricultural pursuits in the countryside, and 'law and order' imposed by effective governments must soon have aborted any tendency for a traditional pattern of lineage grouping to emerge. (Of course, until women emigrated from Fukien and Kwangtung in any considerable numbers – which they did not do until the very end of the nineteenth century – Chinese families could rarely be set up, and any lineage grouping could maintain itself only by a constant stream of migration from the home community.) For this reason the large-scale organization of overseas Chinese on the basis of agnatic kinship has typically taken the form of the clan association and not the lineage.[2] But, in turn, the overseas clan association

dealing with sinicized Min Chia, describes 'clan' organization in a small Yunnan market town. In contrast, the village studied by Osgood seems to show a very weak form of lineage structure: *op. cit.*, pp. 131 f., 354 f.

[1] See J. J. M. De Groot, *Het Kongsiwezen van Borneo . . . met eene Chineesche Geschiedenis van de Kongsi Lanfong*, The Hague, 1885; G. Schlegel, 'Het Kongsiwezen van Borneo . . .' (*compte rendu* of De Groot's book), *Revue Internationale Coloniale*, vol. I, 1885; B. E. Ward, 'A Hakka Kongsi in Borneo', *Journal of Oriental Studies*, Hong Kong, vol. I, no. 2, July 1954; Victor Purcell, *The Chinese in Southeast Asia*, London, 1951, pp. 489–94; Lo Hsiang-lin, *A Historical Survey of the Lan-fang Presidential System in Western Borneo Established by Lo Fang-pai and other Overseas Chinese*, Hong Kong, 1961 (in Chinese with English summary); and my paper 'Immigrants and Associations: Chinese in Nineteenth-Century Singapore', *Comparative Studies in Society and History*, vol. III, no. 1, October 1960.'

[2] The literature on associations among the Overseas Chinese is now too large to be cited in a mere footnote. See e.g. G. William Skinner, *Chinese Society in Thailand*, and *Leadership and Power in the Chinese Community of Thailand*, Ithaca, N.Y., 1958, especially p. 59; my *Chinese Family . . . in Singapore*, especially pp. 92 ff., and 'Immigrants and Associations'.

(in which men of a common surname are grouped together for limited purposes) is a development of a form of grouping found in the large towns and cities of China itself;[1] and it follows that, in tracing the fate of agnatic kinship in the Chinese diaspora, we are to a considerable extent watching the general reaction of the lineage to 'unsuitable' conditions, wherever they may be.

It would be worth looking carefully at the few exceptions to the rule that lineage organization is not visible in modern overseas Chinese communities. My attention has been drawn to one such exception in, of all places, Singapore.[2] The 'lineage', consisting of over two hundred members, is the main occupant of one section of a village in the northern part of the Island. In many of the Singapore villages there are concentrations of people from particular lineages in southeastern China; in this case the 'concentration' seems to be not only high but, more important, organized, for it appears to have formed itself into a kind of extension of the lineage at home (in Nan-an county, Fukien). Up to fairly recently the main source of village income was vegetable gardening, but now the men for the most part work outside the village in industrial occupations.

Some thirty years ago the committee of the temple (which, as we shall see in a moment, seems to double in a strange way as local temple and ancestral hall) raised enough money to buy a few plots of land from their landlords, and there are now some thirty acres of 'lineage' land, on which stand most of the houses of the members of the 'lineage'. Tenants of the 'lineage' land, both members and non-members, pay rent to the temple; the accumulated funds have been used for several purposes: ritual, setting up a school, providing assistance to the needy, and the establishment of a loan fund for providing credit to members and non-members.

[1] Men living in the cities and cut off from their home lineages had recourse to ritual centres connected with their surnames. Cf. E. H. Parker, 'Comparative Chinese Family Law', *The China Review*, vol. VIII, 1879, pp. 71 f. fn. 26: 'In the provincial Metropolis of Canton there are ancestral shrines open to all persons in the Province who bear the same surname, and have contributed to the general fund, irrespective of race or origin (i.e. *Hakka*, *Punti*, etc. etc.). Tls. 200 are frequently paid for the privilege of placing a tablet therein, and grand sacrifices and feasts are held in the spring and autumn of each year.'

[2] I am very grateful to Mrs Ann Wee, of the Department of Social Studies, Univ. of Singapore, for making available to me an extract from the following dissertation written in the Department (1960?): Chang Soo, *Chinese Lineage Villages in Singapore*. It is from this extract that I have drawn the facts in the discussion which follows.

It would appear that the temple fund reached some Straits $30,000 (over £3,000) before the Second World War, part of it being sent back to China to pay for the repair of the ancestral hall. There seem to have been strong sanctions brought to bear on debtors to meet their obligations to the temple loan fund.

Members of the 'lineage' are grouped into four *fang*. These are the primary segments of the lineage at home, so that the genealogical point of reference has not shifted overseas. The solidarity of the 'lineage' is (or at least until recently was) to be seen at *rites de passage* and on the birthday of 'the ancestor'. This last is grandly celebrated by common worship in the temple, theatrical performances, and feasting. 'The ancestor' is represented in the temple by a 'statue', and from the descriptions given us of the ritual connected with it, it becomes clear enough that we are dealing with a situation in which a deified ancestor (he is said to have been a member of the lineage at home) serves both as a ritual focus for a 'lineage' and as temple god for a local community – because the non-'lineage' inhabitants of the village, although never being allowed on to the temple committee, take a full part in the temple worship. (Domestic ancestor worship is carried on before photographs, as is commonly the case in modern Singapore.) In addition to being organized as a 'lineage', its members seem also to take an active part in a clan association which includes members of many different Chinese 'dialect' groups.[1]

This 'lineage' is not a lineage, but it comes so close to being one that it is important to stress the difference. Neither is it a segment of a lineage, although superficially it may have this appearance. It is a group of émigrés who have formed themselves into a kind of colonial replica of the home lineage in which they continue to hold membership. They are not an independent lineage or lineage segment in the making, because they have not chosen a genealogical point of reference to define themselves as a unit within a larger unit. Now, it may very well be that, although the circumstances of overseas migration were different from those in which movement took place by land to other parts of Fukien

---

[1] There is an additional fact worth reporting which underlines the distinctiveness of the members of the 'lineage' in their local setting: of the four shops in the village, three are owned by members of the 'lineage'; of these three, the only one which appears to prosper deals mainly with people who are not members of the 'lineage'; while the one shop owned by an outsider and which serves members of the 'lineage' is a successful business.

and Kwangtung, some new settlements in southeastern China came about in much the same fashion – that is to say, by being formed by a group of people drawn from different main segments of a lineage. Then, in order to coalesce and constitute a genealogically coherent unit, the genealogical framework had ultimately to be reworked – and it is possible that some of the vagueness in the oral genealogies of poor lineages is due to a failure to achieve an agreed reformulation. The members of the Singapore 'lineage' could not reshape their genealogy; they continued to be entered on the written genealogy kept at home.

The terms 'patriliny' and 'lineage' have a precise usage in anthropology – and yet they are ambiguous.[1] What is conveyed by the statement that the Chinese are 'patrilineal' and have 'lineages'? I think it will be clear from some of the things said in this book that Chinese are not all patrilineal in one simple sense, and that different lineages in China take on different forms, fulfil different tasks, and are differently articulated with society at large. It is perfectly legitimate to work with a generalized model of Chinese kinship (for example, when we are comparing Chinese society with some other), but as soon as we begin to survey the ethnography of China we see that there are important problems in the variations we can detect – from region to region, from period to period, from 'dialect' area to 'dialect' area, and so on. Why is divorce more common in some areas than others? Is a high divorce rate connected with a greater control exercised by her own agnates over a married woman? If the rights over a married woman are more evenly divided between the family which bore her and that which received her as a bride, what consequences flow for the relations between her children and their mother's agnates? If these relationships are strong, what bearing do they have on the internal order of the lineage? This is one abbreviated example of a series of interlocking questions directed to the discovery of systematic differences (not mere random variations in custom) in different places or times.

The importance of paying attention to differences will be obvious as soon as we ask the question, what has happened to the

[1] See the powerful arguments deployed in I. M. Lewis, 'Problems in the Comparative Study of Unilineal Descent', in *The Relevance of Models for Social Anthropology* (= M. Banton, ed., *A.S.A. Monographs*, vol. 1), London, 1965. Dr Lewis has used the southeastern Chinese evidence in conjunction with the more usual kind of anthropological data.

Chinese lineage in modern China? What kind of Chinese lineage are we referring to? To a proud higher-order lineage of tens of thousands of people spread over a hundred square miles? To a small group embedded in a multilineage village? Politically, economically, and ritually the two extremes have very different implications, and the fate of the two kinds of lineage in the modern world must vary accordingly. Of the first kind we may say that the coincidence within it of political, economic, and ritual hierarchies will make it very sensitive to the involvement of its members in some new external hierarchy; its balance as a traditional entity is easily disturbed. But the same influence brought to bear on the small and humble lineage has less to disturb; its internal hierarchies are weak, and it has long since accustomed itself to interference from outside and the control of its fortunes by people and agencies lying beyond its own limits.

This book is not a study of 'social change' in the conventional sense of the term, but I think it may be interesting to end the enquiry by considering the response of lineage organization in general to the gross changes that China has experienced in the recent period during which it has been modernized. Admittedly the data are scarce, but there is no harm in our speculating.

It is paradoxical that, as Professor Lucy Mair has succinctly put it, the 'very forces which have broken up lineage solidarity elsewhere are the ones that reinforced it in southeastern China'.[1] The world over, people pursuing modern opportunities often turn away from their ancestral lands. Land vested in a lineage tends to be divided up among component families. But in Fukien and Kwangtung, even when people left the village to seek their living elsewhere, they took back wealth to invest in land at home; while the endowment of ancestral halls as an assertion of high social status kept going a system of (in principle) indivisible common estates. By some such argument we can explain, at least in part, why what has tended to disappear in other parts of the world when commercial life and extreme social differentiation have entered the scene, should have survived so sturdily in southeastern China. Certainly, there were many lineages – I tried to characterize them by properties built into model A[2] – which had few commercial or bureaucratic opportunities and where there was little sign of common property. They were, in fact, as I have

[1] *New Nations*, London, 1963, p. 68.   [2] *Lineage Organization*, pp. 131 f.

suggested earlier in this book, relatively unstable. If their members did by good fortune come to prosper, they began the process of investment in land and the building up of ancestral estates which turned small unstable lineages into large lineages retentive of their members.

The conditions environing this system persisted in part into our own day, even in the New Territories of Hong Kong. But in mainland China since 1949 the conditions have, of course, no longer held, while in the New Territories there have been signs since about the end of the Second World War that the old processes would not work themselves out so regularly. (For Taiwan, unfortunately, I cannot speak. It would be very interesting to know how the intensive government and the economic changes – especially those entailed in land reform – of recent years have affected the areas of the island where lineage organization was traditionally strong.)

I am reluctant to say very much about the fate of New Territories lineages before we can study the published results of the field investigations made by the anthropologists who have recently been at work in them. But a few general points can certainly be put now.[1] The first is that, while old segmentary divisions remain (although in some rich lineages their estates are being dismantled) and minor common estates are constantly being formed, new ancestral halls are no longer being built. (The only new ancestral hall I myself saw in 1963 was in fact an old one rebuilt – and paid for largely out of money earned in Chinese restaurants in Britain. To go by this one example, it is perhaps just as well from an aesthetic point of view that no new halls are being put up nowadays.) In many lineages the new commercial and industrial markets for land (products of the Hong Kong post-war economic revolution which has brought factories and workshops into the New Territories and turned large area of rice fields into vegetable gardens)[2] have made people anxious to dispose of their holdings or rent them out to strangers at a good price. (An

[1] Cf. my paper 'Shifts of Power in the Hong Kong New Territories'.
[2] Cf. Marjorie Topley, 'Hong Kong' in R. D. Lambert and B. F. Hoselitz, eds., *The Role of Savings and Wealth in Southern Asia and the West*, Paris, 1963, and 'Capital, Saving and Credit among Indigenous Rice Farmers and Immigrant Vegetable Farmers in Hong Kong's New Territories', in R. Firth and B. S. Yamey, eds., *Capital, Saving and Credit in Peasant Societies, Studies from Asia, Oceania, the Caribbean, and Middle America*, London, 1964.

interesting complication sometimes arises when an attempt is made to realize the market value of an estate: the many owners fail to agree on the principle for sharing the money to be received. The members of larger branches of the estate-owning unit naturally favour a straightforward *per capita* division of the assets, while the members of smaller branches seek a division *per stirpes* in the first place in order that their ultimate *per capita* shares may be larger.[1]) Some lineages in the southern part of the New Territories have entirely disappeared beneath the incoming tide of industrialization, new urban areas swallowing up their land. Many lineages have ceased to be the sole occupants of their traditional territories, having admitted immigrant market gardeners to their fields and strange tenants to their houses.

A very rough guide to the position reached is afforded by some of the statistics gathered in the 1961 census of Hong Kong. If we confine our attention to 'master farmers' whose principal crop was rice, we can see that those who farmed 'ancestral land' (i.e., land belonging to groups of agnates of which the farmers were members) still made up a sizeable proportion, as the following table shows.[2]

Tenure of land	Master farmers
own land	3,297
ancestral land, no rent	990
ancestral land, rent pay	511
long leased, money rent	365
long leased, grain rent	825
long leased, mixed rent	79
short leased, money rent	291
short leased, grain rent	678
short leased, mixed rent	44
own and ancestral land	509
any other combination	725
total	8,314

[1] Cf. p. 52 above.
[2] K. M. A. Barnett, *Report on the 1961 Census*, vol. III, Hong Kong [1962], p. 59, Table 408. Of course, some farmers, while not cultivating 'ancestral land', will have drawn benefit from it when it is cultivated by others. The master farmers whose principal crop was rice may be assumed to have been nearly all old-established New Territories people. Of the total of 14,266 farmers whose principal crop was rice, 10,607 gave Hong Kong as their 'place of origin' and 11,949 as their birthplace. See *ibid.*, pp. 77, 79, Tables 424, 425.

The changes in landholding and land-use are among the more obvious features of the modern New Territories. Shifts in power are no less important but more difficult to detect. To understand them one would need to consider the whole span of British rule, beginning, for example, with the administrative acts which undermined the position of some of the dominant lineages by depriving them of the right to levy 'taxes' on the land farmed by other lineages.[1] The legal powers of lineage elites were diminished by British officers assuming a chief part in social control, for in this regard the colonial administrators did not pattern their activity on that of their Chinese predecessors. An effect of this divergence from Chinese imperial practice is that nowadays, when the government is trying to get Village Representatives and the Rural Committees on which they sit to take on a major responsibility for the settlement of disputes, the District Officers and their staffs are still looked to as chief arbiters. But precisely because the new government was more benign and less partial than the one it replaced, it could no longer be used to bolster up the position of ambitious individuals and lineages. Except in minor posts, the Chinese had no place in the new administration. No longer could government be fended off or invoked according to the pleasure of interested and powerful parties. Peace having been established in the countryside,[2] local leaders and strong lineages suffered a loss of power and influence. As for education, ambition could not now be satisfied by success in classical scholarship, for politically it led nowhere. Some men began to think of advancement through urban occupations, and at the present day it seems to be generally true of the New Territories that progress up the educational ladder is seen more as a means of escape from rural life than as a way of creating high social status within the village community. In a few words, it has become less and less likely that men will seek to invest capital, power, and talent in traditional institutions.

None of this means that all, or most, lineages in the New Territories are dead or moribund. They are being transformed, and the point at which we shall no longer be able to recognize

[1] See *Lineage Organization*, p. 76.

[2] Very soon after they assumed power in the New Territories, the British began to make roads (there had been only paths hitherto) and set up police posts. It took a few years to clear the area of bandits, but violence between settled villagers was much more easily suppressed.

them as versions of the 'traditional' southeastern Chinese lineage is yet far off.[1] Certainly, in the political conditions created by the British, the old elite of higher-order lineages have not managed to survive in any effective manner, but their component localized lineages live on. Their power to dominate their lesser neighbours has been abridged; they cannot now speak with the voices of the literati; their leaders can no longer so effectively control the affairs of the lineage as a whole; but many of them have profited from Hong Kong's commercial economy and, more recently, from the opportunity to act as landlords to the new Chinese population from across the international border. On their side, the humbler lineages of former times have probably suffered less disturbance of their internal order than their more powerful neighbours; fewer leaders have needed to be displaced, and it has been easier for the rising business man to seize the new opportunities for local power and defend the interests of his lineage against its former masters.

But a few miles away, in China itself, we should expect to find (if we were allowed to look) the results of a much faster decline. Whatever interpretation we may choose to put upon Communist policy towards the family, of its hostility to the lineage there can be no doubt. In Communist eyes the lineage was one of the bonds holding the peasant in subjection[2] – or, as we should probably say as outsiders looking on, it was a barrier to the exercise of new central power. In the nature of things, there are few detailed accounts of how the Communist state set about and succeeded in breaking the backs of the lineages that stood in its path; but it is self-evident that first land reform and then collectivization were by themselves enough to put an end to a system of which differential wealth and the ownership of estates by lineages and their segments were crucial parts.

The title of *Revolution in a Chinese Village, Ten Mile Inn*, by Isabel and David Crook[3] raises some expectations which are not fulfilled by the book; for, although it was published a decade after the establishment of Communist power on the mainland, it in

---

[1] Potter, *P'ing Shan*, presents a very interesting analysis of the changes which have taken place in the Tang lineage he studied – changes which, for all their importance, still leave Ping Shan a clearly recognizable version of the powerful and large lineage discussed at many points in *Lineage Organization* and this book.

[2] See *Lineage Organization*, p. 111, fn. 1.

[3] London, 1959.

fact deals with a village in a northern area of China which had been under the control of the Communists since 1940, and it takes the story of social change only up to 1947, the year in which the Crooks arrived in the village. Ten Mile Inn, a community of some 1,500 souls, was composed almost entirely of three lineages ('clans' as the authors call them). By 1947 (if I may reinterpret evidence which the authors present in aid of a different thesis), land reform had cut out both the possibility and hope of social mobility; power had been centralized in the village in a way that would have been impossible when lineage, secret society, and other sectional interests had crossed the division between those who had much land and those who had less land than they wanted; and the village had ceased to be relatively independent of the state. After 'eight years of democratic reforms' the temple association and the lineages could no longer 'make even a pretence of serving a useful function', because the village government collected the taxes, education was a matter for the village school, 'and new social and economic relationships had been formed in the mutual-aid groups'. No more was it common village practice to carry out ancestor worship or care for old graves. On the other hand, 'the age-old inter-clan rivalries' were not completely dead, and when the village cadres erred, older men of the Li or Fu lineages 'might be heard to mumble that most of the cadres were Wangs'. But, the Crooks assure us (political tastes differ but the following fact must be welcome to many kinds of reader), the 'Communist Party members and other leading spirits of the village were constantly on the watch against a possible re-emergence of clan-factionalism which had once helped to keep the peasants divided and to maintain the feudal landlords and rich peasants in power'.[1]

When we turn to C. K. Yang's study, *A Chinese Village in Early Communist Transition*, we are in the part of China that primarily concerns us here, and in the presence of a Communist government victorious throughout the mainland. But, as the title of the book indicates, it deals only with the initial period of Communist control, and little can be drawn from it about the full impact of the new regime. As one would expect, Yang stresses the enhancement of the social standing of women and speaks of the coming to power of young people. The 'formal

[1] *Op. cit.*, p. 166.

structure of clan authority' broke up, not because of specific government orders against lineages as such but as a result of 'the whole devastating revolutionary process of remaking the village's political and economic life'. The lineage 'elders' councils' were helpless in the face of the new situation; they ceased to convene. Since there was no longer any lineage property, the position of lineage business manager was 'practically abolished'. (The Communists arrested many lineage managers in other villages, accusing them of embezzling lineage funds; official directives on land reform castigated lineage financial management as a 'system of "feudalistic exploitation"' of lineage members.) Rites in the ancestral halls were greatly reduced. 'Our observation in Nanching confirmed the impression that the clan was unlikely ever to recover its traditional importance in the operation of village life. . . .'[1] In a companion study to this book, Yang offers a much more general account of the decline of the lineage under Communism, but the points he makes in this regard are pretty much the same in both studies.[2]

Another writer, W. R. Geddes,[3] was able in 1956 briefly to restudy the village first described in Fei Hsiao-tung's *Peasant Life in China*.[4] But since in Fei's account of the village, lineages were shown to be very shallow, small, and unimportant, what Geddes can now tell us about them is not highly significant from our present point of view, even when he says that 'the *tsu* has declined to a state of very little importance indeed'.[5]

None of these accounts effectively deals with the fate of lineages after the coming of the communes in 1958. In order to handle the most recent phase of the modern history of the Chinese lineage we need to have as much trust in our own imagination as suspicion of the few 'facts' offered to us.

In the initial period of commune-ization one might well have been tempted to assert that the lineage had disappeared for ever on the mainland. Its material and religious apparatus having been dismantled, what could remain of it? How could it survive as a political entity once it had been submerged in the massive commune? But some part of the underlying structure of Chinese

[1] *Op. cit.*, pp. 178–80.
[2] *The Chinese Family in the Communist Revolution*, pp. 191–6.
[3] *Peasant Life in Communist China.*
[4] London, 1939.
[5] Geddes, *op. cit.*, p. 30.

12

society has again been allowed to become apparent in recent years. According to Skinner's argument,[1] the area of the individual commune has been revised to make it coincide with, or at least approximate to, that of the 'standard marketing community'. And we know that since 1960 economic and administrative rights and duties have been transferred downwards from the commune to its component units – first to the 'production brigades' and then (in 1961) to the 'production teams' – in such a way as to underline the significance of traditional social entities. The teams have on the average some thirty households in them; and while there may be as many as ten teams in a brigade, the latter unit often seems to coincide with a village.[2] I think we may assume, therefore, that in the southeastern part of the country the very small lineages as teams and the moderately large ones as brigades have often been given some organizational expression within the latest social framework devised for rural China.[3] Of course, the large local lineages, both on account of their sheer size and because of their history of power, will have suffered greatly, while higher-order lineage organization must have vanished very quickly from the map.

Groups of male agnates still occupy the villages inhabited by their forefathers[4] and are regarded by the state as forming legitimate units in economic and political life. But how lineage-like

[1] See the third instalment in *The Journal of Asian Studies*, vol. xxiv, no. 3, May 1965, of 'Marketing and Social Structure', pp. 395 ff.

[2] There would be no point in my trying to cite all the literature on the communes – much of it is in any case of little sociological value. On the statements I have made above see John Wilson Lewis, 'The Leadership Doctrine of the Chinese Communist Party: The Lesson of the People's Commune', *Asian Survey*, vol. iii, no. 10, October 1963, pp. 460 ff., and Joan Robinson, 'The Chinese Communes', *The Political Quarterly*, vol. 35, no. 3, July–September 1964, p. 288.

[3] Lewis, *op. cit.*, pp. 462 f., suggests that village and lineage solidarity was increased by the land policy of the early 1950s (the period of the co-operatives), and that there was a 'reestablishment of many formal functions associated in the past with the traditional lineage and village organizations . . . before party leaders had trained a sufficient number of basic-level cadres to staff rural posts.' I am sure Professor Lewis is right to stress the importance of local particularism and its unintended strengthening by Communist policy, but it takes more than pooled land and village solidarity to make a lineage – which must have both solidarity and internal competition at the same time.

[4] Goode, *World Revolution and Family Patterns*, pp. 298 f., enumerating the means taken by the Communists to destroy the *tsu*, says that people have been moved about in order to disrupt the local ties uniting members of one lineage; but he cites no evidence, and I myself know of none for a widespread breaking up of lineage populations by administrative fiat.

are they? To what extent may the lineage in its new guise as brigade or team display some of its old solidarity vis-à-vis its neighbours and the state and show its former inner differentiation? How far, in recovering from the upsets of the first impact of the commune system, has the lineage been able to reconstruct its own mechanisms of internal control?

The state has not, of course, abandoned its determination to watch over and intervene in village affairs (although in reality it may sometimes fail to control local leaders to its own satisfaction). It is unlikely that a lineage will be able to offer effective political resistance to the state. It will surely be prevented from forming dangerous alliances with other lineages. Where all land is common (save for the small private plots, which cannot be used to build up heritable estates[1]), segmentation and power on the basis of some common land is ruled out. It is possible that individuals may, through education and by dint of acquiring political experience and standing, create positions for themselves which rest on their ties with the external world of power, and having done so, strive to assert themselves and their families against their fellows. But it is unlikely that they would be able for long to escape the sanctions of a vigilant political apparatus designed to repress unwanted social differentiation and dangerous local power.

If men go on living where they were born, the lineage as a local group can maintain its continuity through time. Has marriage reform (a key feature of the remaking of Chinese society by the Communist state) disrupted the pattern of patrilocal residence by formally equalising the rights of men and women? Has the lineage remained an exogamous unit? Are marriages still 'arranged' and therefore political? If we try to think our way through the Chinese propaganda and the information supplied by indifferent reporting, we may perhaps guess that the marriage system is still of a kind to link some local lineages within a restricted geographical range and express the state of relations between them. 'Free choice' in marriage is an established legal right; it is another matter to assume that it is a constraining social fact.[2]

---

[1] It would seem that the total area to be set aside for private plots may not exceed 7 per cent of the land cultivated by the brigade or team, as the case may be. In addition, people may use the courtyards of their houses for growing vegetables. See Robinson, op. cit., p. 290. It is not clear to me how rights in houses are allocated and transmitted.

[2] Cf. my paper 'The Family under Chinese Communism', pp. 346 f.

Ancestral halls are now public buildings of another sort, usually schools;[1] their ritual function has been undermined by the removal of economic supports and attacked by ideological campaigning – ancestor worship is feudal superstition and genealogical records dangerous literature. Of course, it would be sociologically naive to assume that the customs by which crucial institutions and groupings were expressed have been completely swept off the cultural map of China; and we should be politically simple-minded to imagine that the state in Communist China can have its way entirely with traditional practices. The customs and practices go on and need (from the point of view of the ultimate controllers) constantly to be reprobated.

Consider the following examples from the area of the country we are primarily concerned with.

'The Winter Solstice is a greater event than the Chinese New Year.' This just about sums up a traditional practice hitherto prevalent in some localities of the Yünt'an commune in our Kaochou *hsien*. The Winter Solstice Festival is meant to be more important than the traditional Chinese Spring Festival. Every Winter Solstice here in pre-liberation days saw the general masses busy with sacrifices to gods and ancestors and with courtesy calls on relatives. Conformity with tradition compelled some already hard-pressed poor peasants to ask for loans. This only got them deeper into difficulties.

Such a traditional approach to the Winter Solstice has been continuously carried on after Liberation. As far as the last few years are concerned, a year-by-year production improvement has enabled some production brigades to mark the Winter Solstice Festival with increasing pomp and ceremony. They take this day off every year *en bloc*, killing chickens, ducks and pigs and fixing glutinous rice dumplings as sacrifices to the ancestors and local deities. With the bountiful late crops obtained this year, some production brigades are now cooking up something big for the coming Winter Solstice (December 22) in celebration of the good year.

. . . People's pre-liberation god-worshipping act is just a superstition preying upon their minds. Such a superstitious act should not be carried on. Attention to this problem by the production brigades and the commune members in all localities is therefore urged. . . .[2]

---

[1] In former times (and now in the New Territories) ancestral halls often doubled as schools. In Communist China they have been turned unambiguously into schools.

[2] *Nan-fang Jih-pao*, Canton, 18 December 1964. This and other extracts given below from Chinese newspapers are taken from the American *Survey of the China*

In the Spring Festival each year, many workers of our unit return to the countryside to visit their relatives and friends. Last year, after the workers returned to their hometowns, some of them took a lead in breaking down superstitions. This is quite important. For instance, a worker by the surname of P'eng returned to his home during the Spring Festival last year. Besides giving his family and his relatives and friends a number of superstitious articles, he also personally worshipped the gods and his ancestors by burning joss sticks. He pasted on the door of his house a motto: 'When you step out of this house, peace be with you'. By doing so, he exerted a very bad influence on the masses around him.[1]

In view of the fears expressed that kinship loyalties may distract people from their solidarity with the working class (for 'feudal' elements are said to be on the watch for their chance to do damage by appealing to lineage sentiments), it is understandable that written genealogies are frowned upon. A group of scholars doing field work in Fukien province, and making use of clan and lineage genealogies as sources, found it necessary when publishing their results to counter various objections that might be raised against their recourse to 'feudal' material.[2] But a more telling case is to be found in the Peking *Chung-kuo Ch'ing-nien Pao* in 1963 (26 October). The item begins with a letter addressed to the editor in which the writer raises the problem of whether, in the naming of children, people are right to go on drawing on lineage genealogies for the generation series of personal names. The editor replies at length.

You are right in saying that the clan register is a product of the feudal society. It should be discarded today. Why? Let us discuss the problem from the angle of birth of the clan register and the class interests which it reflected. The birth of the clan register system owed itself to the patriarchal system, which was a gradation system founded on blood relationship. . . . Clannish organization became the basis of feudalism. . . . The laboring people, besides being oppressed by the rule of the feudal state organs, were also bound by the rule of the clannish organizations and by patriarchal thought . . .[3]

Since you are a native of Chekiang, let us take a look at the clan

Mainland Press, and were passed on to me either by Miss Audrey Donnithorne or Mr W. A. C. Adie, to whom I wish to express my gratitude.

[1] *Nan-fang Jih-pao*, Canton, 15 January 1965.
[2] See Chuang Wei-chi *et al.*, 'A Study of the Rural Economy. . . .'
[3] Cf. Mao Tse-tung's views on the subject, summarized in *Lineage Organization*, p. 111 n.

registers kept by families along [sic] Chekiang and Kiangsu in the epoch of the Ming and Ch'ing dynasties. Then you will see that all the articles of 'family regulations' and 'family instructions', without exception, required the clansmen to be loyal to the ruling regime of the landlord class. . . . In numerous 'family regulations', the first requirement was to 'pay state taxes'. . . . Naturally, it was the peasants who would be punished if taxes were not paid. Besides, the peasants had to do uncompensated labor and bear countless feudal obligations, such as building ancestral halls. . . . Some peasants, unable to eke out a living, had to work for people outside the clan or engaged in 'menial jobs'. But then they would be charged with the crime of 'doing disgrace to their ancestors', and 'banished from the clan by the approval of all clansmen'. . . .

Through the above-mentioned examples, we can see that clan registers were used by the ruling classes to cover up the sharp contradictions between them and the subject classes under the slogan of glorifying the ancestors, protecting the honor of their clans and of common interests. . . . Having understood the substance of the clan register, we would naturally not continue to keep it.

As regards the ranking system, it was already initiated in primitive society where marriage was limited to people of the same tribes. After the establishment of the patriarchal system, the problem of rank [i.e. generation status] received particular attention. The situation regarding a poem or certain words you cited which were used to indicate the order of posterity was prevalent in . . . the Ming and Ch'ing dynasties. The aim was to further clarify and maintain the blood relationship between people of the same clan which was getting bigger and bigger and more diffused, so as to carry out control by the patriarchal right. Today, there is of course no need for us to distinguish strictly the ranks of the same clan, or to ascertain whether people with the same surname whom we do not know belong to our clan system, etc. Therefore, I believe that it is unnecessary to indicate the rank and provide names for our distant posterity, nor will our posterity accept them. As for the ranks of close relatives, they are undoubtedly clear without the arrangement of specific words in their names.

To be sure, it is permissible if the relatives are willing among themselves to name their children from the same words or from a meaningful sentence. It is strictly the private affair of parents and their children, and should be distinguished from the keeping of clan registers and observation of the ranking system.[1]

There remains a way in which the solidarity of lineages and

[1] But at times, instead of being completely eliminated, the genealogy books have been converted to suitably written family histories depicting the class struggle. How 'genealogical' can they remain in this new form?

their segments may be ritually expressed. In the plains, the graves seem to have been cleared away to increase the area of cultivable land; but where, as in the south-east, graves generally occupy land unfit for agriculture, they have been left untouched. And it would appear that people still care for their tombs and may, as the next quotation will show, rally at them in such a way as to excite the suspicion that old forms of collective ancestor worship are being practised.

The visit to ancestral tombs by members of clans having the same surname but different ancestors is a feudal, clannish activity. In it, clans having the same surname are regarded as a unit, and only clannish relations are taken into consideration, regardless of class distinctions. In the old society, this kind of activity was a means employed by the feudal ruling class for benumbing the laboring people. . . . Its aim was to make the laboring people believe that 'people having the same surname belong to the same family' and that it would be a matter of course to observe the 'clan system' and 'family rules', and make us obey willingly the rule and exploitation of the feudal class. Now, the evil landlord class has been defeated, but remnant feudal clannish ideas . . . have not been thoroughly eliminated. Some people hold that visits to ancestral tombs by clans having the same surname but different ancestors are 'a matter of course'. . . .

Today, the activity of visiting ancestral tombs by clans . . . is still very harmful.

First, this activity may deepen the feudal clannish ideas cherished by the laboring people, and blur our class distinctions. . . . As we know, there are among people of the same clan or having the same surname laborers as well as members of the exploiting class, and poor and lower-middle peasants as well as landlords and rich peasants. If we go with the landlords and rich-peasant elements to visit the ancestral tombs and claim relationship with them, what class viewpoints are we still holding? This is most agreeable to the landlords and rich-peasant elements, because they generally are older and belong to a senior generation, so that they will eventually be 'elders of the clan'. This will . . . weaken the dictatorship of the proletariat and impede the progress of class struggle. . . . We must also hold our class viewpoint in dealing with dead persons. In the old society, class exploitation existed and some of the ancestors of the laboring people might also be landlords, bullies and rogues. If we look at the memory of our ancestors simply with clan affection and worship all ancestors alike, we shall be lacking a class viewpoint. To visit tombs of the landlords will make us lose our class standpoint. . . .

Secondly, the class enemy in the rural areas may also make use of this tomb-visiting activity for carrying out sabotage activities. . . .

Thirdly, according to old custom, when visiting tombs of their ancestors, people of the same clan or having the same surname gather from places far and near, bringing with them sacrifices and enjoying themselves in feasts. This wastes a great deal of manpower, material power and time. . . .[1]

On the other hand, new graves in the old style (normally the culmination of two-stage burial) are unlikely nowadays to be made, and even if the services of geomancers are available, there would appear to be little incentive for people to avail themselves of them – unless advancement in the new political and educational hierarchies of Communism is thought to fall within the range of the success controlled by 'winds and waters'.

This last statement is not so outrageous as it may seem. Consider the following two letters-to-the-editor.

Dear Comrade Editor,

I am a youth. Last year I returned to my home village to take part in agricultural production. Before I did so, my aged father had passed away. Because of his death, coupled with my return for agricultural production, after failing to pass the examination to enter a senior middle school, my mother has been grumbling all day long saying that the family's fortunes have been declining. She has also been talking about our house being geomantically bad. She wants to move away and build a new house. I have been very much upset. Some old villagers have expressed agreement with her and they seem to have some ground for their views. Comrade editor, is there any connection between geomancy and the rise and fall of a family's fortunes?[2]

Dear Comrade Editor,

I am a worker. My home is in the country. Some time ago, my grandfather died and I got leave to return home. My grandmother told me that we should engage a 'geomancer' to find a place for the departed grandfather to settle in – a site for the grave which must be geomantically good so as to bring prosperity to the offspring. I was also advised by many old villagers that in view of the scarcity of descendants in the family (I am the only male descendant in four generations) misfortune would befall us if I did not solicit the assistance of a geomancer. In my view, this is superstition. I do not believe in it but can find no reason to offer, especially when the cases cited by the villagers

[1] *Nan-fang Jih-pao*, Rural Edition, Canton, 18 April 1964.
[2] *Nan-fang Jih-pao*, Canton, 26 July 1962.

seem to substantiate the claims of geomancy. Please, therefore, tell me what 'geomancy' really is. What shall I do to convince these country people?[1]

What is particularly interesting in the first letter is the reference to the writer's having failed to get through the examination for admission to senior middle school. The editor, having disposed of the superstitious belief in fate and pointed out that it was after all only natural for the writer's father to have died 'from disease at an advanced age', goes on to comment on the academic misfortune.

As to your failure to enter a higher school, naturally there must have been various concrete reasons. Every year only a small proportion of the graduates of junior middle schools succeed in winning promotion to senior middle schools. For those who fail, the principal outlet is to return to the countryside to undertake agricultural production. This is also a normal phenomenon. Moreover, the development of agricultural production is precisely the primary task of socialist construction. Therefore, the few things that have happened to your family are by no means abnormal phenomena. Much less can it be said that the fortunes of your family are declining, especially where there is no basis for the superstitious belief in 'geomancy' and 'fate'.

The various references to geomancy in the Chinese mainland press (I have seen cuttings for the years 1962 to 1964) make it plain that, while the regime may think, or pretend to think, that its problem is to eradicate superstition, its real task is to reconcile people to a uniform level of living and to persuade those who have lost in the race for academic and political advancement that their social worth is not thereby diminished. In the traditional society men strove to beat their lineage-mates and other neighbours in riches and standing; in a modified form their preoccupations survive today. There is no need to exaggerate the continuity of institutions and ideas from the old to the Communist society; they still seem to be able to speak for themselves.

None of this provides us with a clear picture of what has remained of the Chinese lineage. Too many questions have to be left unanswered. I ended *Lineage Organization* by referring to the observations that needed to be made in the Hong Kong New Territories; those observations have been made in the last few years and are being continued, so that in the near future we shall

[1] *Kung-jen Jih-pao*, Peking, 22 September 1962.

be able to analyse in detail the adaptation of a wide range of lineages to modern social and economic conditions. I shall end this book, not by saying what needs to be done on the spot in mainland China (after all, it is rather obvious), but by stressing that the interest of young students of Chinese society must constantly be sustained against the time when the mainland will again be open to scholarship. That day (if a messianic note is permissible) will come.

BIBLIOGRAPHICAL POSTSCRIPT

While the manuscript of this book has been in the hands of the printer I have found a few additional bits of evidence, and I have thought it worthwhile to refer to them in a postscript, for they contribute to my argument at several points. I should like in this connexion to acknowledge my debt to various libraries of Cornell University, and to thank Professor John W. Lewis (for drawing my attention to material on present-day southeastern China) and Mr Richard C. Howard, the Curator of the Wason Collection (for his having tracked down and borrowed for me a copy of the article by Fabre to which I shall refer).

It will be convenient to begin with the contemporary scene. We may gain some insight into the social organization of the countryside of Fukien and Kwangtung by studying two sets of documents that have come out of mainland China. The first is a collection of papers relating to Lien-chiang *hsien* in northern Fukien: *Fan-kung yu-chi-tui t'u-chi Fu-chien Lien-chiang lu-huo fang-wen-chien hui-pien* (Collection of [Communist] bandit local documents seized in an anti-Communist raid on Lien-chiang, Fukien), Ministry of National Defence, Bureau of Investigation, Taipei, 1964. A translation of these papers was made available to me by Professor Lewis. The second set consists of official documents issued by the office of the Pao-an *hsien* Party Committee for distribution to cadres. Translations are to be found in *Union Research Service*, Hong Kong, vol. 27, 1962 (mimeo.). Pao-an is the modern name for Hsin-an, the county from which the Hong Kong New Territories were excised in 1898.

The Lien-chiang papers were drawn up in 1962 and 1963. They seem to show, among other interesting things, that party officials were much preoccupied with the problem of traditional ritual and marriage practices. In one commune many new temples are said to have been built and others repaired. A number of ritual specialists are mentioned, geomancers among them. A geomancer is listed in a statistical table on 'Three Bad Practices' in Ch'ang-sha Brigade, 1962. As for marriage, sums of money handed over for bride-price are recorded (ranging from 400 to 2,000 *yuan*), and a local assertion is quoted (1963) to the effect that, the expense of acquiring a wife being so great, people can work themselves half to death in agriculture and still not accumulate enough money to get married. In Hua-wu Brigade the average age of eighteen girls disposed of in marriage was 14 and the average 'price for selling them' 750 *yuan*. The documents deplore the extravagance involved in celebrations for new houses, new ovens (presumably the setting up of new households), new walls (again perhaps connected with the emergence of social units), births, birthdays, and weddings. The objection raised does not appear to be to 'money marriages' in general, but rather to those which smack of trafficking in women. The Pao-an papers offer one scrap of evidence on the persistence of the rule of patrilocal marriage. The following recommendation is included among the suggestions for the distribution of rations in Chin-chieh Brigade (1961): 'Newly wed wives, on principle, should get their share of distribution from the production units to which they originally belonged; if the shares were too small, their work points might be transferred and accounted for in the distribution for the team to which they had become affiliated.'[1]

Both sets of documents offer some figures on the composition of brigades and teams.[2] Shan-keng Brigade in Lien-chiang county (1962) has 'only one natural village of 138 households with 552 persons'. It is composed of six production teams, ranging in size from 19 to 26 households. In the context of a discussion of decentralization in Hung-t'ang Brigade (1962), there is a reference to a proposal by the central government that a team consist of 20 to 30 households in the plains. Hung-t'ang Brigade itself has 12 production teams with an average of 27 households per team. In Pao-an, P'ing-huan Brigade (1961) has 168 households and a population of 653;[3] Ch'ih-shih-kang Production Team, of Lung-tung Brigade, has 46 households (1961).[4] The flexibility in social units (permitting some adjustment to the boundaries of pre-existing local groups) is conveyed in the Lien-chiang documents (1962) where reference is made to the fact that, while a commune ordinarily corresponds

---

[1] *Union Research Service*, vol. 27, no. 8, 27 April 1962, p. 160.
[2] See p. 176 above.
[3] *Union Research Service*, vol. 27, no. 7, 24 April 1962, p. 127.
[4] *Ibid.*, vol. 27, no. 8, 27 April 1962, p. 132.

to a *hsiang*, in some cases it may cover less than a *hsiang*, and may have two levels (commune and team) or three (commune, brigade, and team).

From these tantalizing glimpses into the present we may turn to the somewhat less fragmentary evidence on the past. The most important source to be considered is 'Avril au pays des aïeux' by the missionary Alfred Fabre,[1] a remarkably informative account of ancestor worship and burial practices in relation to the festival of Ch'ing Ming. The paper is based in the main on the author's experiences in Shun-tê, Kwangtung. It casts some light, in the first place, on lineage segmentation and on the possibility that coherent lineage units were formed by men of different origins.

In Fabre's account the central ancestral hall of a lineage is said to hold the tablets of only the first three, four, or five generations. 'Le chef en tête avec son ou ses épouses, les fils, les petit-fils ensuite sur autant de lignes que de générations. Le nombre étant complété, les ancêtres de générations médiates sont exclus, comme ils le sont aussi du logis familial.'[2] The tablets of ancestors of lower generations are cared for in lesser halls, some of which were still being put up in Fabre's day (the early thirties). 'Cette érection est en fonction du nombre, de la richesse des descendants d'un même aïeul intermédiaire, lesquels se cotisent pour la constitution d'un fonds commun.'[3] Such an intermediate hall will in turn, apparently, hold the tablets of some four generations of ancestors.[4] It is of interest that Fabre points out in this last context that there is a tendency for the Catholic churches founded in Shun-tê to follow the model of the ancestral halls, the worshippers often seeking to organize themselves in 'families'.

When he speaks of worship at the tombs, Fabre says that the grave of the first ancestor need be no more than a cenotaph. 'Ce tombeau du premier ancêtre peut même être purement fictif et n'être qu'un symbole, un signe de ralliement.' And he goes on to speak of the case of a group of settlers who, five hundred years earlier, 's'échappa de Namhong pour fuir la vengeance impériale. Ils vinrent coloniser le *Sheuntak, Yungky, Kwaichow*, etc. Six ou sept de ces fuyards, frères, cousins proches ou éloignés, ou même point parents du tout, se groupèrent en une société de défense, société de secours mutuel, pour le défrichement du pays couvert

---

[1] *Collectanea Commissionis Synodalis*, Catholic Church in China, vol. 8, 1935, Peking. [2] *Op. cit.*, p. 115. [3] *Ibid., loc. cit.* [4] And cf. *ibid.*, p. 131.

encore de maigres plages de sables. Ils se donnèrent un aïeul commun, purement nominatif, dont ils se dirent les fils. L'aïeul n'est que fictif, fictif aussi le tombeau. La réalité ne commence qu'aux associés en chair et en os, descendants putatifs, ascendants réels.' Even today descent is reworked to enable a man to be incorporated into a lineage. 'Il y aurait incardination d'individus à tel ou tel clan de même nom sans doute, mais de sang totalement différent. Moyennant $500, 1000 dollars, tel étranger au pays, tel barquier, [Tanka] de race vile, enrichi, se fait agréger à un groupe de son nom. C'est une sorte de naturalisation. Il apporte sa mise au fonds commun, légué par les ancêtres, accru par les descendants, et obtient en retour les avantages de la protection du clan. *Ejusdem nominis, fit quasi ejusdem generis.*'[1]

It will have been noticed that Fabre refers to a lineage being formed by men coming together to clear land 'couvert encore de maigres plages de sables'. The remark seems to be significant in relation to the argument[2] that lineage estates often came into being as a direct result of pioneer settlement and the bringing into cultivation of new tracts of land. I have found a further source bearing on the matter. In 'A General Descriptive Survey of the Honan Island Village Community'[3] Rui Feng and Ping-hang Yung mention the existence of dyke farms on the island (which is in P'an-yü, opposite the city of Canton). 'The dyke farms, which are usually a combination of fruit and rice, may be as large as 116 acres (1,000 *mow*) each [in contrast to the very small individual farms], and are the permanent property of the clan.'[4] Again: 'The construction of dykes is a permanent or longtime improvement of the farm.' It would not pay to make such an investment in a small farm. 'Some of the large dyke farms belong to, and are the permanent property of the clan. The interest yielded by them is used for the expenses of the clan. The rich farmers also sometimes own these large dyke farms, but rarely.'[5] Some references to 'sand fields' in Kwangtung (especially Shun-tê) will be found in Sasaki Masaya, 'The Gentry of Shun-tê *Hsien* and the Tung-hai District',[6] a study which also has a bearing on local organizations, *yüeh*[7] among them.

---

[1] *Ibid.*, p. 117.   [2] See pp. 160 f. above.
[3] *Lingnan Science Journal*, vol. 10, nos. 2 and 3, August 1931, Canton.
[4] *Op. cit.*, p. 155.   [5] *Ibid.*, p. 173.
[6] *Kindai Chugoku Kenkyu*, no. 3, Tokyo, 1959 (in Japanese).
[7] See pp. 82 ff. above.

Fabre's paper is an extremely valuable source on funeral practices, especially in regard to disinterment and reburial.[1] He makes the common point that burial is often delayed by the search for propitious sites, a search which the rich are especially likely to engage in. The geomancers (charmingly rendered as 'docteurs ès vents et eaux') exact their price, and good sites come dear. 'Le pied de terrain pour tombeau en telle colline de *Kwaichow* ou du *Youngki* peut y avoir la valeur qu'il aurait au beau milieu de Paris.'[2]

The bones of the dead are disinterred because some sort of misfortune has befallen the descendants or when the tomb is physically defective (for example, when it is infested by white ants). In addition, a body is normally exhumed when the death was caused by certain diseases or by violence.[3] And Fabre offers some fascinating details on the techniques and rituals of disinterment and the placing of the bones in funerary urns.[4] It would seem to follow from this account that the majority of graves are reopened, and indeed Fabre proceeds to tell us that in the region of Yung-kwai the remains of fifty out of every ninety buried adults are dug up (ten per cent of coffins never having been buried in the first place). The bones removed from both exhumed and unburied coffins are put into urns; so that sixty per cent of people who die as adults reach this funerary stage. 'Des ces 60 urnes, 48 seront réin-humées, parfois après 10, 15, 20 ans. Une douzaine ne le seront jamais. Une superstition, la pauvreté, l'incurie seront la cause de ce retard temporaire ou définitif.'[5] The unburied urns are sometimes stored at the undertaker's or arranged round the tomb of some major ancestor, but most often they are scattered over the hill-sides where they lead an existence even more precarious than that of unburied coffins.[6]

Some further information on burial in Fukien is to be gathered from Floy Hurlbut, *The Fukienese, A Study in Human Geography*[7] and from Grace Steinbeck and Susan Armstrong, 'Social and Religious Life.'[8] Hurlbut describes the normal pattern by which graves are set on the hillsides, but goes on to say that in the sandy

---

[1] See pp. 118 ff. above. [2] *Op. cit.*, p. 132. [3] *Ibid.*, p. 134.
[4] *Ibid.*, pp. 134 ff. [5] *Ibid.*, p. 137. [6] *Ibid.*, p. 138.
[7] Published by the author, n.p., 1930, Ph.D. thesis, Univ. of Nebraska; at pp. 79 f.
[8] In The Anti-Cobweb Club, *Fukien, a Study of a Province in China*, Shanghai, 1925; at pp. 27 ff.

stretches along the coast, where hills are of course rare, the dead belonging to poor farmers are buried in the fields and after a few years sink into oblivion.[1] The poor, that is to say, are prevented from making use of their dead. As for geomancy, yet another 'dialogue' appears in J. Thomson, *The Land and the People of China*.[2]

This last book also contains some interesting data on vendettas in Kwangtung, reinforcing a point made at p. 109 above: 'The most singular feature in these contests remains to be told. The fighting-men are professional braves in the pay of the hostile parties ... These braves are a scourge even to those whom they are employed to succour, and a constant drain upon their resources, for if not actively engaged in warfare they distribute their attentions impartially over the different villages, committing depredations when and where they please.'[3]

It is possible, finally, to tie together the two themes of vendetta and the significance of the dead by calling on an early nineteenth-century account: Charles Gutzlaff, *China Opened: or, A Display of the Topography, History, Customs, Manners, Arts ... of the Chinese Empire*.[4] There was an old rivalry 'between the clans of the Chung and Chuy families, who live in the neighbourhood of Canton'. One of the patriarchs of the Chung, disappointed in revenge, bit off his finger and wrote his wrongs on a scroll, placing a solemn charge on his descendants to seek vengeance. 'Unhappily, the rival clan had their cemetery inhabited by the other, and it was upon the remains and tombs of the deceased that the Chung family avenged themselves. They defaced the graves, and even threw putrid bodies upon them, when the feast of the tomb approached. No greater insult can be offered to the Chinese than this.'[5]

Ithaca, New York   M.F.
December 1965

---

[1] *Op. cit.*, p. 80.   [2] London, 1876; at pp. 209 ff.
[3] *Op. cit.*, p. 113.   [4] Revised by A. Reed, London, 1838, vol. I, p. 474.

[5] An article on 'Changing Habits and Customs' in mainland China (*China News Analysis*, no. 601, 25 February 1966, Hong Kong, pp. 3 f.) refers to both geomancy and burial practices at the present time. (See above, pp. 181 ff., 185.) The evidence is drawn from the mainland press and wireless. The article appears too late for me to make adequate use of it here.

LIST OF WORKS CITED

AMYOT, J., 1960. *The Chinese Community of Manila: A Study of Adaptation of Chinese Familism to the Philippines Environment*, Research Series no. 2, Philippines Studies Program, Dept. of Anthropology, Univ. of Chicago (mimeo.).

BAKER, H., [1965.] 'Burial, Geomancy and Ancestor Worship', in Royal Asiatic Society, Hong Kong Branch, *Aspects of Social Organization in the New Territories.*

BALAZS, E., 1964. *Chinese Civilization and Bureaucracy*, trans. H. M. Wright, ed. A. F. Wright, New Haven and London.

BALFOUR, S. F., 1941. 'Hong Kong before the British', *T'ien Hsia Monthly*, vol. XI, nos. 4, 5, Shanghai.

BALL, J. D., 1904. *Things Chinese, or Notes Connected with China*, 4th edn., London.

BARCLAY, G. W., 1954. *Colonial Development and Population in Taiwan*, Princeton, N.J.

BARNETT, K. M. A., 1956. *Hong Kong Annual Departmental Report by the District Commissioner, New Territories for the Financial Year 1955–56*, Hong Kong.

—— 1957. 'The People of the New Territories', in J. M. Braga, compiler, *Hong Kong Business Symposium, A Compilation of Authoritative Views on the Administration, Commerce and Resources of Britain's Far Eastern Outpost*, Hong Kong.

—— [1962.] *Report on the 1961 Census*, vol. III, Hong Kong.

BEATTIE, J., 1964. *Other Cultures: Aims, Methods and Achievements in Social Anthropology*, London.

— 1964. 'Feud', in J. Gould and W. L. Kolb, eds., *A Dictionary of the Social Sciences*, London.

BODDE, D., 1957. *China's Cultural Tradition, What and Whither?*, N.Y.

BOHANNAN, P., 1963. *Social Anthropology*, N.Y.

BOYD, A., 1962. *Chinese Architecture and Town Planning, 1500 B.C.–A.D. 1911*, Chicago.

BUCK, J. L., 1937. *Land Utilization in China*, Nanking.

BURGESS, E. W. and LOCKE, H. J., 1953. *The Family, from Institution to Companionship*, 2nd edn., N.Y.

CHANG CHUNG-LI, 1955. *The Chinese Gentry, Studies on their Role in Nineteenth-Century Chinese Society*, Seattle.

—— 1962. *Income of the Chinese Gentry*, Seattle.

CHANG SOO, [1960?] *Chinese Lineage Villages in Singapore*, unpublished dissertation, Dept. of Social Studies, Univ. of Singapore.

CHAO CH'ENG-HSIN, 1940. 'Familism as a Factor in the Chinese Population Balance', *Yenching Journal of Social Studies*, vol. III, no. 1, October.

CHEN HAN-SENG, 1936. *Agrarian Problems in Southernmost China*, Shanghai (also published as *Landlord and Peasant in China*, N.Y.).

CHEN TA, 1939. *Emigrant Communities in South China, A Study of Overseas Migration and its Influence on Standards of Living and Social Change*, London and N.Y.

'Chinese Clans and their Customs, etc., The', 1865. *The Chinese and Japanese Repository*, no. XXIII, June 1.

CH'Ü T'UNG-TSU, 1957. 'Chinese Class Structure and its Ideology', in J. K. Fairbank, ed., *Chinese Thought and Institutions*, Chicago.

—— 1959. *Law and Society in Traditional China*, Paris and The Hague.

—— 1962. *Local Government in China under the Ch'ing*, Cambridge, Mass.

CHUANG WEI-CHI, LIN CHIN-SHIH, and KUEI KUANG-HUA, 1957. 'Investigation into the History of the Overseas Chinese of Ch'üan-chou', *Hsiamen Ta-hsüeh Hsüeh-pao, She-hui K'o-hsüeh Pan*, no. 1, Amoy (in Chinese).

COHEN, M., [1963]. *The Hakka or 'Guest People': Dialect as a Sociocultural Variable in Southeastern China*, unpublished M.A. thesis, Columbia Univ., N.Y.

COLLINS, C., 1952. *Public Administration in Hongkong*, London and N.Y.

Correspondence (June 20, 1898, to August 20, 1900) respecting the Extension of the Boundaries of the Colony, 1900. Confidential Print, Eastern no. 66, Hong Kong, Colonial Office, London, November.

CREEL, H. G., 1964. 'The Beginnings of Bureaucracy in China: The Origin of the *Hsien*', *The Journal of Asian Studies*, vol. XXIII, no. 2, February.

CROOK, I. and CROOK, D., 1959. *Revolution in a Chinese Village, Ten Mile Inn*, London.

DE GLOPPER, D. R., 1965. *The Origins and Resolution of Conflict in Traditional Chinese Society*, unpublished M.A. thesis, Univ. of London.

DE GROOT, J. J. M., 1885. *Het Kongsiwezen van Borneo . . . met eene Chineesche Geschiedenis van de Kongsi Lanfong*, The Hague.

—— 1892, 1894, 1897. *The Religious System of China*, vols. I, II, III, Leiden.

DICKINSON, J., 1924. *Observations on the Social Life of a North China Village*, Peking.

DUKES, E. J., n.d. *Along River and Road in Fuh-Kien, China*, N.Y.

DURAND, J. D., 1960. 'The Population Statistics of China, A.D. 2–1953', *Population Studies*, vol. XIII, no. 3, March.

EBERHARD, W., 1959. 'Mobility in South Chinese Families', *Sinologica*, vol. VI, no. 1.

—— 1962. *Social Mobility in Traditional China*, Leiden.

EITEL, E. J., 1873. *Feng-Shui: or, The Rudiments of Natural Science in China*, London.

ENDACOTT, G. B., 1964. *Government and People in Hong Kong*, Hong Kong.

ESCARRA, J., 1949. *La Chine, passé et présent*, Paris.

EVANS-PRITCHARD, E. E., 1940. *The Nuer, A Description of the Modes of Livelihood and Political Institutions of a Nilotic People*, Oxford.

FABRE, A., 1935. 'Avril au pays des aïeux', *Collectanea Commissionis Synodalis*, Catholic Church in China, vol. 8, Peking.

Fan-kung yu-chi-tui t'u-chi Fu-chien Lien-chiang lu-huo fang-wen-chien hui-pien (Lien-chiang documents), 1964. Ministry of National Defence, Bureau of Investigation, Taipei.

FEI HSIAO-TUNG, 1939. *Peasant Life in China, A Field Study of Country Life in the Yangtze Valley*, London.

FEI HSIAO-TUNG and CHANG CHIH-I, 1949. *Earthbound China, A Study of Rural Economy in Yunnan*, London.

FENG RUI and YUNG PING-HANG, 1931. 'A General Descriptive Survey of the Honan Island Village Community', *Lingnan Science Journal*, vol. 10, nos. 2 and 3, August, Canton.

FEUCHTWANG, S. D. R., 1965. *An Anthropological Analysis of Chinese Geomancy*, unpublished M.A. thesis, Univ. of London.

FIELDE, A. M., 1885. *Pagoda Shadows, Studies from Life in China*, 4th edn., Boston, Mass.

—— 1894. *A Corner of Cathay, Studies from Life among the Chinese*, N.Y.

FORTES, M., 1959. *Oedipus and Job in West African Religion*, Cambridge.

—— 1961. 'Pietas in Ancestor Worship', *Journal of the Royal Anthropological Institute*, vol. 91, pt. 2, July–December.

—— 1965. 'Some Reflections on Ancestor Worship in Africa', in M. Fortes and G. Dieterlen, eds., *African Systems of Thought*, London.

FORTUNE, R. F., 1935. *Manus Religion* (= *Memoirs of the American Philosophical Society*, vol. III) Philadelphia.

FRANKE, W., 1960. *The Reform and Abolition of the Traditional Chinese Examination System*, Center for East Asian Studies, Harvard Univ., Cambridge, Mass. (mimeo.).

FREEDMAN, M., 1957. *Chinese Family and Marriage in Singapore*, London.

—— 1958. *Lineage Organization in Southeastern China*, London, reprinted with minor corrections, London, 1965.

—— 1960. 'Immigrants and Associations: Chinese in Nineteenth-Century Singapore', *Comparative Studies in Society and History*, vol. III, no. 1, October.

—— 1961. 'Problems in the Analysis of the Chinese Family', *Bulletin, Philadelphia Anthropological Society*, vol. XIV, no. 2 (mimeo.).

—— 1961–2. 'The Family in China, Past and Present', *Pacific Affairs*, vol. XXXIV, no. 4, Winter.

—— 1963. 'The Chinese Domestic Family: Models', *Actes du VIe Congrès International des Sciences Anthropologiques et Ethnologiques, Paris, 1960*, tome II, Ier volume, Paris.

—— 1963. 'A Chinese Phase in Social Anthropology', *The British Journal of Sociology*, vol. XIV, no. 1, March.

—— 1963. *A Report on Social Research in the New Territories*, Hong Kong (mimeo.).

—— 1964. 'What Social Science can do for Chinese Studies', *The Journal of Asian Studies*, vol. XXIII, no. 4, August.

—— 1964. 'The Family under Chinese Communism', *The Political Quarterly*, vol. 35, no. 3, July–September.

—— 1966. 'Shifts of Power in the Hong Kong New Territories', *Journal of Asian and African Studies*, vol. 1, no. 1, Leiden.

FRIED, M. H., 1957. 'The Classification of Corporate Unilineal Descent Groups', *Journal of the Royal Anthropological Institute*, vol. 87, pt. 1, January–June.

FRIED, M. H., 1962. 'Trends in Chinese Domestic Organization', in E. F. Szczepanik, ed., *Symposium on Economic and Social Problems of the Far East*, Hong Kong.

FUKUTAKE TADASHI, 1951. *The Structure of Chinese Rural Society*, Tokyo (in Japanese).

GALLIN, B., 1959. 'A Case for Intervention in the Field', *Human Organization*, vol. 18, no. 3.

—— 1960. 'Matrilateral and Affinal Relationships of a Taiwanese Village', *American Anthropologist*, vol. 62, no. 4, August.

—— 1963. 'Cousin Marriage in China', *Ethnology*, vol. II, no. 1, January.

—— 1963. 'Land Reform in Taiwan: Its Effect on Rural Social Organization and Leadership', *Human Organization*, vol. 22, no. 2.

—— 1963. 'Chinese Peasant Values towards the Land', *Proceedings of the 1963 Annual Spring Meeting of the American Ethnological Society*, Seattle.

GAMBLE, S. D., 1963. *North China Villages, Social, Political and Economic Activities before 1933*, Berkeley and Los Angeles.

Gazetteer of Place Names in Hong Kong, Kowloon, and the New Territories, A, [1960.] Hong Kong.

GEDDES, W. R., 1963. *Peasant Life in Communist China*, Monograph no. 6, Society for Applied Anthropology, Ithaca, N.Y.

GEERTZ, C., 1963. *Agricultural Involution, The Process of Ecological Change in Indonesia*, Berkeley and Los Angeles.

GENÄHR, F., 1864. 'Ueber chinesische Geomantie', *Berichte der Rheinischen Missionsgesellschaft*, no. 6, January, Barmen.

GILES, H. A., 1896. *A Chinese Biographical Dictionary*, London and Shanghai.

GOODE, W. J., 1963. *World Revolution and Family Patterns*, Glencoe, Ill.

GOODY, J., 1958. ed., *The Developmental Cycle in Domestic Groups*, Cambridge Papers in Social Anthropology, no. 1, Cambridge.

—— 1962. *Death, Property and the Ancestors, A Study of the Mortuary Customs of the LoDagaa of West Africa*, London.

GRANET, M., 1951. *La religion des Chinois*, Paris.

GRANT, C. J. [1960?]. *The Soils and Agriculture of Hong Kong*, Hong Kong.

GRAY, J. H., 1878. *China, A History of the Laws, Manners and Customs of the People*, ed. W. G. Gregor, London.

GROVES, R. G., [1965.] 'The Origins of Two Market Towns in the New Territories', in Royal Asiatic Society, Hong Kong Branch, *Aspects of Social Organization in the New Territories*, Hong Kong.

GUTKIND, E. A., 1946. *Revolution of Environment*, London.

GUTZLAFF, C., 1838. *China Opened: or, A Display of the Topography, History, Customs, Manners, Arts . . . of the Chinese Empire*, revised by A. Reed, London.

HAYES, J. W., 1962. 'The Pattern of Life in the New Territories, in 1898', *Journal of the Hong Kong Branch of the Royal Asiatic Society*, vol. 2, Hong Kong.

—— 1963. 'Cheung Chau 1850–1898: Information from Commemorative Tablets', *Journal of the Hong Kong Branch of the Royal Asiatic Society*, vol. 3.

—— 1963. 'Movement of Villages on Lantau Island for *Fung Shui* . . . Reasons', *Journal of the Hong Kong Branch of the Royal Asiatic Society*, vol. 3.

—— 1965. 'Peng Chau between 1798 and 1899', *Journal of the Hong Kong Branch of the Royal Asiatic Society*, vol. 4, 1964.

—— [1965.] 'The Settlement and Development of a Multiple-Clan Village,' in Royal Asiatic Society, Hong Kong Branch, *Aspects of Social Organization in the New Territories*, Hong Kong.

—— [1965.] 'A Mixed Community of Hakka and Cantonese on Lantau Island', in Royal Asiatic Society, Hong Kong Branch, *Aspects of Social Organization in the New Territories*, Hong Kong.

HENRY, B. C., [1885?]. *The Cross and the Dragon; or, Light in the Broad East*, London.

HICKEY, G. C., 1964. *Village in Vietnam*, New Haven and London.

HO PING-TI, 1959. *Studies on the Population of China, 1368–1953*, Cambridge, Mass.

—— 1959. 'The Examination System and Social Mobility in China, 1368–1911', in V. F. Ray, ed., *Intermediate Societies, Social Mobility, and Communication*, American Ethnological Society, Seattle.

—— 1959. 'Aspects of Social Mobility in China, 1368–1911', *Comparative Studies in Society and History*, vol. I, no. 4, June.

—— 1962. *The Ladder of Success in Imperial China, Aspects of Social Mobility, 1368–1911*, N.Y. and London.

HOLMES, D. R., 1960. *Hong Kong Annual Departmental Report by the District Commissioner, New Territories for the Financial Year 1959–60*, Hong Kong.

HSIAO KUNG-CHUAN, 1960. *Rural China, Imperial Control in the Nineteenth Century*, Seattle.

HSU, F. L. K., 1949. *Under the Ancestors' Shadow, Chinese Culture and Personality*, London.

—— 1963. *Clan, Caste, and Club*, Princeton, N.J.

HU CHANG-TU et al., [1960?]. *China, its People, its Society, its Culture*, London.

HU HSIEN-CHIN, 1948. *The Common Descent Group in China and its Functions*, N.Y.

HURLBUT, F., 1930. *The Fukienese, A Study in Human Geography*, n.p. (Ph.D. thesis, Univ. of Nebraska).

KRONE [R.], 1859. 'A Notice of the Sanon District', Article V, *Transactions of the China Branch of the Royal Asiatic Society*, pt. VI, Hong Kong.

LAAI YI-FAAI, MICHAEL, F., and SHERMAN, J. C., 1962. 'The Use of Maps in Social Research: A Case Study in South China', *The Geographical Review*, vol. LII, January.

LANG, O., 1946. *Chinese Family and Society*, New Haven.

Laws of Hong Kong, The, n.d. vol. III, Hong Kong.

LEACH, E. R., 1961. *Rethinking Anthropology*, London.

LEVY, M. J., 1949. *The Family Revolution in Modern China*, Cambridge, Mass.

LEWIS, I. M., 1965. 'Problems in the Comparative Study of Unilineal Descent', in *The Relevance of Models for Social Anthropology* (= M. Banton, ed., *A.S.A. Monographs*, vol. I), London.

LEWIS, J. W., 1963. 'The Leadership Doctrine of the Chinese Communist Party: The Lesson of the People's Commune', *Asian Survey*, vol. III, no. 10, October.

LIANG CH'I-CH'AO, 1956. *History of Chinese Culture*, Taipei (in Chinese).

LIM, J., 1958. *Sold for Silver, An Autobiography*, London.
LIN, PETER WEI, 1922. *The Social Effects of Ancestor Worship in a South China Town*, unpublished M.A. dissertation in the Faculty of Pol. Science, Columbia Univ., N.Y.
LIN YUEH-HWA, 1948. *The Golden Wing, a Sociological Study of Chinese Familism*, London.
LIU HUI-CHEN WANG, 1959. 'An Analysis of Chinese Clan Rules: Confucian Theories in Action', in D. S. Nivison and A. F. Wright, eds., *Confucianism in Action*, Stanford, Calif.
—— 1959. *The Traditional Chinese Clan Rules*, Locust Valley, N.Y.
LO HSIANG-LIN, 1961. *A Historical Survey of the Lan-fang Presidential System in Western Borneo* . . ., Hong Kong (in Chinese, with brief English summary).
LO HSIANG-LIN et al., 1963. *Hong Kong and its External Communications before 1842, The History of Hong Kong prior to British Arrival*, Hong Kong.
London Missionary Society Archives, Fukien Reports, 1866–1891 (MS.).
McALEAVY, H., 1958. 'Varieties of *Hu'o'ng-hoa* . . .: A Problem of Vietnamese Law', *Bulletin of the School of Oriental and African Studies*, vol. XXI, pt. 3.
MACGOWAN, J., 1897. *Pictures of Southern China*, London.
—— 1907. *Sidelights on Chinese Life*, London.
—— 1909. *Lights and Shadows of Chinese Life*, Shanghai.
MADAN, T. N., 1963. 'The Joint Family: A Terminological Clarification', in J. Mogey, ed., *Family and Marriage*, Leiden.
MAIR, L., 1963. *New Nations*, London.
MARSH, R. M., 1961. *The Mandarins, The Circulation of Elites in China, 1600–1900*, Glencoe, Ill.
—— 1961. 'Formal Organization and Promotion in a Pre-industrial Society', *American Sociological Review*, vol. 26, no. 4, August.
—— 1962. 'The Venality of Provincial Office in China and in Comparative Perspective', *Comparative Studies in Society and History*, vol. 4, no. 4, July.
MENZEL, J. M., ed., 1963. *The Chinese Civil Service, Career Open to Talent?*, Boston, Mass.
MIDDLETON, J., 1960. *Lugbara Religion, Ritual and Authority among an East African People*, London.
MIYAKAWA HISAYUKI, 1960. 'The Confucianization of South China', in A. F. Wright, ed., *The Confucian Persuasion*, Stanford, Calif.
MORGAN, W. P., 1960. *Triad Societies in Hong Kong*, Hong Kong.
NEEDHAM, J., 1956. *Science and Civilization in China*, vol. 2, *History of Scientific Thought*, Cambridge.
NEEDHAM, R., 1962. *Structure and Sentiment, A Test Case in Social Anthropology*, Chicago.
NEWELL, W. H., 1962. *Treacherous River, A Study of Rural Chinese in North Malaya*, Kuala Lumpur.
NG, P. Y. L., 1961. *The 1819 Edition of the Hsin-an Hsien-chih, A Critical Examination with Translation and Notes*, unpublished M.A. thesis, Univ. of Hong Kong.
OKADA YUZURU, 1949. 'Kinship in South China: Village Life on Amoy Island', in Okada Yuzuru, *Kiso Shakai*, Tokyo (in Japanese).

OSGOOD, C., 1951. *The Koreans and their Culture*, N.Y.

—— 1963. *Village Life in Old China, A Community Study of Kao Yao, Yünnan*, N.Y.

PARKER, E. H., 1879. 'Comparative Chinese Family Law', *The China Review*, vol. VIII.

PITCHER, P. W., 1909. *In and about Amoy*, Shanghai and Foochow.

PLATH, D. W., 1964. 'Where the Family of God is the Family: The Role of the Dead in Japanese Households', *American Anthropologist*, vol. 66, no. 2, April.

POTTER, J. M., 1964. *P'ing Shan: The Changing Economy of a Chinese Village in Hong Kong*, unpublished Ph.D. thesis, Univ. of California, Berkeley, Calif., September.

—— [1966?]. 'The Structure of Rural Chinese Society in Hong Kong's New Territories', in press.

PRATT, J. A., 1960. 'Emigration and Unilineal Descent Groups: A Study of Marriage in a Hakka Village in the New Territories', *The Eastern Anthropologist*, vol. XIII, no. 4, June–August, Lucknow.

PURCELL, V., 1951. *The Chinese in Southeast Asia*, London.

ROBINSON, J., 1964. 'The Chinese Communes', *The Political Quarterly*, vol. 35, no. 3, July–September.

Royal Asiatic Society, Hong Kong Branch, [1965.] *Aspects of Social Organization in the New Territories*, Week-end Symposium, 9th–10th May, 1964.

SASAKI MASAYA, 1959. 'The Gentry of Shun-tê *Hsien* and the Tung-hai District', *Kindai Chugoku Kenkyu*, no. 3, Tokyo (in Japanese).

SCHEINFELD, D. R., 1960. *A Comparative Study of Ancestor Worship, with Special Reference to Social Structure*, unpublished M.A. thesis, Univ. of London.

SCHLEGEL, G., 1885. 'Het Kongsiwezen van Borneo . . .' (*compte rendu* of De Groot's book), *Revue Coloniale Internationale*, vol. I.

SCHOLZ, H., 1951. 'The Rural Settlements in the Eighteen Provinces of China', *Sinologica*, vol. III, no. 1.

SHAH, A. M., 1964. 'Basic Terms and Concepts in the Study of Family in India', *The Indian Economic and Social History Review*, vol. I, no. 3, January–March.

SKINNER, G. W., 1951. 'A Study in Miniature of Chinese Population', *Population Studies*, vol. V, no. 2, November.

—— 1957. *Chinese Society in Thailand: An Analytical History*, Ithaca, N.Y.

—— 1958. *Leadership and Power in the Chinese Community of Thailand*, Ithaca, N.Y.

—— 1959. Review of *Lineage Organization*, *Pacific Affairs*, vol. XXXII, no. 2, June.

—— 1964. 'What the Study of China can do for Social Science', *The Journal of Asian Studies*, vol. XXIII, no. 4, August.

—— 1964-5. 'Marketing and Social Structure in Rural China', *The Journal of Asian Studies*, vol. XXIV, nos. 1, 2, 3, November 1964, February 1965, May 1965.

SMYTHE, L. S. C., 1935. 'The Composition of the Chinese Family', *Nanking Journal* (*Chin-ling Hsüeh-pao*), vol. 5, no. 2, November.

SPRENKEL, O. B. VAN DER, 1959. *New Light on the Chinese Gentry Clan from Genealogical Registers*, paper read in the Anthropological Section, A.N.Z.A.A.S., Perth, W.A. (mimeo.).

—— 1961. 'The Geographical Background of the Ming Civil Service', *Journal of the Economic and Social History of the Orient*, vol. IV, pt. 3.

—— 1964. 'Max Weber on China', *History and Theory*, vol. III, no. 3.

SPRENKEL, S. VAN DER, 1962. *Legal Institutions in Manchu China*, London.

STEINBECK, G. and ARMSTRONG, S., 1925. 'Social and Religious Life', in *Fukien, A Study of a Province of China*, The Anti-Cobweb Club, Shanghai.

SUNG HOK-P'ANG, 1935, 1936, 1938. 'Legends and Stories of the New Territories', *The Hong Kong Naturalist*, vol. VI, no. 1, May, nos. 3 and 4, December 1935; vol. VII, no. 1, April, no. 2, June, nos. 3 and 4, December 1936; vol. VIII, nos. 3 and 4, March 1938.

TAGA AKIGORO, 1960. *An Analytic Study of Chinese Genealogical Books*, Toyo Bunko Publications, series A, no. 45, Tokyo (in Japanese).

THOMSON, J., 1875. *The Straits of Malacca, Indo-China and China*, London.

—— 1876. *The Land and the People of China*, London.

TOPLEY, M., 1954. 'Chinese Women's Vegetarian Houses in Singapore', *Journal of the Malayan Branch of the Royal Asiatic Society*, vol. XXVII, pt. 1 (no. 165), May, Singapore.

—— 1955. 'Ghost Marriages among the Singapore Chinese', Article 35, *Man*, February.

—— 1956. 'Ghost Marriages among the Singapore Chinese: A Further Note', Article 63, *Man*, May.

—— 1963. 'Hong Kong', in R. D. Lambert and B. F. Hoselitz, eds., *The Role of Savings and Wealth in Southern Asia and the West*, Paris.

—— 1964. 'Capital, Saving and Credit among Indigenous Rice Farmers and Immigrant Vegetable Farmers in Hong Kong's New Territories', in R. Firth and B. S. Yamey, eds., *Capital, Saving and Credit in Peasant Societies, Studies from Asia, Oceania, the Caribbean, and Middle America*, London.

TREGEAR, T. R., 1958. *A Survey of Land Use in Hong Kong and the New Territories*, Hong Kong.

TREWARTHA, G. T., 1939. 'Field Observations on the Canton Delta of South China', *Economic Geography*, vol. XV, no. 1.

TUAN CHI-HSIEN, 1958. 'Reproductive Histories of Chinese Women in Rural Taiwan', *Population Studies*, vol. XII, pt. 1, July.

TWITCHETT, D. C., 1959. 'The Fan Clan's Charitable Estate, 1050-1760', in D. S. Nivison and A. F. Wright, eds., *Confucianism in Action*, Stanford, Calif.

—— 1960. 'Documents on Clan Administration, I: The Rules of Administration of the Charitable Estate of the Fan Clan', *Asia Major*, n.s., vol. VIII, pt. 1.

Union Research Service, 1962. Vol. 27, nos. 7 and 8.

WANG GUNGWU, 1959. *A Short History of the Nanyang Chinese*, Background to Malaya Series, no. 13, Singapore.

WARD, B. E., 1954. 'A Hong Kong Fishing Village', *Journal of Oriental Studies*, vol. I, no. 1, January, Hong Kong.

—— 1954. 'A Hakka Kongsi in Borneo', *Journal of Oriental Studies*, vol. I, no. 2, July, Hong Kong.

—— 1959. 'Floating Villages: Chinese Fishermen in Hong Kong', Article 62, *Man*, vol. LIX, March.

—— 1962. Review of *Lineage Organization*, *The British Journal of Sociology*, vol. XIII, no. 4, December.

—— 1965. 'Varieties of the Conscious Model: The Fishermen of South China', in *The Relevance of Models for Social Anthropology* (= M. Banton, ed., *A.S.A. Monographs*, vol. I), London.

WILHELM, H., 1958. 'The Concept of Time in the Book of Changes', in J. Campbell, ed., *Man and Time, Papers from the Eranos Yearbooks*, London.

—— 1961. *Change, Eight Lectures on the I Ching*, trans. C. F. Baynes, London.

WILHELM, R., 1928. *The Soul of China*, trans. J. H. Reece, N.Y.

—— 1951. *The I Ching or Book of Changes*, trans. C. F. Baynes, London.

WILLIAMS, S. W., 1883. *The Middle Kingdom*, vol. II, London.

WILLOUGHBY-MEADE, G., 1928. *Chinese Ghouls and Goblins*, London.

WILSON, B. D., 1960–1. 'Chinese Burial Customs in Hong Kong', *Journal of the Hong Kong Branch of the Royal Asiatic Society*, vol. I, Hong Kong.

WOLF, A. P., 1964. *Marriage and Adoption in a Hokkien Village*, unpublished Ph.D. thesis, Cornell Univ., Ithaca, N.Y.

WRIGHT. A. F., 1965. 'Chinese Studies Today', *Newsletter of the Association for Asian Studies*, vol. X, no. 3, February.

WRIGHT, M. C., 1957. *The Last Stand of Chinese Conservatism: The T'ung-chih Restoration, 1862–1878*, Stanford, Calif.

YANG, C. K., 1959. *The Chinese Family in the Communist Revolution*, Cambridge, Mass.

—— 1959. *A Chinese Village in Early Communist Transition*, Cambridge, Mass.

YANG, M. C., 1948. *A Chinese Village, Taitou, Shantung Province*, London.

—— 1963. 'The Traditional Market-Town Area as a Modern Rural Community in China', *Journal of Sociology*, no. I, National Taiwan Univ., Taipei, December.

YAP, P. M., 1958. *Suicide in Hong Kong, with Special Reference to Attempted Suicide*, Hong Kong.

INDEX